SOME GOD!

SOME GOD!

A Christian Companion to Charlotte's Webs of Hope

A Through-the-Year Devotional

AMANDA J. CHAMBERS

Some God!
Copyright © 2024 by Amanda J. Chambers
All rights reserved.

Published in the United States of America by Credo House Publishers,
a division of Credo Communications LLC, Grand Rapids, Michigan
credohousepublishers.com

ISBN: 978-1-62586-284-6

Cover and interior design by Frank Gutbrod
Editing by Suzanne U. Rhodes and Elizabeth Banks

All Scripture quotations, unless otherwise noted, are taken from the ESV® Bible (The Holy Bible, English Standard Version®), copyright © 2001 by Crossway, a publishing ministry of Good News Publishers. Used by permission. All rights reserved.

Scripture quotations marked BSB are taken from The Holy Bible, Berean Standard Bible, which is produced in cooperation with Bible Hub, Discovery Bible, OpenBible.com, and the Berean Bible Translation Committee. This text of God's Word has been dedicated to the public domain.

Scripture quotations marked GNT are taken from the Good News Translation (Today's English Version, Second Edition), copyright © 1992 by American Bible Society. Used by permission.

Scripture quotations marked NASB are taken from the New American Standard Bible®, copyright © 1960, 1971, 1977, 1995, 2020 by The Lockman Foundation. Used by permission. All rights reserved.

Scripture quotations marked NET are taken from the NET Bible®, copyright © 1996, 2019 by Biblical Studies Press, LLC. http://netbible.com. Used by permission. All rights reserved.

Scripture quotations marked NIV are taken from the Holy Bible, New International Version®, NIV®. Copyright © 1973, 1978, 1984, 2011 by Biblica, Inc.™ Used by permission of Zondervan. All rights reserved worldwide.

Scripture quotations marked NIrV are taken *from* the Holy Bible, New International Reader's Version®, NIrV®. Copyright © 1995, 1996, 1998, 2014 by Biblica, Inc.™ Used by permission of Zondervan. All rights reserved worldwide.

Scripture quotations marked NLT are taken from the Holy Bible, New Living Translation, copyright © 1996, 2004, 2015 by Tyndale House Foundation. Used by permission of Tyndale House Publishers, Inc., Carol Stream, Illinois 60188. All rights reserved.

Scripture quotations marked MSG are taken from *The Message*, copyright © 1993, 2002, 2018 by Eugene H. Peterson. Used by permission of NavPress. All rights reserved.

Scripture quotations marked RSV are taken from the Revised Standard Version of the Bible, copyright 1946, 1952, and 1971, Division of Christian Education of the National Council of the Churches of Christ in the United States of America. Used by permission. All rights reserved.

Scripture quotations marked NRSVUE are taken from the New Revised Standard Version Bible, Updated Edition. Copyright © 2021, National Council of Churches of Christ in the United States of America. Used by permission. All rights reserved.

Scripture quotations marked KJV are taken from the Authorized (King James) Version. Rights in the Authorized Version in the United Kingdom are vested in the Crown. Reproduced by permission of the Crown's patentee, Cambridge University Press.

Scripture quotations marked NKJV are taken from the New King James Version®. Copyright © 1982 by Thomas Nelson. Used by permission. All rights reserved.

Printed in the United States of America
First Edition

Some God! A Christian Companion to Charlotte's Webs of Hope is a discipleship tool for educational, spiritual, and emotional growth and is based on the concept of the cultural redemptive analogy; the book is not affiliated with *Charlotte's Web* by E. B. White nor endorsed by White Literary LLC.

Some God! is dedicated to my true Friend who saved me
from eternal death and gives me abundant life.

And to my mother, a true friend and a good writer,
who encouraged me to write.

And to my family, David, David M., and Luke,
cheerleaders for good progress.

And to my own Charlotte, Suzanne U. Rhodes, mentor,
faithful editor, radiant friend.

And to the ones

Who,
like Wilbur,
feel alone, afraid, runty, rusty, wobbly of heart,
but whom God names "Priceless" and whom He desires to draw near
to give them hope, home, a future of peace, and freedom from fear.

> *A bruised reed he will not break,*
> *and a faintly burning wick he will not quench.* (Isaiah 42:3)

> *Because of the tender mercy of our God, . . . the sunrise shall*
> *visit us from on high to give light to those who sit in darkness*
> *and in the shadow of death, to guide our feet into the way of*
> *peace.* (Luke 1:78–79)

CONTENTS

Foreword *1*
Preface *3*
Introduction *4*
Synopsis and Guide *6*
The Plan for the Year *8*
The Plan—Month by Month *9*
A Quick-Start Guide for Looking Up and Becoming Unstuck *12*

January: *Personality* *13*
February: *Relationships* *35*
March: *Transition and Struggle* *57*
April: *Roots of Faith* *78*
May: *Branching Out, Budding, and Blooming* *104*
June: *Preparing to Launch* *126*
July: *Freedom and Thinking* *147*
August: *Farm and Work* *168*
September: *Trials and Victory!* *191*
October: *Writing and Nature* *212*
November: *Gratitude, Rest, and Reflection* *233*
December: *Promise and Prophecy* *255*

Acknowledgments *278*
Radiant Actions *280*
Bibliography *282*
Index *289*
Endnotes *295*

FOREWORD

A February 1939 essay by E. B. White is set against the backdrop of a radio preacher's sermon while the stubbled writer reclines in his living room, settled in comfortably for a Sunday with his paper at home, not church. "In this house we cling to a few relics of religious observance, but there is no heart in it," he writes. "If we possess faith (and I guess we do) it is of a secret and unconsecrated sort ill at ease in church." Later, he confesses that "for the most part, religion is tucked away in a bottom drawer, among things we love but never use."[1]

Those snippets from "Sabbath Morn" may be as close as one gets to White's religion. His writing was rarely confessional; he held back his inmost thoughts. He essayed through his day with wit and quip, comfortable with description but guarding his privacy. Only from his correspondence would the wider world later gain some insight into his personal challenges—the depression and anxiety that dogged him. He likely had his religion and knew the Bible like he did all great literature, yet either kept it to himself or believed in God as a watchmaker, the one who set it all up and then bowed out, showing up only now and then. "The Lord is persistent and lingers in strange places," he concluded—enchanting what the world so busily disenchants.[2]

White was an astute observer of that other Book—Creation, the natural world in which he seemed most at home. And in that world, he excelled in the capacity to observe and describe. In the corridors and towers of Manhattan, readers of *The New Yorker* or *Harpers* could follow White through a day on the farm or witness the death of a pig or imagine with him the conversation among a barn spider, pig, goose, and rat.

On another Sunday in 1939, the "sermon" he heard was one more typical for the writer. "Woke to find the wind blowing from the sea, and the sky overcast," he recorded. "Three starlings sat gloomily in the Balm o' Gilead tree, awaiting better times, and in the plowed field some crows held a special meeting and took a vote. In an hour it was snowing."[3]

It is in White's astute observation of creation that Amanda Chambers finds his unwitting testimony to the One who made it all and initiated a plan to save it all: God in Christ, redeeming the world. In this collection of reflections inspired by White's beloved *Charlotte's Web,* Amanda does not so much put words in White's mouth as she lets his words and characters inspire her to reflect on applications which flow from her own Christian belief that a loving God made the universe and is at work in Christ setting it right, making all things new—even a tiny spider named Charlotte.

Both deep faith in Christ and attentiveness to His world shape these devotions. I've known Amanda for over forty years as a prayerful observer of the world with a childlike wonder at its beauty and a playful approach to life. She once chose a different snack or dessert for each of her friends to remind her to pray for them.

1

It may be her first book, yet she's been penning poems and stories and journaling for much of her life.

So it is no surprise that in these reflections Amanda makes rich use of metaphor—runty pig, tiny spider, roguish rat, and wordy geese—to shine insight into relationships, faith, struggle, provision, and things to come. She offers a short devotion followed by an application and prayer as well as a web of related entries, engaging the reader with prose and wit that reveals her love of words. One would benefit most by reading and rereading the book that inspired it as these spiritual insights are slowly savored through the year.

Amanda has been mining for the truths reflected here for a lifetime—quoting theologians from Spurgeon to Tillich to Schaeffer, writers from Flannery O'Connor to Madeleine L'Engle to David Brooks, and directing us to classic hymns, contemporary music, and art that enriches mind and soul and body in a richly sensual experience. Yet more than anything, these reflections brim with Scripture, offering a practical theology to apply in the everyday world.

Don't get too bogged down in arrangement, as thoughtful and enriching as it is. Drop in anywhere for sustenance, for both encouragement and holy provocation. Take this entry on a timeless midway ride: "The Ferris wheel's axis is like the still point in time," Amanda writes. "Use your imagination to see the center axis of a Ferris wheel as a symbol of the eternal, inextinguishable Life in the center of your being that gives foundation, direction, and energy to *your* seasons." She compares the wheel to a clock. "Time, cycles, and seasons of earthly life are like spokes in the wheel. It is a symbol of time progressing, a crossroads of time. But God is ageless, outside of time, ever present." In her prayer, she bids us to remember that "praise is the still point of our souls."

Amanda is well-placed for these kinds of meditations. Her prayerful seeking of the Lord often gives her unique insights. In looking below the surfaces of everyday life, she mimics a master, White himself, who often turned his eye and typewriter to the eternally charged mundane, to earthly realities that, when described so aptly, spoke of a deeper, spiritual reality.

"Very dark here today—just enough light in the sky to strike a match by," wrote White to his writer friend Edmund Ware Smith on New Year's Day, 1958, a rich evocation of a nearly pitch-dark day and of a time when people carried matches for, as they say, "their matchless friends," when lighting up after a meal was common.[4]

This book will provide more than enough light for any of your days. It's a match for a gray or dark room. Light it up.

Steve West
Reporter, WORLD Magazine and *The World and Everything in It*

PREFACE

Charlotte's Web by E. B. White is a story of the impossible: a fragile spider, who with its gossamer web, saves a pig. This devotional book, drawn from the beloved classic, discovers many such echoes of the gospel, the impossible story of God becoming a man and offering redemption to all people for eternity. Truly, with Him "all things are possible" (Matt. 19:26).

Consider also White's depiction of the selfless servant heart of one friend for another. Charlotte wants Wilbur to have life, and she gleans no glory for herself as she weaves words in her web. In this we can recognize Jesus, the ultimate servant. He laid down everything to come from heaven to wretched earth to reclaim us from the mud and manure.

Impossible salvation, friendship, servanthood—these are themes of *Some God! A Christian Companion to Charlotte's Webs of Hope (A Through-the-Year Devotional)* that you will encounter month by month, themes that are platforms for faith reflections on many topics—such things as hope, friendship, justice, deliverance, truth, freedom, imagination, story, mentoring, and teamwork. Even Templeton, the despicable rat, is not without a scrap of grace that inspires. You'll certainly want to revisit *Charlotte's Web,* or read it for the first time, to gain full benefit from these devotions.

While God isn't mentioned directly in *Charlotte's Web* (and neither is He spoken of in the Old Testament book of Esther), we discern His shadow. The light in White's story is filtered light from the gospel, as its images whisper rumors of sacrifice and resurrection. Indeed, *Charlotte's Web* illustrates many biblical truths that when taken to heart make for spiritual, mental, and emotional growth, and even improved physical health.

I wrote *Some God!* to encourage you while you're "waiting for the dawn" (see Luke 1:78–79) when troubles feel like an endless night and you long for relief. Often bewildered, Wilbur, like us, has emotional "wobblestacles" and muddles. He is struck many times with stark terror. But he becomes a Wilbur Force, courageously acting to save his friend Charlotte's magnum opus. At the end, he's a rock and at peace. His story provides encouragement for all of us who tend toward piggly-wiggly emotions and need the strengthening force of grace to endure and overcome life's severest challenges.

There are twenty devotions per month to correlate with the average number of workdays in a month.

"May the God of hope fill you with all joy and peace in believing so that by the power of the Holy Spirit you may abound in hope" (Rom. 15:13).

INTRODUCTION

Who will deny that spiritual insight could come from a barn in a children's story? E. B. White himself said, "Children can sail easily over the fence that separates reality from make-believe. A fence that can throw a librarian is nothing to a child."[5] Using fiction to illustrate spiritual truths is a way of crossing a boundary between the imagined to eternal reality. Jumping over the fence from one to the other enables the mind to grasp more firmly what is true. Even C. S. Lewis quotes *The Wind in the Willows* to illustrate the presence of the divine in the natural world.[6]

White admits that *Charlotte's Web* has greater meaning than just a child's tale. In his essay "Death of a Pig" he tells how he nursed a sick pig that died a day or so later, an experience that led to his idea for a book about a pig.[7] He was troubled by the suffering and loss of his pig and wrestled with the implications it had for his own life. He writes: "The pig's imbalance (became) the man's vicariously, and life (seemed) insecure, displaced, transitory."[8] He also said that "to confront death . . . is to identify with the victim and face what is unsettling and sobering . . . I knew that what could be true of my pig could be true also of the rest of my tidy world."[9]

Echoes of this truth are found in the old sheep's words to Templeton: "Wilbur's destiny and your destiny are closely linked."[10] *Charlotte's Web* is more than just a children's tale; it reveals much about life, mortality, the heart, the mind, identity, relationships, courage, selflessness, and selfishness. There is much to gain in wisdom for living by closely examining its themes. White's vibrant details carry the flame of eternity within them.[11]

White's philosophy reflects God's character as revealed in the Bible:

White said, "All I hope to ever say is that I love the world."[12] John writes in his gospel, "God so loved the world" (John 3:16).

White's delight in the "glory of everything"[13] parallels the thought that all creation declares God's glory. "For his invisible attributes, namely, his eternal power and divine nature, have been clearly perceived, ever since the creation of the world, in the things that have been made" (Rom. 1:20).[14]

Wonder implies "amazement, awe, marvel, astonishment, surprise."[15] Miracles fascinated White, even just ones of everyday life. Dr. Dorian advises Mrs. Arable to "always be on the watch for the coming of wonders."[16] God is known as the God of wonders (see Acts 12-13; Ps. 75:1). "You are the God who works wonders; You have made known Your might among the peoples" (Ps. 77:14). He performs extraordinary works and miracles beyond our comprehension.

Jesus said of His own parables that if one wants to understand them, he will.[17] Childlike imagination, like Fern's in *Charlotte's Web*, will need to rise to find inspiration in White's story. The book of Hebrews explains that the Jewish rites were shadows of what was to come. *Charlotte's Web* is a book of shadows that play from the realities of God and the natural world He made, where a web pulls us into truth.

As for now, we humans, inhabitants of a fallen world, see only through a glass darkly. But consider how shafts of light streak into dark waters of a pool and shatter. If we peer into those waters to admire the glorious disarray, refracted radiance plays both downward and ricochets upward toward the surface. Light from a parable is like that display of light in a pool. Prisms of faith, imagination, and inspiration allow us to detect the brilliance of grace hidden in the barnyard.

SYNOPSIS AND GUIDE

Summary of *Charlotte's Web*: Fern Arable, an eight-year-old girl, saves a runt pig named Wilbur from execution. He moves from a pen under an apple tree in her yard to a farm down the road belonging to Fern's uncle. Extremely lonely, the pig meets a spider named Charlotte, who befriends him and later saves his life. Charlotte spins words in her web to attract attention to Wilbur's specialness. The wordy geese and Templeton, the resident roguish rat, suggest words for the web. Wilbur wins the top prize at the fair and gains future security because of Charlotte's efforts. She dies alone at the fairgrounds, but Wilbur rescues her egg sac. He goes home to the farm, continues to live peacefully, and enjoys the companionship of Charlotte's progeny.

You may be asking, why should I read this book? After all, time is our most valuable asset.[18] Ask yourself the following questions to see if your time will be well-spent by using this resource:

What is the purpose of this book?
Characters, conversations, and scenes from *Charlotte's Web* spark discussions of spiritual truths.

How can this book help me?
Wisdom from the Scriptures is the foundation for each devotion, while the crisp and concrete illustrations from *Charlotte's Web* expand understanding. Ultimately, my prayer is that you will become "unstuck" and launched into a deeper faith to increase in your fruit-bearing for God. Note that Arable, Fern's family name, means "suitable for crops."

Some God! also can be used as a guide for intercessory and personal prayer.

When should I use this book?
Some God! is organized by themes for each month of the year, and each month contains twenty devotions for a year-long journey. I like to think of it as giving you, the reader, a walking tour along a river—a river of grace, where each entry is a stop to provide a fresh supply of encouragement. The apple tree through the year is a metaphor for the seasonal groupings of the devotions.

Structure
Each entry includes a Prayer, a Radiant Action, Webs, and Gleanings. The term "Radiant" is one of Charlotte's descriptive terms for Wilbur. Radiant Actions are practical applications. Webs are related entries to explore to help you think

through matters more thoroughly. For example, the entry in March on Vision includes these Webs: Discipline (Apr.), Balance (May), and Ferris Wheel (June). The web entries are listed alphabetically at the end of the book for easy reference. Gleanings conclude many devotions and include additional Scripture verses, poems, and meaningful quotes.

Preparations

Invest in a journal. The Radiant Actions often are suggestions for journal entries. It's your home for reflections, to record struggles, and victories. Reflection is the way to catch an updraft and get unstuck! You also need a Bible and probably a copy of *Charlotte's Web*.

THE PLAN FOR THE YEAR

These devotions are crafted to be specific and useful invitations to listen to God's voice. Together, they comprise a monthly discipleship manual to help you find peace, calling, equipping, hope, and a fruitful life in Him as the Holy Spirit directs.

The apple tree symbolizes the journey through the year.[19] White described the pigpen on his farm like this: "There is a pleasant yard to move about in, shaded by an apple tree which overhangs the low rail fence."[20] An apple tree appears in every season in *Charlotte's Web* as a means of picturing the passing of time as the story develops. The apple tree is a shelter for Wilbur's nursery in the spring and resplendent with fruit in the triumphant fall.

In winter, for example, an apple tree's branches are barren, but its structure and strength are exposed, with the trunk and bare limbs like structures of the human personality. In January we will consider significant qualities in Fern, Wilbur, Templeton, and Charlotte: their emotions, thinking patterns, identities, relationships, and boundaries. In turn, these traits will provide a foundation to take frank inventory of ourselves with a view toward personal growth. Later months look at the characters' obstacles and growth.

Come to the barn. Turn an old milking stool upside down to listen as sunlight pours in on dusty streams. The radiance from the manger is all around, and you may hope to hear God's voice above the garrulousness of the present world.

THE PLAN—MONTH BY MONTH

January: Personality
February: Relationships
March: Transition and Struggle
April: Roots of Faith
May: Branching Out, Budding, and Blooming
June: Preparing to Launch
July: Freedom and Thinking
August: Farm and Work
September: Trials and Victory!
October: Writing and Nature
November: Gratitude, Rest, and Reflection
December: Promise and Prophecy

January explores some of the basic structures of human personality (emotions, thinking patterns, identity, relationships, and boundaries) by briefly probing these aspects in Fern, Wilbur, Templeton, and Charlotte. We look to the apple tree in winter as a metaphor to aid understanding. The tree's bare-bones branches and the trunk that gives supporting strength represent certain basic aspects of human personality. Through honest self-examination, we can evaluate our own character qualities, with God's power, to understand and strengthen our spiritual limbs.

February is a month of formation. The apple tree will be budding before long! An apple can be an affectionate reference to a loved one, as in "He is the apple of my eye." This is the month to consider relationships to oneself and others, such as close friends or a marriage partner, and to the people we encounter in the community. We ponder the joys and hindrances that can accompany these connections.

March is a month of transition. The weather is moody and unstable, as emotions can be. The apple tree's limbs thresh the air as it stretches and bends with the wind. In March we may find ourselves struggling with heart challenges, but there is nothing to do but keep marching. It can be a time of pruning—of removing unproductive branches before full blooming begins.

April is a time of planting, as the unseen roots grip tightly to the soil to suck in the needed nutrients. April's devotions are based on the roots of faith: sin, deliverance, Easter, and changed lives.

May is the month when an apple tree usually blossoms. The tree awakens fully from dormancy, producing petals that seem to laugh in dew, rain, and sunlight. This is a season of new life, of exploring personal direction and purpose. These new buds are like new hopes and cheerful songs—clear signs of renewal. They nourish the heart, as vital as sap in a living tree. It's a time to celebrate motherhood and delight in the gifts of the God who gives life.

In *June*, when apple blossoms turn pink, the gardener must watch for pests and disease, just as we as believers need the Holy Spirit to search us for unhealthy habits and sinful behaviors. June's devotions include listening to God, just as Fern listened in the barn. Other themes include courage and preparation for launching out.

In *July*, apples are on the way. Now is the time for swinging and swimming, and for thinking through the meaning of real freedom in community, personal life, and the mind.

In *August*, summer's green leaves and ripening fruit invite discussion of a fruitful harvest. Here is a collection of inspirations from farm life, including thoughts on time, management, work, and fatherhood.

September is the month of victory. At last, there are round, delectable apples hanging like ornaments on the tree. Tears and trials precede a great heart harvest.

In *October*, earth is pivoting from one season to another. The apple tree begins a fluttery shedding, throwing off its last flings of splendor. These devotions are all about the human ability to wield the powerful gift of writing and communication—tools for persuasion and change. And here are devotions on creatures like the wild fox and the barn inhabitants of geese, pigs, and sheep whom we think have no speech.

In *November*, our apple tree begins its rest. This is the season for quiet reflection—a time to sift through the graces that proffer strength in the testing, to examine one's heart for generosity, to foster gratitude for food and unlikely gifts which may appear.

Come *December*, an apple tree's finery has fallen like rags to the ground, but a first snow may clothe its nakedness. December is a month for waiting, for promise and prophecy as the Christmas season descends with its rich and royal goodness to unfurl the hopeful time when all will be made well and right. The aging year dwindles and passes by in farewell. The Grand Weaver, the One who enables frail humans to stitch and knit and spin, weaves time and facts, thoughts, hurts, and events into the truth of His redemptive plan.

Jesus Christ the Apple Tree[21]

The tree of life my soul hath seen,
Laden with fruit, and always green:
The trees of nature fruitless be
Compared with Christ the apple tree.

His beauty doth all things excel:
By faith I know, but ne'er can tell
The glory which I now can see
In Jesus Christ the apple tree.

For happiness I long have sought,
And pleasure dearly I have bought:
I missed of all: but now I see
'Tis found in Christ the apple tree.

I'm weary with my former toil,
Here I will sit and rest awhile:
Under the shadow I will be
Of Jesus Christ the apple tree.

This fruit doth make my soul to thrive,
It keeps my dying faith alive;
Which makes my soul in haste to be
With Jesus Christ the apple tree.

A QUICK-START GUIDE FOR LOOKING UP AND BECOMING UNSTUCK

If you need clarity for direction in life, the following lists provide helpful pointers for discernment and follow-through. The titles are entries found in the different months.

Discernment for Life Goals:

January: All (Devotions on Personality)
February: Identity, Self-Sacrifice
March: Vison (Timing), Crisis (Wisdom), Mission: Specific Assignments, Callings (Roles)
April: Holy Spirit, Faith, Changed
May: Passion, Anointing, Direction, Life Goals, Dreams II, Purposes, Equipping and Design, Energy and Hope, Lament to Creativity
June: Look Up!, Glory!
July: Liberty, Clean and White: Moral Freedom, Truth, Childlike, Imagination, Justice
August: Land, Specific Goals

Follow-Through for Depth and Maturity

March: Waiting
April: Unstuck with an Updraft: Out of the Deep Freeze
May: Balance, Flight
June: Courage and Risk, Puddle Jumping, Wilbur's Wobblestacles, Charlotte's Entanglements
July: Play, Thinking, Faithfulness
August: Decisiveness, Work and Diligence, Initiative, Grace
September: Failure, Death of a Vision, Magnum Opus, Victory
October: Rest
November: Gratitude, Mustard Seed's Journey II
December: Joy, Established, Trough

May these devotions help you know the great God who gives passion and purpose for life. May you discover wisdom and nurture that increase your love for God and others while heightening your desire for justice and change. May you will grow more hopeful and energetic and gain initiative and inquisitiveness. May you become unstuck and launch to fly!

Employ a journal for your Radiant Action reflections.

JANUARY
PERSONALITY

Heart, Mind, Identity, Relationships, and Boundaries

January devotions focus on Fern, Wilbur, Templeton, and Charlotte, and consider five aspects of their personalities relatable to us as well. The apple tree in January is bare, with its structures exposed, providing us with a good metaphor for the bare branches of human personality. Abraham Lincoln loved looking at a winter tree. "The branches and crotches of trees interested him more in the wintertime, stripped of leaves and naked in design, than in the summer, when covered; he searched for basic anatomy of structure."[1]

The structures of personality included in January are emotions, thinking patterns and beliefs, identities (will, purpose, and preferences), relationships, and boundaries. This probe of inner dynamics is a useful way to promote emotional health within the context of learning to live through God's grace. January is traditionally the time when people set goals, and wholeness of personality is one worthy objective that affects all others.

Emotions are often the most powerful influencers when it comes to making decisions. However, thoughts and beliefs are strategic and weightier, for they give perspective, rein in emotion, and clarify identity. Insight about our identity—who we truly are in our will, preferences, and purposes—can reshape emotions and beliefs. Emotions, beliefs, and identity influence our relationships and help to form boundaries in those relationships. All these personality branches impact our goals for living. Ignoring them will undermine healthy growth in our personalities and our actions.

Fern's personality components are listed as Fern's Heart, Fern's Mind, Fern's Will, Purposes, and Preferences, Fern's Who, and Fern's Fences. The other three characters also have titles that correlate to their personas.

WEEK 1: FERN
Emotions and Motivations: Fern's Heart, *p. 15*
Thoughts and Beliefs: Fern's Mind, *p. 16*
Identity: Fern's Will, Purposes, and Preferences, *p. 17*
Relationships: Fern's Who, *p. 18*
Boundaries: Fern's Fences, *p. 19*

WEEK 2: WILBUR
Emotions and Motivations: Wilbur's Achy-Breaky Heart, *p. 20*
Thoughts and Beliefs: Pig Brains, *p. 21*
Identity: Wilbur's Will, Purposes, and Preferences *Hoof Am I?*, *p. 22*
Relationships: Pork Links, *p. 23*
Boundaries: Wilbur's Pen, *p. 24*

WEEK 3: TEMPLETON
Emotions and Motivations: The Rat's Nest, *p. 25*
Thoughts and Beliefs: Templeton's Dump, *p. 26*
Identity: Templeton's Will, Purposes, and Preferences, *p. 27*
Relationships: Strings Attached, *p. 28*
Boundaries: Templeton under the Trough, *p. 29*

WEEK 4: CHARLOTTE
Emotions and Motivations: The Heart of Charlotte, *p. 30*
Thoughts and Beliefs: Thinking Upside Down with Charlotte, *p. 31*
Identity: Charlotte's Will, Purposes, and Preferences, *p. 32*
Relationships: Charlotte's Web, *p. 33*
Boundaries: Charlotte's Outlook on Emotions, Time, and Talents, *p. 34*

DAY 1

Emotions and Motivations: Fern's Heart

"Control Myself?" yelled Fern.[2]

Fern's character bursts with intensity and diversity. Furious, she runs after her father to save Wilbur. Gentle, she gives Wilbur a bottle. Patient, she sits beside Wilbur on an old milk stool, listening to the animals. Playful, and like her emotions, she swings high and low with Avery from the barn loft.

Fern's emotional range is true for most of us. Emotions can grip us with the force of a wave rolling in from the outer seas in high wind. Or they can creep in subtly like foxes for a surprising but muted ambush. Whether sudden and forceful or subtle like morning mist, emotions can evolve, revolve, and resolve. They aren't bad in themselves, and they aren't to be denied, pushed down, and relegated to some nether inner world space where they fester.

Acknowledging negative emotions and restructuring them through scriptural perspective and counsel brings forth healing growth. The love and light of God can touch and redirect unhealthy feelings. As feelings come to the light for untangling, life springs up and out.

Jesus did not deny His grief over the death of Lazarus—John 11:35 tells us that He wept—yet in the depths of that grief He was motivated to bring life out of mourning. Jesus, both God and man, was and is outraged against sin, death, and the devil—those things that destroy people made in His image. He can laugh as well as cry with us. He empathizes with all our human feelings, weaknesses, and temptations. He gathers our tears and longs to shelter us under His wings (Heb. 4:15; Ps. 56:8; 91).

Jesus came to lift us up to a life we never dreamed of having—a life of fellowship with the Father who is the source of joy and peace. He is the spring of redeemed emotion, the orchestrator of hearts righted and in cadence with God and each other.

> *"The fruit of the Spirit is love, joy, peace, forbearance, kindness, goodness, faithfulness, gentleness and self-control"* (Gal. 5:22–23 NIV).

Prayer: Dear Lord, help me be aware of my feelings and offer them to You. Make me steadfast, not wavering like a fern in the breeze. Help me be aware of certain times of day, seasons, or situations that may trigger unwieldly emotions, for disaster can unfold if emotions rule unrestrained.

Radiant Action: Journal entry: What triggers my negative and positive feelings? Include a prayer.

Webs: Love (Feb.), Emotional Self-Control (Mar.), Unstuck (Apr.)

DAY 2

Thoughts and Beliefs: Fern's Mind

"The truck is rolling away, Papa," said Fern.[3]

Good thinking harnesses feral emotions. Fern is rational. She warns her distracted father about the truck for literally there was "no one at the wheel."[4] (This scene is a picture of the mania on the farm since Charlotte began weaving words and it is another critical moment in the plot—no truck, no fair, no prize, no more Wilbur). Fern's ability to glean facts from observation and from listening attentively in the barnyard form the foundation of her beliefs and a solid capacity to think clearly and decisively. She knows animals can talk because she's heard them. She uses this knowledge to persuade her skeptical mother to finish listening as she recounts Charlotte's colorful fish story. She can even go to combat and argue fiercely with her practical father about the life of the runt piglet.

Christians who observe the facts of Scripture and allow them with grace to shape beliefs, will find their thinking capacities growing. As we listen to God's voice in the Bible, we discover who God is and who we are in Him and our faith blossoms. As we grow in faith and biblical knowledge, our thinking, choosing, and ability to wisely channel emotions will be renewed. As Paul says, "Be transformed by the renewal of your mind, that by testing you may discern what is the will of God, what is good and acceptable and perfect" (Rom. 12:2).

Prayer: Dear Father, Jesus has promised us the Spirit of truth who will teach us all things. Shape my beliefs to Your truth and align my emotions under this truth. Thank You for Your armor for victorious living, specifically the helmet of salvation to protect my mind and the belt of truth around my being. These tools keep me out of the mud of fads and fantasies of this faltering, fading earth. These temptations sometimes call to me like Lurvy announcing the delivery of slops.

Radiant Action: Journal entry: What is my reading or listening Bible plan? I'll try to read or listen at least five minutes a day. My notes are treasures I will review.

Webs: Crisis (Mar.), Unstuck (Apr.), Courage (June)

Gleanings: "Whatever is true, whatever is honorable, whatever is just, whatever is pure, whatever is lovely, whatever is commendable, if there is any excellence, if there is anything worthy of praise, think about these things" (Phil. 4:8).

DAY 3

Identity: Fern's Will, Purposes, and Preferences

Fern raced off.[5]

Fern's purpose at age eight is to save and nurture a helpless piglet and enjoy the peaceful companionship of her barnyard friends. Fiercely passionate about Wilbur, her baby, she sits for hours with him. At nine she grows up; her identity matures. She gives up her animal companions. Fern isn't disloyal to Wilbur—rather, she moves naturally into a more grown-up stage, as Dr. Dorian predicts. Fern's identity changes its outer appearances, but her unique core identity of personality and giftings remains constant.

Like Fern, our priorities change as we mature and discover more of who we are. Circumstances and the original core personality underpin an individual's natural identity. A *believer's eternal* identity changes. The Christian has exchanged the old nature for a brand-new one. We become a new creation. Jesus's grace and redemption change the course of our preferences and purposes. Our identity of personality and giftings doesn't change, but it is redeemed. It flows from Whose we are and from what the Father says about us. He honors our personality and identity, shaping them into what He intended them to be, and one day, He will perfect us.

Paul reflects on this new identity, exclaiming, "Therefore if anyone is in Christ, he is a new creation. The old has passed away. Behold, the new has come" (2 Cor. 5:17)! In Christ you and I are forgiven and thus accepted, adopted, and chosen as His beloved children. We are called to His purpose and have become citizens of heaven. In this sense, we have a completely new mission as a friend to the Almighty who says nothing can separate us from Him, our Abba, our Daddy.

> "For we are his workmanship, created in Christ Jesus for good works, which God prepared beforehand, that we should walk in them" (Eph. 2:10).

Prayer: Father, thank You for making me Your child. You have made me a new creation. Help me to know who I am and Whose I am.

Radiant Action: Journal Entry: Study Ephesians 2:10, Romans 7 and 8. When I see a fern, I will ponder my purposes, giftings, specific missions, and new identity as a child of God.

Webs: Identity (Feb.), Calling "Here Pig" (Mar.), Purpose Series (May), Names (May)

Gleanings: "And they sang a new song, saying . . . You have made them a kingdom and priests to our God, and they shall reign on the earth" (Rev. 5:9–10).

DAY 4

Relationships: Fern's Who

Fern couldn't take her eyes off the tiny pig.[6]

Relationships shape identity, and identity shapes relationships. Fern has many stable and affecting bonds: her family, her community, Dr. Dorian, Wilbur, Charlotte, her barnyard friends, the Zuckermans, and Henry Fussy. Dr. Dorian influenced Mrs. Arable for good. Fern's friendships with the animals shaped her for good. Relationships, like right thinking, can help us get unstuck and into healthy thinking, doing, and being: "As iron sharpens iron, so one person sharpens another" (Prov. 27:17 NIV).*

God is the only powerful source of constructive core redemption. We cannot choose our birth families—our parents and siblings—who form so much of our soul. But knowing God as our best friend and knowing what He says about who we are changes us for good and forever.

> "You are my friends if you do what I command you. No longer do I call you servants, for the servant does not know what his master is doing; but I have called you friends, for all that I have heard from my Father I have made known to you" (John 15:14–15).

Prayer: God, You who call Your followers friends, help me to examine my relationships and the health of them. Shape my heart to be unselfish in learning to love others and soften my will to be accountable to those I can trust. Help me to put You first in all things. Convict me when I'm not allowing You to be the most important relationship. It is by loving You that I'm able to love others. You are my Father, my Brother, my Helper, my Guide.

Radiant Action: Journal Entries: 1. Relationship evaluation: Whom I am influencing and who is influencing me? Who is in my inmost circle? 2. Are these friends primarily positive or negative? Are they faithful? Do they have integrity? 3. Do they hold me accountable? 4. Am I faithful and have integrity? 5. Who is in my next broadest circle? 6. To whom do I go for comfort? Who comes to me? 7. Am I someone who seeks the good of another, or am I someone who seeks the other to do me good? 8. What about the social media factor?

Webs: Friendship (Feb.), Love (Feb.), Teamwork (Feb.)

*But relationships can also be negative influences. "Do not be misled: 'Bad company corrupts good character'" (1 Cor. 15:33 NIV).

DAY 5

Boundaries: Fern's Fences

"I'm just telling you the facts."[7]

Outwardly Fern seems to be a quiet, uncomplaining child. Although she obeys her mother and sets the table for breakfast, she stands up to her father and argues with her mother. Fern has boundaries for what she will allow others to do in her life.

Boundaries keep our identity and personhood separate from another's. As Cloud and Townsend explain, "You do not exist in a vacuum; you exist in relation to God and others. Your boundaries define you in relation to others."[8] Boundaries mark where one person ends, and another begins.

A good understanding of one's identity is part of building good boundaries. Misunderstanding the core of who we are leads to a crisis in boundaries and to behaviors of either assuming too much or too little responsibility. Sometimes, after caring for a helpless parent for an extended period, one may be prone to continue taking on disproportionate responsibility for others. On the other hand, one might be on the receiving end of too much help and remain passive and irresponsible for making their own choices.

Good boundaries keep out enemies as did the walls of ancient cities where broken walls meant death or captivity (see Amos 1:10; 4:3). Nehemiah took time to examine the walls of Jerusalem and then, because of their critical significance, to rebuild them with urgency despite targeted opposition. And so, we need to examine our own identity, walls, and boundaries and repair what may be damaged.

Knowing we are made in God's image and that He loves us helps us understand that it's okay to set healthy limits on the negative behavior of others. Knowing Him gives us wisdom about our capacities; He helps us build and maintain healthy boundaries, so we know where we end, and others begin.

Prayer: Father, teach me what is appropriate in giving support and receiving help. Examine the walls of my identity and see if there are any holes in my understanding of who I am and for what I am responsible. Rebuild my walls where they are damaged.

Radiant Action: Journal entries: 1. What are my responsibilities or roles? 2. How am I nurturing myself? 3. Do I take on responsibility that belongs to others? 4. Am I too prone to help another at the expense of my own good? 5. Am I letting someone else take up my responsibilities?

Webs: Expectations of Others (Feb.), Emotional Self-Control (Mar.), Equipping (May)

Gleanings: "The prudent see danger and take refuge" (Prov. 27:12 NIV).

DAY 6

Emotions and Motivations: Wilbur's Achy-Breaky Heart

[Wilbur] would . . . gaze at her with adoring eyes.[9]

Wilbur is vibrantly emotional. He is fainting and hyperexcitable. But when he's bored, he tires of living. When given bad news, he dramatically throws himself down. He ping pongs between feeling horrified, sad, full of energy and hope, embarrassed, in love with life, and radiant. He worries excessively, blushes, cries, trembles, and displays exuberance.

It is good to feel. It is how we are made. But how can we wrestle our emotions into moderation when they overwhelm? It is worth the struggle, the straining effort, to find emotional balance and the abundant life Jesus promises. He sets the captives free, unbinding them from tentacles of fear, shame, inordinate sadness, disconsolate despair, or other feelings that rupture equilibrium.

The first step toward freedom is to acknowledge enervating emotions. Then talk to Jesus about them. He invites us to come to Him however we feel: "Come to me, all you who are weary and burdened, and I will give you rest. Take my yoke upon you and learn from me, for I am gentle and humble in heart, and you will find rest for your souls. For my yoke is easy and my burden is light" (Matt. 11:28–30 NIV).

Prayer: Dear Creator of the universe, nothing is too hard for You, and nothing too small. I ask You to recreate my fallen emotions and give me hope and perspective. Cleanse me of what is negative and give me power to control and direct my feelings in healthy ways. Thank You for forgiving me when I swerve too far emotionally. I'm so grateful that You understand me. Help me balance my physical self to help stabilize my emotions.

Radiant Action: Journal Entries: 1. Am I often frustrated, maybe overly so? 2. Am I anxious much of the time? 3. Do I feel dominated by another person? 4. Am I thankful? Joyful? 5. Why am I feeling this way? 6. Do these feelings reflect truths that anchor me, such as the certainty that God is working on my behalf? 7. Do they reflect that He is with me and will never leave me?

Webs: Belonging and Adoption (Feb.), Holy Spirit (Apr.), Energy and Hope (May)

DAY 7

Thoughts and Beliefs: Pig Brains

"Who's going to save me? . . . How?"[10]

All too often, Wilbur fails to use his brains in situations, reacting instead with pure emotion and great grunts of desperation. He faints rather than embrace adventure and opportunity. He chooses scraps over freedom and security over open fields.

Yet, like Fern, he is gifted with curiosity and a strong intellect, and throughout the story we see him advance in mental prowess. He's an observer. He forms opinions. He asks questions. He defines vocabulary words ("frolic" for Templeton). He makes judgments, complaining that Templeton is "destroying other people's property"[11] and doesn't behave like a decent animal. He considers Charlotte cruel and bloodthirsty. Later, he reconsiders the concept of a web and ascertains that it's a good thing. He allows Charlotte to tutor him in thinking and education. He becomes increasingly thoughtful and can even assess when he's not thinking of much. He names Charlotte's offspring according to logic.

Wilbur asks questions when trying to spin a web: "How do I start?"[12] He uses his brains to make some solid choices. He chooses to trust in Charlotte and her plan. He turns from raw drama and despair to a position of reasoning with Templeton, persuading the rat to thrust his bloated body up the wall. He carries Charlotte's egg sac, unnoticed and protected, in the only logical place—his mouth.

God created humans to be thinking beings. He expects us to develop and use our minds. "Jesus replied, 'Love the Lord your God with all your heart and with all your soul and *with all your mind*'" (Matt. 22:37 NIV—emphasis mine). In Isaiah 1:18, the Lord extends an invitation to exercise our minds, saying, "Come now, let us reason together."

Prayer: Father, like You, I can think. How grateful I am for the life of my mind. Please help me to develop my mental capacity and reasoning ability. Shape my beliefs with truth from Your Word and not from ragged, unfettered, scattered emotions. Enable me to renew my mind each day with Your Word that is sharper than a two-edged sword and can help me to think clearly and truthfully. Unfetter my mind by the power of Your Spirit.

Radiant Action: Journal entries: 1. What makes me foggy? Sharp? 2. How do the fruits of the Spirit, love, joy, peace, patience, kindness, goodness, faithfulness, gentleness, self-control, affect my thinking?

Webs: Thoughts and Beliefs Series (Jan.), Energy and Hope (May), Unseen (June)

DAY 8

Identity: Wilbur's Will, Purposes, and Preferences: *Hoof Am I?*

He loved life and loved to be a part of the world.[13]

Wilbur sees his ideal self as wild and free, snuffling for truffles. The farmers see Wilbur as a runty spring pig destined to become bacon, chops, and ribs. As Wilbur comprehends this ill intent, he resists. He inwardly knows that he is more than a side of pork. Charlotte, too, knows Wilbur is much more than breakfast. He has the capacity to be a loyal and winsome friend— "Some Pig," "Terrific," "Radiant," and "Humble."

Finding one's identity and defining the strong components in it that give fire to life is not easy. Instead of being rooted in what we can achieve or even do for others, identity for the believer derives from our relationship with the Creator of everything. When we rest in His love for us and in the confidence that we can do nothing to earn His love, we can be secure enough to begin to know ourselves truly. We are new creations, set free to walk in newness of life.

Who then or what can stop us from becoming who God intends us to be? We *can* become who God intends for us to become. Consider Peter. Jesus turned this cowering disciple—the one who melted under the stare of a servant girl—into the rock upon which He built His church.

> *"Fear not, for I have redeemed you; I have called you by name, you are mine"* (Isa. 43:1).

Prayer: God, You are the One who guides my life and makes a way for me, whether in triumphs or troubles. You root me in who You are and in what Your Son has done for me. You seal and fill me with Your Spirit. You mold me into who I need to be and save me from the purposelessness of a merely material world. Help me to trust how You made me, and free me from any limitations designed by the enemy.

Radiant Action: Journal entries: 1. Do I trust God for how I am made: scars, weaknesses, strengths, and gifts? 2. Do I accept family origin, gender, skin color, features? 3. When I look into a mirror, I will remind myself of Hoof (Who and Whose) I am. I will say, "I am a child of God and I have a future. My value is not in what I can do, but in the fact that God loves me."

Webs: Identity (Feb.), Humble (Feb.), Calling: "Here Pig" (Mar.), Mission (Mar.), Vision (Mar.)

DAY 9

Relationships: Pork Links

He realized that friendship is one of the most satisfying things in the world.[14]

Wilbur is Fern's baby, complete with bottle and nipple. Lurvy, Farmer Zuckerman, and Mrs. Zuckerman shelter him. The sheep, Templeton, Charlotte, the geese, and later, Charlotte's babies, are his companions. Wilbur's identity is bound up in those relationships.

Charlotte believes in Wilbur from the start. Of all the pig's community, Charlotte best envisions his potential. She sees Wilbur not only as a pig, but a friend and a hub who can bring people together and nurture hope for all.

This friendship between pig and spider brought life to both. Wilbur's worst day of rain, boredom, and loneliness crashed in upon him after a futile search for a friend. Then, "out of the darkness, came a small voice he had never heard before."[15] Wilbur realizes his future depends on Charlotte. In turn, her future generations in the barn depend on Wilbur.

Identity and destiny, although molded by the Creator, are bound to and influenced by other earthly creatures. As believers, our relationships carry divine significance. God calls us to belong to His group of friends, the body of believers. His will is for us to love one another and be an active part of His body, the church.

Wilbur is a promise keeper, telling Charlotte's offspring who remained in the barn that he will always be their friends. This faithfulness is a key quality for anyone who belongs to Christ: "Now you are the body of Christ, and each one of you is a part of it" (1 Cor. 12:27 NIV).

Prayer: Thank You for calling me to be a member of Your group of friends. Make me a good friend to You and to others. Teach me how to be a helpful part of the church.

Radiant Action: Journal entries: 1. Who is drawing me into their web of motivations and thinking, molding my identity by what they say about me or to me and by their actions towards me and their expectations of me? 2. Is there someone I can befriend and build up to see themselves in a new light that could release an unexpected potential?

Webs: Friendship (Feb.), Teamwork (Feb.), Communication in Community (Mar.), Barnyard Disciples (Mar.)

DAY 10

Boundaries: Wilbur's Pen

Wilbur felt queer to be outside his fence.[16]

A boundary can be physical as well as a part of the intangible personality. Wilbur's physical boundary is a pen equipped with a trough on the lowest level of an old barn. Although he experiences a short-lived escapade into the wild farmyard beyond his pen, he discovers that the outrageous freedom outside it offers nothing but confusion and anxiety. Despite the cheers of the goose and the admiration of the other animals, Wilbur resolutely chooses the quiet and safe, if boring, confines of the place where he is fed. The boundaries of his physical location mold Wilbur's emotions, thinking, identity, and relationships.

Charlotte trains Wilbur to have emotional boundaries. At times she forbids him to plunge into despair. "Be quiet, Wilbur!"[17] She coaches him on how to handle rudeness and self-centered behavior. She trains him to think of himself as "Some Pig," a "Terrific" pig, and a "Radiant" pig. At last, he knows that being humble and low to the ground is better than being a gigantic bumpkin of a hog.

We can establish healthy emotional boundaries by using good tools such as Christian counselors, and good books like Cloud and Townsend's *Boundaries* series and the Scazzero's *Emotionally Healthy Spirituality* series. Asking yourself hard questions is also a helpful way to assess the health of your emotional boundaries. It isn't fruitful to be confused about identity in close relationships.

God can train the mind and heart so that positive thoughts replace negative ones, and we let wisdom rule in relationships. Jesus taught us to be servants, but not all serving is within the boundaries of what is God-honoring.

Prayer: Dear God, give me grace and wisdom to know how to preserve my own healthy boundaries without selfishness or self-promotion. Help me to think healthy thoughts about myself.

Radiant Action: Journal Entries: 1. Do I know where "I" end and others begin? Am I enmeshed in certain close but detrimental relationships? 2. Am I able to say "no" to requests that are harmful or not in the path God has for me? 3. Can I say "yes" to relationships that nurture my well-being remembering that self-sacrifice is required in committed relationships?

Webs: Boundary Series (Jan.), Direction (May), Balance (May)

DAY 11

Emotions and Motivations: The Rat's Nest

"I'll appeal to his baser instincts, of which he has plenty."[18]

Templeton resents Charlotte for inconveniencing him when she requests him to fetch words, even though the rat routinely goes to the dump and woodshed. He mocks Wilbur for failure to spin a web. He disparages Wilbur at the fair when the hog called Uncle wins the blue ribbon. He delights in biting the curly tail when Wilbur faints. Templeton cleverly exploits the crisis of Charlotte's impending death to pontificate on the lack of appreciation due him. He has what James calls "bitter jealousy and selfish ambition" in his heart (James 3:14). Paul's words are true of Templeton as well as the Cretans: "Their god is their belly, and they glory in their shame" (Phil. 3:19).

Who are the Templetons in your life? Who is it who sucks out all your positive emotions? Can you believe that God can use this person or group of persons for your good? He can and will. After all, it's the Templetons of the world, the Judases, who move forward the plans of God. In Genesis, Joseph testifies to his brothers who had sought his harm, "As for you, you meant evil against me, but God meant it for good, to bring it about that many people should be kept alive, as they are today" (Gen. 50:20; see also Prov. 16:4; Rom. 8:28).

Or, an even deeper question, what Templeton lurks inside of you, and what triggers it?

Prayer: Father, purge me of rank self-glory and indulgence. Help me believe that You will take care of those who trouble me. May the grace they see in my life draw them to You. Help me to be wise and not naïve by putting my confidence in untrustworthy people having Templeton's characteristics. "Like a bad tooth or a lame foot is trust in a faithless person in time of trouble" (Prov. 25:19 NRSVUE).

Radiant Action: Journal Entries: 1. What "rats" are in my own "attic" of mind and heart? Self-interest and self-pity? Pride or self-absorption? Reflect on the the cross, our powerful means of deliverance. The Templeton in me is crucified with Christ and new life arises through the Spirit (Rom. 8). 2. What is ugly about others that might really be a blessing?

Webs: Enemies (Mar.), Surprising Deliverers (Apr.), Captured: Sin (Apr.)

DAY 12

Thoughts and Beliefs: Templeton's Dump

"I'll tell you what I'll do . . ."[19]

Rats are intelligent, and Templeton is intelligent in his own surly way. He can think things through. He plans. He fixes his nest for winter. He reasons that that there must be a goose egg that didn't hatch and that losing weight is not worth longer life. He understands causality, admitting that Wilbur will die if nothing is done to save him. Templeton gives opinions. He is even conscious of what motivates him to act.

Although he's a slick bargainer, Templeton's selfishness makes him easily manipulated with promises of food. He is shrewd, and shrewdness, often perceived as craftiness with deceitful intent, can also indicate the ability to apply wisdom to navigate in this world. Jesus commends a dishonest manager for this trait. He tells us to be alert, perceptive, and worldly wise like Templeton because we live amid wolves (see Matt. 10:16; Luke 16:8).

Prayer: Lord, make me shrewd in the right ways—thinking things through before acting, planning, being resourceful and curious, asking the right questions, and recognizing my places of temptation. Cleanse me of the need for recognition and projecting on others my own faults.

Radiant Action: Journal Entries: 1. What challenging situations am I in that require shrewdness and care? 2. Do I have difficult, Templeton-like people in my life? 3. What are two strategies from God's wisdom that will help manage their attempts to cower, shame, exploit, or harm me?

Webs: Thoughts and Beliefs Series (Jan.), Smelling (Mar.), Captured: Sin (Apr.)

DAY 13

Identity: Templeton's Will, Purposes, and Preferences

"You know how he is—always looking out for himself."[20]

Templeton is a useful example of the old nature, the human heart before redemption. As a biblical character, the rat would likely be a soldier gambling greedily for Jesus's clothing or a Herod dealing death to the innocents in pursuit of power. He could be a Judas creeping along the wall to inform the Jews of Jesus's location. His motto is always, "What's in it for me?"

Yet Templeton has some good in him. He has gifts. He can tie knots, climb, reason, and forage. He has sharp teeth that are useful. He is resourceful. He stashes away bits of string that Wilbur will use, though unsuccessfully, in his silly attempt to spin a web. He finds trash in the woodshed that ironically leads to the third winning web word— "Radiant."

Templeton uses the discarded, the insignificant, the disgusting. One writer describes resourcefulness as the "wise use of that which others would normally overlook or discard."[21] This is a trait of our God, who sees potential in us despite our frailty and rebellious unrestraint. God saves us from the dump, cleans us up, and uses us for good.

Despite himself, Templeton is a comical hero who steps in at times of dire need, and ironically, it's always because of his selfishness. He hoards the rotten egg that saves Charlotte. He finds the right word, although reluctantly, through his indulgent revelry. He revives Wilbur from a faint by biting his tail so the pig can get his prize. His long, ugly teeth snip through web thread to rescue the egg sac for Wilbur, but once again, he's self-serving and motivated only by the promise of Wilbur's slops.

Templeton is amusing in some ways, but he also could be considered "a muse" in the sense that he provides Charlotte with words from the dump, and thus he inspires her writing. May the difficult personalities in our lives give us inspiration for achievement.

Prayer: Father, thank You for making a way for us as Your children to change from our basic selfish tendencies. Make me resourceful. Help me also to be resourceful in looking for the good in others. If there's any humor in someone, help me see it.

Radiant Action: Journal Entries: 1. What can help me grow curiosity, creativity, and resourcefulness? 2. How can I develop my sense of humor?

Webs: Small Things (Feb.), Mud and Manure (Mar.), Lament to Creativity (May), Humor (July), Scraps and Slops (Nov.)

DAY 14

Relationships: Strings Attached

"I'm staying right here," grumbled the rat. "I haven't the slightest interest in fairs."[22]

Selfishness abhors relationship. Templeton knows nothing of the warmth or give-and-take of friendship—his narcissism precludes it. He's absent from the barn community meeting on Wilbur's behalf and dismisses the gathering when he finally shows up, creeping along the wall. He's a loner and an outlaw, the Scrooge of the barnyard. Dickens describes Scrooge as resembling a rat creeping along an alley: "To edge his way along the crowded paths of life, warning all human sympathy to keep its distance."[23] Templeton could have exclaimed, "Bah, Humbug!" and not have surprised anyone.

Templeton lived alone and for his own interests. Some people prefer to be alone, but most of us humans prefer some company and suffer at times from loneliness. Understandably, many factors can lead to social isolation, such as moving to a new place, pandemics and quarantines, distrust stemming from abuse, and many others. But often it's sin and our own selfishness that cause us to forgo godly fellowship and settle for shallow acquaintances. After all, that way we can retain our independence and live however we like.

As for our divine connection, we are, in our fallen nature, alienated from God and are not able to reach out for Him. Instead, God saw our helpless situation and reached out for us.

"God shows his love for us in that while we were still sinners, Christ died for us." (Rom. 5:6–8).

Prayer: Make me aware of selfishness in my life and change me to be more like the humble servant Jesus. Thank You for being my Friend and Brother. Help me to be a worthy friend to those around me. Instead of creeping away, guide me to embrace their needs and stick by them.

Radiant Action: Journal Entry: What are examples of God's unselfish love to me? I won't focus on what others have done to hurt or ignore me. "We love because he first loved us" (1 John 4:19).

Webs: Aloneness (Feb.), Loneliness (Feb.), Love (Feb.), Enemies (Mar.)

Gleanings: "Beloved, let us love one another, for love is from God, and whoever loves has been born of God and knows God" (1 John 4:7).

DAY 15

Boundaries: Templeton under the Trough

He did not like being treated like a messenger boy.[24]

Templeton keeps his boundaries fixed as stone and keeps everyone else outside them. He easily says "no" to anything that inconveniences him. Being able to say "no" is an integral part of setting healthy emotional boundaries. But Templeton always refuses anything requiring sacrifice. At the moment of desperate need, refusing to comply with Wilbur's desperate pleas, the rat lays back in the straw and spurns Wilbur's cry as he laments with reeking self-pity the lack of appreciation due him.[25]

Templeton's physical boundaries or places he likes to inhabit include the dump, a nest under a pig's trough, an old shed, the perimeter of the barnyard, and pathways to and fro for foraging through rubbish. By the end of the story, his body is as large as a woodchuck because of his greedy gobbling.

In direct contrast to the egotistical, self-absorbed, socially isolated rodent, Jesus broke through the boundaries of heaven and the limitations of earth to bring us life far more abundant than hoarding stuff and running the rat race. Jesus understood our isolation and loneliness; He knew our need for belonging, forgiveness, a new heart, and a new start.

Prayer: Father, I praise You for sending Jesus down from heaven to live as we do on our earthly plane. I marvel that the members of the Trinity—Father, Son, and Holy Spirit—have lived in fellowship throughout time and eternity. The triune God is the essence of love, sending the Son to die and rise for us, and the Holy Spirit to empower and guide us.

Help me, dear Lord, to see where I need to break through emotional or physical boundaries by the power of Your Spirit, to love You, love my brother and my sister, and to minister fruitfully and faithfully to others. By Your grace, may I not be like the seed that keeps its shell intact but dies only with itself for comfort, nor be like the rat sneaking and creeping through life concerned solely with its rat self. Change my "I won't" to "I will."

Radiant Action: Journal Entry: Who is the Spirit nudging me to reach out to today? I'll write down the name, put the note where I will see it, then "do good to" that other.

Webs: Identity (Feb.), Captured: Sin (Apr.), Life Goals (May)

DAY 16

Emotions and Motivations: The Heart of Charlotte

"Never hurry and never worry!"[26]

Like her eight legs, Charlotte's heart is complex. She is no-nonsense, loyal, hardworking, confident, persevering, and undemanding of attention. She is bloodthirsty, yet wise. She is sometimes moody, sometimes sweet, sometimes delighted, sometimes proud, and sometimes sad (but rarely).

She doesn't indulge in tears when torn between her need and Wilbur's. Will she make her egg sac at the fair or stay in the secure and comfortable barnyard? Her concern is for his best interest. Despite her weakened state, she decides to uproot herself and go to the fair—all for love of Wilbur.

Charlotte casts a microscopic shadow of the self-sacrifice and love God has toward us. In His great, tenderhearted love for us, God took pity on the weak. Caring more for our future than His comfort, Jesus uprooted Himself from heaven—His perfect haven. He now sends out His own people by the power of the Spirit to uncomfortable places. Mark 4:35–41 tells the story of Jesus sending his disciples directly into a storm. Their journey would bring only one person, the demoniac, to faith. But the demoniac became the missionary to his region.

Prayer: God, train my motivations to align with the cross. Every time self-pity and self-indulgence tempt me, or the desire for public honor or private wealth draw me, help me to remember Jesus's sacrifice and His will to love me with everything He is. Help me make the right choice when for someone else's sake I need to risk something and reach out and go. Don't let me choose to stay comfortable in my pleasant harbor.

Radiant Action: Journal Entries: Jesus chose to do the Father's will in laying down His life for me. "My Father, if it is possible, may this cup be taken from me. Yet not as I will but as you will" (Matt. 26:39 NIV). 1. How does His sacrifice impact me? 2. What does it mean for me in terms of radical transformation?

Webs: Self-sacrifice (Feb.), Love (Feb.), Teamwork (Feb.)

DAY 17

Thoughts and Beliefs: Thinking Upside Down with Charlotte

"I have to be sharp and clever . . . I have to think things out."[27]

Charlotte's tiny spider brain holds an immense world of thought. She lives by her wits and keeps her mind sharp by not eating too much. She hangs upside down to think so blood goes to her head, allowing her to reflect carefully and without distraction. She's not in a hurry. She waits for her thoughts to congeal in the same way her sting congeals her prey.

Her vocabulary is superb, her speech refined. She teaches words. She teaches processes, telling Wilbur how to spin a web. She's a gifted storyteller. Like a philosopher, she assesses her trick to fool Mr. Zuckerman (Was White crafting a pun with the farmer's name—*Sucker*man?) by convincing him that Wilbur was a special pig who should be spared from becoming a Christmas ham—and she thinks the plan will work.

Charlotte's trick started with her keen observation of Zuckerman whom she discerned was gullible and craved recognition. She thought and thought, then devised a plan based on insight into his character. With Wilbur and his fate, she discerned the limits and scope of the problem, and weighed the possibilities, then waged war with brilliant intelligence against certain tragedy.

Her upside-down thinking suggests that we, too, should look for upside-down solutions and perspectives that are outside the box of standard. As a wise and resourceful teacher, she makes Wilbur think, learn the meaning of words, question and ask why, and consider the future.

Every day, Charlotte reworks her web. Like webs, minds can fray. Like Charlotte, it is good to take time to reknit the threads of thoughts tattered from weariness, confusion, despair, or waywardness: "Be transformed by the renewal of your mind." (Rom. 12:2).

Prayer: God, give me clear thinking and strategies for difficult situations. Help me to think "upside down" if necessary and avoid eating too much.

Radiant Action: Journal Entries: 1. New vocabulary word every day to help me be more articulate. (See Merriam-Webster's Word of the Day.) 2. How does Charlotte change Wilbur's future by thinking, planning, and commitment? Is it possible to prepare for an impending or future crisis or conflict by observing the facts, weighing the possibilities, knowing the nature of my opponent, and being willing to look at unusual solutions?

Webs: Friendship (Feb.), Mission (Mar.), Vision (Mar.)

DAY 18

Identity: Charlotte's Will, Purposes, and Preferences

A true friend and a good writer.[28]

The name Charlotte means "free man" or "petite." It's the perfect name for the tiny heroine who gains Wilbur's freedom. Charlotte is both educated and educator. She's a writer, a storyteller, and a clear communicator. Although she's a fictional character, Charlotte has glimmers of traits we can recognize in each person of the Trinity.

The Father is omniscient and aware of our need. God plans our escape from eternal death. Charlotte knows all about her world and Charlotte thinks and plans Wilbur's rescue.

Jesus is called the Word. Charlotte is passionate about words.

Jesus chooses to lay down His life. For all of mankind, there is only one Savior: "For there is one God, and there is one mediator between God and men, the man Christ Jesus" (1 Tim. 2:5). Charlotte is Wilbur's one savior, sacrificing comfort and convenience for him. (She, however, does not have any choice in her death, only her place of death.)

Jesus went ahead to prepare a heavenly future and home for us. Charlotte prepares a future on a farm for Wilbur. Jesus was born in a manger; Charlotte's home is in the barn, and she delivers her egg sac in a shed.

Jesus is Immanuel—God with us. Charlotte is Wilbur's friend and faithfully accompanies him through his trials to the end.

All scatter at Jesus's death except for a few women and the disciple John. The Arables and Zuckermans, Wilbur, and Templeton depart for the farm. Charlotte dies alone.

The Holy Spirit is called Comforter, Paraclete, Advocate, the Helper. The Holy Spirit reproves and empowers; He makes the believer brave. He is the Spirit of wisdom and understanding. He spotlights Jesus and remains in the background. We also observe Charlotte's loving acts as she helps, comforts, reproves, and empowers Wilbur but keeps a low profile. The spotlight is on Wilbur, not the clever spider.

The Holy Spirit desires our freedom and empowers it (see Eph. 3:14–19); Charlotte works tirelessly for Wilbur's freedom and peaceful future.

Prayer: Almighty God, as we consider Charlotte to be a merely microscopic shadow of the Trinity, give us spiritual sight and the imagination to recognize glimmers of Your perfect nature in things great and small in our world.

Radiant Action: A small spider will remind me of the Trinity.

Webs: Motherhood (May), Equipping and Design (May), Purpose Series (May)

Gleanings: "The spider taketh hold with her hands and is in kings' palaces" (Prov. 30:28 KJV).

DAY 19

Relationships: Charlotte's Web

"Your success in the ring this morning was, to a small degree, my success." [29]

Charlotte is a leader. To lead, one must have relationships with followers. The barnyard community cooperates with her, and Wilbur trusts her. She communicates well with those under her influence and is intelligent and persuasive.

Charlotte is a protector. Spiders have eight legs like the ribs of a large umbrella. As an umbrella protects from sun and rain, Charlotte shields Wilbur from loneliness and death while finding success and satisfaction for herself. Life, she believes, is built by lifting others up.

Charlotte is faithful. She never leaves Wilbur until the task is done. She accepts Wilbur for who he is. Likewise, God loves us as we are. This love doesn't stop with us—Jesus commands us to love one another.

"Therefore welcome one another as Christ has welcomed you" (Rom. 15:7).

Prayer: Dear God, open my eyes to see those near me, and show me how I can lift them up even though it might be inconvenient. Help me to build solid relationships with You and others so I can learn to love as You have loved me.

Radiant Action: Journal Entries: 1. How I can find meaning and purpose through community? What is my identity within my ring of relationships? 2. How can I uplift others with the resources I've been given?

Webs: Teamwork (Feb.), Communication in Community (Mar.)

DAY 20

Boundaries: Charlotte's Outlook on Emotions, Time, and Talents

> *"If they would hang head-down at the top of the thing and wait quietly, maybe something good would come along."*[30]

Charlotte exercises emotional boundaries by curbing excessive emotion. She has a New Englander's practical approach to feelings, seen in her directness when she rebukes Wilbur and reprimands the lamb for shaming Wilbur. She tells Templeton in no uncertain terms that if he plans to sneak off at the fair to indulge his greedy appetite, he'd better bring back a word.

She can say "no" in a healthy way. To conserve energy, she refuses to sing a song for Wilbur so she can make something for herself.[31] The goose proposes she weave "Terrific, Terrific, Terrific." But Charlotte refuses to take on such an impossible task, declaring that she would have to do the St. Vitus dance.[32]

Charlotte has physical boundaries. She is limited by time—after laying her eggs, she will die. A boy almost kills her with a stick.

In considering Charlotte's limitations, we find compelling parallels with Jesus. The One without physical boundaries and with limitless love bound Himself in a fragile human body of flesh to give us unlimited access to God, unlimited grace while living, and unlimited, unseen riches forever as our inheritance. The all-powerful Creator—born as a baby—living with human frailty—dying by crucifixion.

Charlotte would not let rats, inconvenient timing, or physical weakness deter her. Neither did Jesus allow religious leaders, the failures of His followers, or the devil's schemes deter Him from the purpose He came to fulfill.

Prayer: Dear Savior, be magnified in my life. Despite my weakness, be glorified. You can do more than I can even think or imagine. Make me willing to go beyond my comfort levels to follow You. Help me to be wise in how I use my limited emotional and physical capabilities.

Radiant Action: Journal Entries: 1. How can God's grace shine through my weaknesses? 2. What limitations do I have that I am using as excuses for not serving?

Webs: Insignificance (Feb.), Mission (Mar.), Purpose Series (May), Equipping and Design (May)

Gleanings: "Not that we are sufficient of ourselves to think anything as of ourselves; but our sufficiency is of God" (2 Cor. 3:5 KJV).

FEBRUARY
RELATIONSHIPS

February is a month of formation. The apple tree will be budding before long! An apple can be an affectionate reference to a loved one, as in "He is the apple of my eye." This is the month to consider relationships to oneself and others, such as close friends or a marriage partner or the people in your community. In these devotions, we ponder what joys and hindrances may arise in these connections.

RELATIONSHIP TO SELF
Identity, *p. 36*
Some Pig, Some People, *p. 37*
Terrific, *p. 38*
Radiant, *p. 39*
Humble, *p. 40*
Runtiness, *p. 41*
Small Things, *p. 42*
Insignificance, *p. 43*
Weakness, *p. 44*
Loneliness, *p. 45*
Aloneness, *p. 46*

RELATIONSHIP TO OTHERS
Teamwork: The Power of Together, *p. 47*
Friendship, *p. 49*
Love, *p. 50*
Marriage, *p. 51*
Belonging and Adoption, *p. 52*
Finding the Good in the Bad, *p. 53*
Self-Sacrifice, *p. 54*
Waiting for the Dawn, *p. 55*
Expectations of Others: Do What?, *p. 56*

DAY 1

Identity

"Well, you're a good little pig, and radiant you shall be."[1]

Wilbur imitates Charlotte by trying to weave a web but discovers he's ill-equipped. Despite his sincerest exertions, being a web weaver is simply not a part of his identity. Happily, the words Charlotte cast become the foundations of who Wilbur really is. He becomes the "Some Pig" that turns the community upside down. He acts "terrific" and "radiant" once he is named as such, and in the end, is the essence of a humble personality that wins the grand prize.

Some Pig | Terrific | Radiant | Humble

God speaks words of life over His children as well. We are who He says we are. The time is now to jettison lies formed in us from others and to embrace what God says about us. If we don't, we will flop around in life without direction like Wilbur outside his pen. Without the security of knowing that our true identity is found in Christ, we will be prone to more defensiveness, jealousy, and even resentfulness of others we perceive as being more intelligent, talented, attractive, or more accomplished than we are.

But if you know the Lord your Maker, you'll gain a growing understanding of your intrinsic value. Your identity and calling are based on what or in whom your trust lays. Knowing you are eternally and completely loved by the Almighty Creator, redeemed by His Son, and sealed for heaven roots you in the solid soil of a secure identity. Having these truths planted deep in the innermost self allows our true personality to blossom and the lies of the enemy to wither away. Nourished by God's words of life, we are becoming who we are meant to be.

After Jesus rose from the dead, He talked to Peter privately by the shore. He called him by his old name, Simon, to emphasize that he was no longer held by the old identity. He became Peter, the rock, and that meant getting busy doing what his new identity compelled. This, too, is our charge.

Prayer: Awesome Designer, I trust that You know me and love me. You made me in Your image. Show me who I am in You and how to refute the negative voices from the devil, myself, and others who would say I am not who *You* say I am.

Radiant Action: I will listen on Youtube.com to the song "You Say" by Lauren Daigle.

Webs: Identity Series (Jan.), Equipping and Design (May), Purpose Series (May)

Gleanings: "O Lord, you have searched me and known me!" (Ps. 139:1).

DAY 2

Some Pig, Some People

"It's the pig that's unusual."[2]

Wilbur needs a miracle. Charlotte performs four of them: four words that not only secure his future but shape his character. She gives Wilbur a superior identity by what she writes about him. He is *some* pig because "it says so, right there."[3]

Like Wilbur, we need a miracle for our future too. And we have one. Jesus has made the way for forgiveness and reconciliation with God. We are new creations. We are *some people* in Christ. And God says so about us, right there in His Word.

We are . . .
new creations (2 Cor. 5:17)
sealed by the Holy Spirit (Eph. 1:13)
loved by Him first (1 John 4:19) and greatly loved (Rom. 1:7)
adopted (like Wilbur) into God's family (Eph. 1:5)
protected (2 Thess. 3:3)
complete through union with Christ, who is the head over every ruler and authority (Col. 2:10 NLT)
equipped with powerful armor (Eph. 6:10–18)
the salt of the earth (Matt. 5:13)
citizens of heaven (Phil. 3:20)
given the ministry of reconciliation (2 Cor. 5:18)
comforted (2 Cor. 1:4)
at peace with God (Rom. 5:1)
ambassadors (2 Cor. 5:20)

We have . . .
the Spirit of power, love, and self-control (2 Tim. 1:7)
authority over the enemy (Luke 10:19)
an inheritance in heaven waiting for us (1 Peter 1:4)
our names written in the book of life (Rev. 3:5)
knowledge that God is working all things out for His purpose (Rom. 8:28; Eph. 1:11)
salvation and eternal life (John 17:3)

Prayer: Dear Father, thank You for saying we are Some People right there in Your Word because of Jesus. Remind me of this often and help me listen to Your whispers and Your Word.

Radiant Action: I will set a reminder on my phone to review three times a day who I am in Christ.

Webs: Identity Series (Jan.), Identity (Feb.), Small Things (Feb.)

DAY 3

Terrific

"Terrific!" breathed Zuckerman.[4]

Just as we read of Zuckerman's enthusiastic admiration for Wilbur in this story, so does our God joyfully admire us. We are terrific in His eyes, not because of what we have done, but because He sees us through His Son. God breathes His Spirit into our lives when we know Jesus, and that is *terrific*!

We're terrific because we are . . .

able to quench the enemy's fiery darts (Eph. 6:16)
able to do all things through Him (Phil. 4:13)
called by His name (Isa. 43:1)
complete in Christ (Col. 2:10, NLT)
empowered to witness (Acts 1:8)
God's possession (1 Cor. 6:19–20)
His children (John 1:12)
His chosen (Eph. 1:4)
His temple (1 Cor. 3:16–17)
His workmanship (Eph. 2:10)
invited to approach the throne (Rom. 5:2, Heb 4:16)
living stones (1 Peter 2:5)
more than conquerors (Rom. 8:37)
possessing the mind of Christ (1 Cor. 2:16)
reigning in life (Rom. 5:17)
reigning with Him (2 Tim. 2:12)
seated with Christ (Eph. 2:6)
set apart for His use (2 Tim. 2:21)
strengthened with all power (Col. 1:11)

Terrific, don't you think?

Prayer: Father, I praise You for these gifts that are so wonderful, they surprise me in my daily living. Thank You for the grace to believe and stand on who You say I Am, what I have, and what I can do.

Radiant Action: Journal Entries: 1. Name one reason God is terrific and one thing about myself that He made terrific, then I will thank Him for both. 2. What is terrific about those close to me?

Webs: Identity Series (Jan.), Identity (Feb.), Small Things (Feb.)

Gleanings: "He will take great delight in you; . . . he will . . . rejoice over you with singing" (Zeph. 3:17).

DAY 4

Radiant

"That pig is radiant."[5]

Radiant means "sending out light, shining, and glowing brightly." Wilbur himself isn't radiant, but the word Charlotte wove into the web says he is. Her web molds the community's perception of who Wilbur is.

Likewise, the Scriptures mold us and tell us the truth about who we are and who our family in Christ is as well. Who we are for all eternity is not written on a fragile thread that will fade in time but is established in the infallible Word of God. It is written that we are the light of the world because He is the light in us.

Our radiance means we . . .

can flee evil desires (2 Tim. 2:22)
can endure hardship (Heb. 12:7)
can declare His praises (1 Peter 2:9)
can reflect His glory (2 Cor. 3:18)
can set our hearts on things above (Col. 3:1)
can share in His glory (2 Thess. 2:14)
are rescued from the kingdom of darkness (Col. 1:13)
are justified freely by His grace (Rom. 3:24)
are purified by His blood (1 John 1:7)
are brought into the kingdom of His Son (Col. 1:13)
are being transformed into His likeness (2 Cor. 3:18)
are the light of the world (Matt. 5:14)
have a genuine tested faith of greater worth than gold (1 Peter 1:7)

Prayer: God, let Your light radiate from me today. Let me walk in radiant actions today, bathed in Your righteousness, cleansed of my sin.

Radiant Action: I will memorize at least one Scripture from the list above.

Webs: Identity Series (Jan.), Identity (Feb.), Small Things (Feb.), Power of One (May)

DAY 5

Humble

"He's not proud and he's near the ground."[6]

"Humble" describes Wilbur's core identity. He's humble enough to know he needs saving and also knows he has no power to save himself. As with Wilbur, the principle of "humility comes before honor" is foundational for humans. St. Augustine wrote, "Do you wish to rise? Begin by descending. You plan a tower that will pierce the clouds? Lay first the foundation of humility."[7]

In God's economy, those who are humble—admitting weakness and sin and knowing their need for the Savior—are the ones who win heaven. Here is what Scriptures has to say about humility: "He crowns the humble with victory" (Ps. 149:4 NIV). "Not by might, nor by power, but by my Spirit, says the LORD of Hosts" (Zech. 4:6). Humility means finding out who I am in the light of God (Deut. 8:3). God is in charge, and so it is He who promotes when we humbly desire to do His will and not our own (see Ps. 75:7; Luke 18:14; James 4:10; 1 Peter 5:6).

Prayer: Lord of the Hosts, we know we can do nothing of ourselves. Let our successes praise You and help us always to give credit to You and others. Thank You for failures to keep us humble.

Radiant Action: Journal Entry: What events have humbled me or made me feel insignificant? Instead of letting them be barbs in my joy, I may even rejoice in them. These humbling moments are pathways to greater grace. The more grace, the more power. The more power, the more ability and influence. "To the humble he gives favor" (Prov. 3:34).

Webs: Insignificance (Feb.), Weakness (Feb.), Runtiness (Feb.)

Gleanings: "Humble yourselves, therefore, under the mighty hand of God so that at the proper time he may exalt you" (1 Peter 5:6).

DAY 6

Runtiness

"The pig couldn't help being born small."[8]

Wilbur is born a small, weak, defenseless piglet destined for slaughter and desperately in need of a savior. He can't help being born a runt, and it's his smallness that creates the crisis and makes a mother out of a young girl named Fern. His size does not determine how much he is loved. Runtiness does not preclude greatness. Consider Charlotte, whose tiny size belies her mighty accomplishments.

We are born with all sorts of runty characteristics—things we wish we didn't have to deal with, but like it or not, we own them. These attributes could be physical features, handicaps, and other difficult circumstances—even certain relatives! How we deal with unchangeable features will affect our relationship with God. If we accept both how we are made and the circumstances we find ourselves in (not recommending complacency here), then we will be able to trust the all-wise God. Self-acceptance is part of having a solid relationship with the Father. Trusting Him for the fearful and wonderful way we are made keeps us from chasing after idols to find the affirmation we want.

We've already noted that Wilbur's runtiness catapulted him to fame. Although he's a fictional character, we can imagine ourselves in his place. How liberating it is when we learn to trust God, knowing that those characteristics we find imperfect and painful are purposeful and will work out to be something that captures grace for abundant life.

> *"Accept one another [and yourself], then, just as Christ accepted you, in order to bring praise to God"* (Rom. 15:7 NIV).

Prayer: God, help me to accept myself with this feature that I do not love. Help me to trust You with how You designed me. Help me accept the grace You give me to overcome runty attitudes like bitterness.

Radiant Action: Journal Entry: Thanks to God who loves me and has me in His hands. How does my own version of "runtiness" or inadequacy give glory to God? John 9.

Webs: Insignificance (Feb.), Humble (Feb.), Small Things (Feb.)

Gleanings: "I praise you, for I am fearfully and wonderfully made. Wonderful are your works; my soul knows it very well" (Ps. 139:14).

DAY 7

Small Things

A tiny spider crawled from the sac.[9]

Charlotte is but the size of a gumdrop, yet using her gifts, she weaves destiny. Her offspring, too, are very small, yet powerful in their presence to affect Wilbur, a much larger creature.

Jesus delights in using small things as frames for His mighty power. A shepherd boy's five smooth stones knocked down a giant for an entire country. A boy's small lunch fed thousands, and a widow's mite has inspired countless gifts. Israel was a small land, but it was the nursery for the gospel. *Pauli* means small or humble. However, the apostle Paul set the world on fire.

Other Small Things

"Leonardo da Vinci began painting tiny brush strokes on a piece of poplar wood in 1503. Fourteen years and hundreds of thousands of brush strokes later, that piece of poplar was the *Mona Lisa*, a masterpiece that experts are still x-raying to figure out how he painted impossibly thin brush strokes."[10]

Jean-Dominique Bauby, paralyzed after a stroke, wrote his entire autobiography by blinking one eyelid, his only working muscle, to a secretary.[11]

Letters, made of edges and negative spaces, form words that make wills, constitutions, and marriage licenses.

Screws in Ikea products make homes where futures grow.

Other small things with consequence include snowflakes, star winks, calories, the corona virus, bathtub stoppers, ticks, trailer hitch pins, the small ring that caused the Challenger explosion in 1986.

> "Whoever can be trusted with very little can also be trusted with much, and whoever is dishonest with very little will also be dishonest with much" (Luke 16:10 NIV).

Prayer: Lord, use small things to bring me closer to You and use whatever small things I have to glorify You—whether experiences or things or gifts.

Radiant Action: I will find five smooth stones and display them as a reminder of David's victory over Goliath. And when I am outside, I'll ponder the pebble and how God sovereignly used smallish stones of His making to overthrow a giant and establish Israel's destiny.

Webs: Insignificance (Feb.), Runtiness (Feb.)

Gleanings: "Do not despise these small beginnings, for the LORD rejoices to see the work begin…" (Zech. 4:10. NLT).

DAY 8

Insignificance

"It's just a common gray spider."[12]

The small spider who reads and writes messages in her web, who changes Wilbur's destiny, dies alone amidst the fair's refuse. Fern is a small girl who becomes a lifesaver. Templeton, the rat, delivers words and saves the egg sac. Wilbur, the pig who frolics in the manure, becomes a symbol of victory and ongoing life.

Insignificance, in God's economy, is an asset. Jesus was born in a stable, a crude place with the heavy smell of animals, hay, and manure. The insignificance of that stable became our stability.

God doesn't give favor to the large, loud, grunting Uncles of the world who parade their presence. Unimpressed with all the outward trappings that we as humans admire, God looks at the innermost part of our being: "For the LORD sees not as man sees: man looks on the outward appearance, but the LORD looks on the heart" (1 Sam. 16:7).

Who knows what God might do with what little you have? And even if you are unrecognized, like Charlotte, and you feel you're dying in the twilight alone too, be assured that the most seemingly insignificant act for God or gift given out of love for Him is worthy of eternal recognition (see Luke 21:2–3). All He asks is that we offer all of ourselves to Him and by faith believe He will take our gift and use it for His wise purposes, even though we may never see the good it does.

An unknown man from Ur became the father of the family of the Messiah. A slave became a prime minister. A peasant girl's womb harbored the Savior of the world. Rough shepherds were among the first to welcome Him, a woman of muddied reputation is the first to witness His resurrection.

> *"But God chose the foolish things of the world to shame the wise; God chose the weak things of the world to shame the strong. God chose the lowly things of this world and the despised things" (1 Cor. 1:27-28 NIV).*

Prayer: Lord, You are the Radiance, the Imminence, the Transcendence, the Alpha and Omega. Take our meager lunches, moments, gifts, talents, and treasure, and work miracles of water into wine, all for Your glory.

Radiant Action: Read Romans 8 and Ephesians 1:3–14.

Webs: Humble (Feb.), Small Things (Feb.), Runtiness (Feb.), Surprising Deliverers (Apr.)

Gleanings: "For he who is least among you all is the one who is great" (Luke 9:48).

DAY 9

Weakness

"It's . . . weak, and it will never amount to anything."[13]

Wilbur's worth is measured by his physical appearance. At first, he is nothing to Mr. Arable but a runty weakling not fit to live. Later he's seen as potential bacon or ham, but considering his small size, that fate seems unlikely. Yet as the story unfolds, we see it's his weakness and vulnerability that become the rudder for his wondrous destiny.

We have no power in our own doing to make ourselves good and earn a way to heaven. We have the most power when we admit our sin, our brokenness, and our inabilities, and rely on Jesus, who gives us that sanctified power. While we were still weak, Christ died for us (see Rom. 5:6). He accepts us as we are, feeble yet stubborn. He is especially good at taking us in our frailties and, with whatever we can offer, showing His mighty strength.

Opposite from the world's perception, weakness can be an advantage. God values the weak. The tower of Babel was conceived and built high in pride apart from God, who destroyed its great strength. Goliath was cut down after his conceited, pompous display. David, a mere shepherd boy, took him out with his five stones and a confidence founded not in himself, but in God.

Paul declared, "'My grace is sufficient for you, for my power is made perfect in weakness.' Therefore, I will boast all the more gladly of my weaknesses, so that the power of Christ may rest upon me. For the sake of Christ, then, I am content with weaknesses, insults, hardships, persecutions, and calamities. For when I am weak, then I am strong" (2 Cor. 12:9–11).

Prayer: Tender Shepherd, I need Your power to stand. Show me Your strength in my weakness.

Radiant Action: Journal Entry: An honest assessment of one or two weaknesses, perhaps with a good friend's help. I will use a concordance or online app like Bible Hub to find two related Scriptures for each need.

Webs: Insignificance (Feb.), Runtiness (Feb.), Suffering (Mar.)

Gleanings: "But we have this treasure in jars of clay to show that this all-surpassing power is from God and not from us" (2 Cor. 4:7 NIV).

> *"He gives power to the faint, and to him who has no might he increases strength . . . But they who wait for the LORD shall renew their strength"* (Isa. 40:29, 31).

DAY 10

Loneliness

Friendless, dejected, and hungry, he threw himself down.[14]

Wilbur suffers from a suffocating loneliness, both before he meets Charlotte and after her death, when her offspring fly away. Loneliness is such a gripping sorrow that the United Kingdom has a Minister of Loneliness. A small retirement home of twelve residents shut down interactions among them during the pandemic. They all died, none of Covid, and most probably of loneliness.

During a Veritas Forum, a platform for university communities to talk about ideas that shape the lives of humans, *New York Times* commentator David Brooks noted, "Isolation can kill."[15] Pastor Brian Frost adds a theological dimension to the subject, explaining that the problem of aloneness was the first condition God called not good, and He sought to remedy the pain. He sees us "feeling unseen and unheard—the absence of 'with.'"[16]

Jesus faced cruel loneliness. Betrayed, alone in prayer in the blood-sweating hour before His arrest, denied by Peter and others, bloodied and in agony on the cross, becoming sin for us, so that His own heavenly holy Father turned away—these events give us certainty that Jesus understands our own "absence of with."

Closer than Charlotte for Wilbur and Wilbur for Charlotte, Jesus promised He will never leave us. Unlike Charlotte, He will never die. He sticks closer than a brother. His friendship is given to anyone who believes in Him. He can pick you up sobbing out of the manure and raise you up to a place in His kingdom on earth and in heaven. Even though sometimes we're like Wilbur when he ran away, Jesus pursues us, wanting us to be with Him forever.

We will respond to Him as did the psalmist, "Nevertheless, I am continually with you; you hold my right hand. You guide me with your counsel, and afterward you will receive me to glory. Whom have I in heaven but you? And there is nothing on earth that I desire besides you. My flesh and my heart may fail, but God is the strength of my heart and my portion forever. But for me it is good to be near God; I have made the Lord God my refuge, that I may tell of all your works." (Ps. 73:25-28).

Prayer: Father to the fatherless, draw us, make us know and lean into Your constant love. Make a way for all who feel alone. Be our Friend who knows our hearts.

Radiant Action: I will pray for a name to call and then call and set a date to practice hospitality to a friend or acquaintance.

Webs: Friendship (Feb.), Aloneness (Feb.), Belonging and Adoption (Feb.)

Gleanings: "I am not alone. I stand with the Father, who sent me" (John 8:16 NIV).

DAY 11

Aloneness

Charlotte and Wilbur were alone.[17]

Aloneness, as opposed to loneliness, can be productive. The barn, free of humans, was a place for listening and observing, a place of delight and satisfaction. When many people flooded the barn after the miracle of "Some Pig," Fern felt uncomfortable. A person can be alone but not lonely. In his acclaimed and lengthy essay, *Here Is New York*, E. B. White wrote that his city gave "the gift of loneliness and the gift of privacy."[18]

There is a holy aloneness, a set-apartness of quiet where peace and insight may be found. When Charlotte and Wilbur are alone the last day before their separation, they talk freely about life. Jesus often withdrew to a lonely place to hear more clearly the voice of His Father. He also gathered His disciples away for rest and private teaching (see Mark 6:31). While John was alone in exile on Patmos, God revealed the destiny of mankind.

The path to fulfill our purpose, complete our mission, renew our strength, or clarify our vision requires aloneness. Quoting 1 Samuel 30:6, pastor and author Bill Johnson remarks that "When he [David] stood completely alone, that is when David (learned to) 'strengthen himself in the LORD his God.'"[19] Solitude made him rely on God alone and taught him how to win victories.

The challenge for us will always be learning to balance the need for connecting with others and the need for solitude to listen to God. While isolation can be due to unavoidable circumstances, it can also signal selfishness, as we read in Proverbs 18:1, but it's also true that constant social immersion can deaden our spiritual ears. We need to listen when the Beloved calls us away from the things of the world: "Arise, my love, my beautiful one, and come away" (Song 2:10).

Prayer: Father, give me wisdom to find the balance between connecting with community and holy, fruitful aloneness.

Radiant Action: I will commit to spending at least fifteen minutes alone with God each day for a week (or five). I can listen to a hymn or praise song, read Scripture, and pray.

Webs: Loneliness (Feb.), Suffering (Mar.), Purpose Series (May)

Gleanings: "Yet I am not alone because the Father is with me" (John 16:32 NLT).

DAY 12

Teamwork: The Power of Together

"Templeton better come, too—I might need somebody to run errands."[20]

What would have happened if neither Charlotte nor Templeton had come to the fair?—if no "Humble" was inscribed in the web, no one saved the egg sac, no one awakened the fainting Wilbur so he could receive his prize? The barnyard community is a team: all the animals gather for Charlotte's meeting; the old sheep persuades Templeton to get words for Wilbur and convinces him to go to the fair. You might say they're a family.

No one lives to himself. Individualism can be overvalued. We were created for community, accountability, responsibility, and work.[21] Geese take turns leading in formation to strengthen the flock. Bestselling author Jim Stovall explains that two draft horses can pull three times the load a single horse can pull. Horses that have trained together can pull four times the weight one of them could pull.[22]

In hearing the gospel, often whole communities move as a unit to accept or reject the good news. The ultimate team is the Trinity: The Father directs the Son to come to save us. Once Jesus had ascended, the Holy Spirit could come to empower His followers to be lights in the darkness, a power we can appropriate today.

> *"But you are a chosen race, a royal priesthood, a holy nation, God's own people, in order that you may proclaim the excellence of him who called you out of darkness into his marvelous light"* (1 Peter 2:9 NRSVUE).

Prayer: To the Trinity, the Ultimate Team: please knit our hearts together in our families, our churches, our friendships, our workplaces, and our communities. Help us realize that relationships are among life's truest treasures.

Radiant Action: Journal Entries: 1. What teams am I on? Family, church, place of employment, neighborhood? 2. How can I improve my ability to work with a team? How can I grow my better communication skills, more concern for the good of others, and develop specific skills and talents?

Webs: Friendship (Feb.), Marriage (Feb.), Communication in Community (Mar.)

Gleanings: University of Virginia basketball coach Tony Bennett stresses the importance of service: "Whatever your role is, be a servant to the team and make your teammates better."[23]

(Illustration by Beth Woessner— UNC-Chapel Hill Crew Team, 2021)

DAY 13

Friendship

"Do you want a friend, Wilbur?"[24]

Charlotte's Web is about friendship. Charlotte is a "true friend and a good writer."[25] Wilbur was delighted when she called to him out of the darkness, and he knew his loneliness was ending. The story is filled with *unlikely* friends. Charlotte's bloodthirsty ways initially shock Wilbur. He sees few redeeming qualities in her. But time proves her virtues. Who would have ever thought a pig and a spider could be best friends?

Many friendships are based on shared values. Wilbur and Charlotte, although physically different, place a high value on faithfulness in relationships. Likewise, our friendship with Jesus is based on shared values. He tells us, "You are my friends if you do what I command you. No longer do I call you servants, for the servant does not know what his master is doing; but I have called you friends, for all that I have heard from my Father I have made known to you" (John 15:14–15). He is friends with those who are open to the truth He embodies, and, as our closest friends do, He reveals His secrets to us. Like with Wilbur and Charlotte, God doesn't demand perfection before we become His friends.

Sometimes our best friends aren't available, but we can find joy in making new friends as Wilbur did with the baby spiders. Human friends may only be for a season, like Fern for Wilbur, but God is never out of season.

Templeton, the complaining, self-pitying, selfish loner wasn't exactly what you'd call a friend—that rat bit Wilbur's tail! And yet it was Templeton who got Wilbur moving to triumph. Sometimes our best friends are not the ones we like, but the ones who are willing to cause us pain to get us where we need to be.

In the coming kingdom, there will also be unlikely friends: "The wolf and the lamb will feed together" (Isa. 65:25 NIV).

> *"Two are better than one, because they have a good return for their labor:*
> *If either of them falls down, one can help the other up"* (Eccl. 4:9–10 NIV).

Prayer: Lord, make me a true friend as You are my true friend. Make me wise in choosing my friends (see Prov. 22:24) and make me faithful.

Radiant Action: I will visit a friend in person, by technology, by note or text or call. I plan to comfort the grieving and rejoice with those who are rejoicing.

Webs: Loneliness (Feb.), Belonging (Feb.), Love (Feb.), Courage and Risk (June)

DAY 14

Love

Wilbur didn't want food, he wanted love.[26]

Wilbur's longing is the same as ours—to be loved. Charlotte loves him faithfully. She reveals to him his inner beauty and great worth. She loves Wilbur just as he is—covered with mud and manure, despairing, needy, and overly emotional. Charlotte's love covers Wilbur's faults.

In many ways, Charlotte illustrates God's love. God loves us before we are cleaned up. "But God demonstrates His own love toward us, in that while we were still sinners, Christ died for us" (Rom. 5:8 NKJV). In her conduct and character, Charlotte exemplifies the true meaning of love as it is embodied in the God who is love: "Love is patient and kind; love does not envy or boast; it is not arrogant or rude. It does not insist on its own way; it is not irritable or resentful; it does not rejoice at wrongdoing but rejoices with the truth. Love bears all things, believes all things, hopes all things, endures all things" (1 Cor. 13:4–7).

In a famous hymn, the nineteenth-century Scottish pastor, George Mattheson, wrote that God's love is a "love that wilt not let me go."[27] Blind, forsaken by his fiancée, he wrote this treasured hymn on the eve of his sister's wedding. Bearing our sorrows and bringing hope to our hearts, Christ loves to fill broken people. Like the prodigal's father, our gracious God seeks to cover our sins. Unlike Charlotte, who lives and dies but lives on in our imaginations, God's love for us is real and forever.

"I have loved you with an everlasting love" (Jer. 31:3).

Prayer: God, You who are Love, ignite me from the inside out to radiate Your love.

Radiant Action: I will read John 17–21.

Webs: Friendship (Feb.), Marriage (Feb.), Communication in Community (Mar.)

Gleanings: Above all, keep loving one another earnestly, since love covers a multitude of sins" (1 Peter 4:8).

DAY 15

Marriage

*Mr. Zuckerman sat down weakly and ate a doughnut . . .
"Edith, you're crazy," mumbled Zuckerman.*[28]

The Arables and Zuckermans have good marriages—with room for growth. The Arables disagree at times, and Mr. Zuckerman occasionally ignores his wife's good sense. When she prepares to give Wilbur a bath before the fair, he argues with her about its necessity. But after Uncle wins the blue prize, Mr. Zuckerman does what his wife did, and steps into action instead of despair, following her example by giving Wilbur another buttermilk bath. A good marriage is defined not by partners who are perfect but by partners who are willing to grow and bring out the best and most beautiful in each other. But often beauty comes by experiencing irritation and then growth in grace.

Marriage is first conceived in the fellowship of the Trinity—the three Persons of God interconnected in perfect harmony. The Trinity is the template for the connection between souls in marriage. Marriage is a mysterious reflection of the love between Christ and His bride, the church. It is sacred.

Marriage is a morally binding pledge, a covenant between a man and a woman, fueled and molded by God's love, power, and grace. "And though a man might prevail against one who is alone, two will withstand him—a threefold cord is not quickly broken" (Eccl. 4:12). Faithfulness, such as we find in Charlotte and Wilbur, is required.

Marriage is between two sinners with brokenness and baggage unique to each. But the grace of God can sustain and renew love and faithfulness. As for Charlotte, "she was determined to keep her promise."[29]

As He hung in excruciating pain on the cross, Jesus demonstrated His complete faithfulness to us.

"The LORD is trustworthy in all he promises and faithful in all he does" (Ps. 145:13 NIV).

Prayer: Lord, help me to be faithful.

Radiant Action: Journal Entries: 1. Revisit my own vows and my vision of marriage. Is it based on Scripture? 2. What has changed? How have we grown in grace?

Webs: Love (Feb.), Friendship (Feb.), Communication in Community (Mar.)

Gleanings: "So God created man in his own image, in the image of God he created him; male and female he created them. And God blessed them" (Gen. 1:27–28).

DAY 16

Belonging and Adoption

He did not know it, but his friend was very near.[30]

Wilbur, during his time of desperation, discovers that he belongs. In a story from another farm, James Herriot writes about a kitten named Moses. The abandoned black kitten finds a family with a gigantic sow who's nursing many piglets. Moses joins in and suckles too. The sow and her offspring happily accept him. The scrap of a kitten has found his place.

As with Wilbur and Moses, humans often feel desperately alone. According to Dr. Kathy Koch, "belonging" is one of five basic human needs.[31] Jesus, who faced the abyss of abandonment on the cross, crying, "My God, my God, why have you forsaken me?" (Matt. 27:46), offers "adoption . . . as sons through Jesus Christ" (Eph. 1:5).

Paul declares that we were "without hope and without God in the world. But now in Christ Jesus you who once were far away have been brought near by the blood of Christ" (Eph. 2:12–13 NIV). God, seeing us trembling and alone, befriends and adopts us despite our great weakness and proclivity to sin. All along, His intention has been and will ever be to tenderly rescue us and save us from destruction.

For those who have lost a parent(s) or a spouse or friends through death or divorce, God offers permanent adoption into His family with perfect love and a perfect forever in His own home.

> "My Father's house has many rooms; if that were not so, would I have told you that I am going there to prepare a place for you? And if I go and prepare a place for you, I will come back and take you to be with me that you also may be where I am . . . I will not leave you as orphans; I will come to you" (John 14:2–3, 18 NIV).

Prayer: Dear Heavenly Father, thank You for making me Your child through Jesus. Thank You for sharing Your family.

Radiant Action: Journal Entry: Have I confirmed my adoption into God's family? Belonging to God is a simple matter of asking God to forgive my sins and then receiving His forgiveness and love.

Webs: Identity (Feb.), Love (Feb.), Loneliness (Feb.), Home (June)

Gleanings: "The Spirit himself testifies with our spirit that we are God's children" (Rom. 8:16 NIV).

DAY 17

Finding the Good in the Bad

He was sad because his new friend was so bloodthirsty.[32]

Charlotte's ways, at first untenable to Wilbur, became the means of his escape from doom. The web that horrified him contained the elements that saved him.

Who has habits you cannot accept? Or what impossible circumstances are you in? Can you begin to imagine how any of those things could be beneficial—the job, marriage, friendship, rejected manuscript, rebellious child, death, infertility, the angered sibling, lost wealth, lost health, lost independence, lost career, the clique, the church division, the cancel, whatever Jesus didn't do as you had expected, hoped for, and counted on?

It's bitterness after disappointment that causes us to lose our way. It's the broken heart and grief, not the event itself, that keeps us from seeing the next step. Grieving shouldn't be dismissed, minimized, or chided by others or by ourselves. Our Lord grieved, and while we're here, we will also experience sorrow—and it may be profound.

But to find our grief eased and to rediscover joy takes perspective, healing, and sometimes the right counselor. In day-to-day life, how we think about things will either lead to the loss of hope or to a hope that makes us flourish and be fruitful. God gives grace for every situation, including the most distressing and perplexing circumstances and even the mundane.

> "See to it that no one fails to obtain the grace of God; that no 'root of bitterness' springs up and causes trouble, and by it many become defiled" (Heb. 12:15).

Prayer: Dear Father, I don't have the faith today to believe this loss or challenge will work for my good. But I do believe *You* are good and that You oversee all things. Give me the faith and clear vision to take the next step. I lay this event at the cross and look for Your way to resurrect goodness in my life. I cry out to You.

Radiant Action: Journal Entry: I will listen to the Holy Spirit for positive ideas for how God can use this bad for good and write them down. I will talk to someone as led and encourage others.

Webs: Templeton Series (Jan.), Disappointment (Mar.), Faith (Apr.), Grief (Nov.)

Gleanings: "God can make any indifferent thing, as well as evil itself, an instrument for good; but I submit that to do this is the business of God and not any human being."[33]

DAY 18

Self-Sacrifice

"I would gladly give my life for you."[34]

Charlotte left home and created her egg sac in a kind of manger. She deserted her preferences and convenience to ensure the well-being of another. Even though her death was inevitable, she essentially laid down her life for her friend. She and Templeton are antitypes.

Even Wilbur knew the pain but also the attendant joy of giving up something vital for the well-being of another. He laid down his most prized treasure: his slops. Charlotte's magnum opus, her egg sac, returns to the barn only because Wilbur is willing to unselfishly give the rat first dibs on his most precious security. He gives up not only the food, but the power to choose which slops he would eat, and on a deeper level, the power to control his world. He lays down his freedom of choice for the good of his relationship with Charlotte.

Jesus laid down his life to complete the Father's plan of redeeming wily and wayward mankind. He gave us His life; He gave up His freedom; He gave up heaven for a time; He laid down His divine attributes; He bore our shame on the cross for the joy set before Him.

> *"Greater love has no one than this, that someone lay down his life for his friends"* (John 15:13).

Prayer: Father, work in my heart so that my hands no longer clutch what I think I own (but what's only on loan)—things like time, possessions, and life occupations. As Jesus laid down His life, work in me the grace and love to lay down my life for the welfare of others.

Radiant Action: Journal Entry: What is God calling me to do for someone that may be inconvenient? I will set a date and time to do it.

Webs: Friendship (Feb.), Teamwork (Feb.), Suffering (Mar.)

Gleanings: "For the love of Christ urges us on, because we are convinced that one has died for all . . . And he died for all, so that those who live might live no longer for themselves but for the one who for their sake died and was raised" (2 Cor. 5:14–15 NRSVUE).

DAY 19

Waiting for the Dawn

Through a small window, a faint gleam appeared.
One by one the stars went out . . . "Oh beautiful day, it is here at last!"[35]

Night had fallen on the melancholiest of days, made even worse with the administration of medicine and molasses. Then a thin but pleasant voice broke through the malaise and offered hope. The challenge: Wilbur had to wait until morning.[36]

The disciples, too, had waited for dawn. They endured the crucifixion of Jesus; despondent, they moved through Easter Saturday, not believing that Jesus would live again. "My soul waits for the Lord more than watchmen for the morning, more than watchmen for the morning" (Ps. 130:6).

Then the day of resurrection dawned.

For what are you waiting? The dawn of justice? For the Lord to act so you're not tempted to take revenge? Waiting for the dawn of resurrection after a loved one passes away? Waiting for the dawn of redemption for a beloved son or daughter caught in chains of savagely hurtful choices? Waiting for God to take away the awful trial before you?

While we wait: the Ferris wheel is turning ever so slowly, and we know the resurrection has already held its victorious day, with time turning toward Christ's return. The dawn of its morning has already been. We see Mary responding to the One who came from death to life calling her name—calling my name and yours. We see Peter and John racing to the empty grave and marveling at the folded linen cloths.

We live because He lives, and all our waiting is caught in His time of now and forever, where our tears are held and our souls connect with eternity, where *all of our hearts' longings will be satisfied*. But for now, the Ferris wheel carrying us through life turns and sways, and we wait for the dawn, the Morning Star.

"Weeping may tarry for the night, but joy comes with the morning" (Ps. 30:5).

Radiant Action: Journal Entry: I will add a picture of a sunrise to my journal to remind me that the dawn of redemption is coming and with it, the renewal of hopes, dreams, and life. The mercies of the Lord are "new every morning" and "great is His faithfulness" (Lam. 3:22–23).

Webs: Mornings (Apr.), Easter (Apr.), Ferris Wheel (June)

Gleanings: "Be strong, and let your heart take courage; wait for the Lord!" (Ps. 27:14).

DAY 20

Expectations of Others: Do What?

Ever since the spider had befriended him, he had done his best to live up to his reputation.[37]

Wilbur tries to look terrific when the spider web says he is. And when it says he is radiant, he runs, jumps, and does backflips with a half twist to live up to what's expected. He even tries to glow.

What other people say about us can mold our identities and futures. What we say to others can shape *their* destinies. And what we say to ourselves determines our course. Somewhere along the line, the Israelites began thinking they were grasshoppers. They couldn't face the giants, so instead they faced forty years of circling the desert.

Prayer: Lord, help me to speak positive words over others and myself. Help me to be discerning when I'm criticized, so I will heed the seed of what is true and blow away the chaff of what I know is invalid. Aid my understanding of what You expect of me and enable me to live up to it.

Radiant Action: Journal Entries: 1. Review some of the entries on identities (January: Fern, Wilbur, Templeton, and Charlotte, and February: Some Pig, Terrific, Radiant, and Humble). What speaks to me now? 2. Is someone labeling me unkindly? I will reject those labels, remembering what matters is what *God* says about me—I am "accepted in the Beloved." 3. I will turn this toward others and think of one or two specific ways I can challenge close friends or family members to be *some person, terrific, radiant, and humble*, even if they do not reveal these qualities yet.

Webs: Terrific (Feb.), Barnyard Disciples (Mar.), Changed (Apr.), Voices (June)

Gleanings: "Then Caleb silenced the people before Moses and said, 'We should go up and take possession of the land, for we can certainly do it.' But the men who had gone up with him said, 'We can't attack . . .; they are stronger'" (Num. 13:30–31 NIV).

MARCH
TRANSITION AND STRUGGLE

March is a month of transition. Just as the weather is moody and unstable, so can our human emotions be. The apple tree's limbs thresh the air as the tree stretches and bends with the wind. In March we may find ourselves struggling with heart challenges, but there's nothing to do but keep marching. It can be a time of pruning, trimming off unproductive branches before full blooming begins.

WOBBLESTACLES: STRUGGLE AND RESOLVE IN TROUGHS OF DIFFICULTY

Vision: God Gives Guidance for Timing, *p. 58*
Crisis: God Gives Wisdom, *p. 59*
Suffering: God Gives Grace, *p. 60*
Darkness: God Gives Light, *p. 61*
Emotional Self-Control: God Gives Discipline, *p. 62*
Bad News, *p. 63*
Disappointment, *p. 64*
Fear, *p. 65*
Mud and Manure, *p. 66*
Smelling, *p. 67*
Uninvited, *p. 68*
Waiting, *p. 69*
Enemies, *p. 70*
Dreams, *p. 71*
Barnyard Disciples, *p. 72*
Division of Responsibility, *p. 73*
Communication in Community, *p. 74*
Calling: "Here, Pig", *p. 75*
Mission: Specific Assignments, *p. 76*
Quarterly Review: January–March, *p. 77*

See also in June Fern's Puddles, Wilbur's Wobblestacles, Puddle Jumping, and Charlotte's Entanglements

DAY 1

Vision: God Gives Guidance for Timing

"There is no time to be lost."[1]

Charlotte's vision for saving her friend has a time limit. The fair comes in September. She has six weeks from the middle of July to preserve Wilbur. She takes baby steps, a total of only four words, to convince Zuckerman to keep Wilbur alive.

Although God Himself is outside of time, time has always been central to His plans. In Genesis, we read that God created the earth in six days and rested on the seventh. The Passover had to be eaten in haste such that no yeast could be used to slow down preparation of the bread. Jesus came at the fullness of time and completed all the Father's will in thirty-three years.

When a certain mission or job ends that you poured yourself into wholeheartedly, there can be grief for the time and work that has passed. It is critical to manage sadness when the mission is completed. Instead of lamenting the old, be thankful for the accomplishment, and welcome the new season and its opportunities.

> *"But one thing I do: Forgetting what is behind and straining toward what is ahead, I press on toward the goal to win the prize for which God has called me heavenward in Christ Jesus."* (Phil 3:13–14 NIV)

Prayer: Dear Lord, please sharpen my vision and let me walk in Your timeline. Let me rejoice in new seasons and be thankful for the old.

Radiant Action: Journal Entries: Take some time in quiet to think. 1. What is my vision? What goals do I have to fulfill that vision within a specific time frame? 2. How does this vision line up with my calling and my larger purpose for the next ten, five and three years, and then one year? 3. How do I see my vision today, one month from today, and then in six months?[2] I will put a lamp or other electrical appliance on a timer to remind me that my life is also on a timer and to not be slack in following God's will.

Webs: Balance (May), Ferris Wheel (June)

Gleanings: "Where there is no vision, the people perish" (Prov. 29:18 KJV).

DAY 2

Crisis: God Gives Wisdom

"'There are a lot of things Wilbur doesn't know about life,' she thought."[3]

Crisis shapes Wilbur's destiny. Before every step forward in the story, there's a problem to resolve that requires wisdom. Before Wilbur meets Charlotte, loneliness stalks. Before Charlotte can help, her life is threatened. Before words can be spun, words must be discovered. Before Wilbur can win the blue ribbon, Uncle wins it. As Charlotte dies, Templeton mocks, and time leaks away.

Despite the challenges, there is grace for each crisis.

God gives Christians His wisdom for every situation, no matter how perplexing. We just need to ask for it, believing He'll answer in His perfect timing. "If any of you lacks wisdom, let him ask God, who gives generously to all without reproach, and it will be given him" (James 1:5). The Lord will give you testimonies of deliverance to encourage others.

God sees the troubles of our human race and is moved by them. Zechariah spoke of "the tender mercy of our God, whereby the sunrise shall visit us from on high to give light to those who sit in darkness and in the shadow of death, to guide our feet into the way of peace" (Luke 1:78–79). In our times of unease, Jesus promises the Helper.

> *"He will call on me, and I will answer him; I will be with him in trouble, I will deliver him and honor him"* (Ps. 91:15 NIV).

Prayer: God of all comfort, help me to trust in You as each crisis tide rolls in. I know You hold the mighty seas of trouble in Your hands. Thank You for being my strong Deliverer, my Helper, my Comforter, my all-knowing Father, the giver of wisdom in showing me how to navigate rough and flat seas. Help me to bleed gold (faith) when the crisis comes.

Radiant Action: Journal Entry: What are the hard questions arising from my trouble? What Scriptures give clarity and comfort? I will pray for others and share the verses I found as the Spirit leads.

As Dianne Bundt writes, "May you receive fresh insight to meet the challenges of each day and discover creative solutions to your problems."[4]

Webs: Waiting for the Dawn (Feb.), Disappointment (Mar.), Suffering (Mar.)

Gleanings: "Then they cried to the LORD in their trouble, and he delivered them from their distress" (Ps. 107:6).

DAY 3

Suffering: God Gives Grace

"I don't want to die!"[5]

In his short life, Wilbur experiences great sorrow, uncertainty, and anxiety. In his intense fearfulness at his bad news (his sure demise unless someone intervenes), in his extreme loneliness, and in his eventual severe grief at the death of Charlotte and then the loss of her children, Wilbur suffers acutely.

In this life, suffering is inevitable. As Spurgeon put it, "Then little wonder is it if I also have changes in my circumstances from the sunshine of prosperity to the midnight of adversity. It will not always be the blaze of noon."[6] Jesus, God's own son was born to suffer, and suffering makes Him one with our humanity. He bore all the darkness of the world in His crucified body.

For Wilbur, ultimately the path of suffering leads to peace and a glorious life. For Christians, suffering is expected. "In the world you will have tribulation. But take heart; I have overcome the world" (John 16:33). Suffering can be the path to knowing God and finding lasting peace. We do know our sufferings will endure only for a time, and then there will be victory. Even Jesus "who for the joy that was set before him endured the cross" (Heb. 12:2).

The suffering of the man born blind became the key to his salvation. David Brooks quotes theologian Paul Tillich who explains that suffering interrupts life and creates a cavity into the deeper self: "Suffering takes people beneath the busyness of life and reminds them that they are not who they thought they were."[7] Suffering unlocks the unknown lake inside us, the deep-down self that Christ intimately knows and loves.

God's grace carries us closer to Him. As Stephen Davey wisely said, "Don't waste suffering. Make the most of what we are facing."[8]

Prayer: God, You alone know my lake of pain. Embrace me as I remember that "the sacrifices of God are a broken spirit; a broken and contrite heart" (Ps. 51:17).

Radiant Action: Kneel, cry out.

Webs: Death (Apr.), Easter (Apr.), Energy and Hope (May)

Gleanings: "Without the burdens of afflictions, it is impossible to reach the height of grace. The gifts of grace increase as the struggles increase." —St. Rose of Lina

DAY 4

Darkness: God Gives Light

Darkness settled over everything.[9]

Light leaps from the dark spaces. Out of the darkness Charlotte came. The womb, though dark, brings life bursting into the light. Daniel received guidance in a night vision. The greatest revelation of all occurred in darkness: "Now on the first day of the week Mary Magdalene came to the tomb early, while it was still dark, and saw that the stone had been taken away from the tomb" (John 20:1).

Darkness can be a nesting place for God's grace. "He made darkness His hiding place" (Ps. 18:11 NASB). The loveliness of light and restoration, of hopeful new beginnings, starts in the stench and tears of the dark. "Even the darkness is not dark to you; the night is bright as the day, for darkness is as light with you" (Ps. 139:12). "Light dawns in the darkness for the upright" (Ps. 112:4).

Besides hardship, darkness is a metaphor for man's natural spiritual state: "This is the verdict: Light has come into the world, but people loved darkness instead of light because their deeds were evil. Everyone who does evil hates the light [like a rat], and will not come into the light for fear that their deeds will be exposed" (John 3:19–20 NIV).

Charlotte calls to Wilbur out of the darkness. God calls to us who are lost in sinful darkness. He beckons the captives to "'Come out,' and to those in darkness, 'Be free!'" (Isa. 49:9 NIV).

> *"I have come into the world as light, so that whoever believes in me may not remain in darkness"* (John 12:46).

Prayer: Father, I am troubled and lie in darkness. Please reveal Your presence. Cleanse me of my inner darkness. I make this confession: "I was once darkness," and this affirmation: "but now I am light in the Lord. I will live as a child of light (for the fruit of the light consists in all goodness, righteousness, and truth), and I will find out what pleases the Lord" (see Eph. 5:8–10). Bring light, freedom, and comfort out of the deep dark that threatens to suffocate me.

Radiant Action: I will set my mind on the truth of my adoption and quiet my heart to hear Your voice of hope. A flashlight will remind me to walk step-by-step in the darkness.

Webs: Waiting for the Dawn (Feb.), Death (Apr.), Shadows of Death (Apr.)

DAY 5

Emotional Self-Control: God Gives Discipline

"Fern, . . . you will have to learn to control yourself."[10]

In the first scene, Fern is furious at her dad the determined executioner. She *seems* out of control because she shouts from a deep sense of justice. But appearances can mislead. Jesus made a whip and raised His voice in righteous anger as He chased the profiteers from the temple. He was very much in control of Himself. With Fern and with Jesus, righteousness led to a just and very public passionate outcry and action. God sanctions outcries over evil.

In Luke 15:11–32, the parable of the prodigal son illustrates the delicacy of understanding outward aspects of emotion. On the one hand there's the son who lost all self-control, and on the other, there is the older son who burned with anger and indignation. Is the younger brother the only one in the wrong for his sensual licentiousness or is the older brother even worse with his self-righteousness and seething rage?[11] Self-gratification, whether through riotous living or rigid self-righteousness, is all about appeasing the self.

The Holy Spirit grants us both the wisdom to know what is appropriate and the power to crucify our flesh and change. Knowing *whose* we are in Christ determines how we think, feel, and act in various situations. When we know we are His—redeemed and embraced as His beloved children—we can be filled with hope for the future, and we can sustain emotional self-control.

Wilbur matures from one who faints, melts with dizziness, and completely loses hope, to one who can think in a crisis and decide on a practical solution. May God give us the wisdom and maturity to know how to act and react.

> *"God gave us a spirit not of fear but of power and love and self-control"* (2 Tim. 1:7).

Prayer: Dear God, help me listen to Your Spirit to control myself, find joy, and avoid emotional lagoons.

Radiant Action: Journal Entry: List (and do) some of my favorite things.

Webs: Boundary Series (Jan.), Identity Series (Jan.), Identity (Feb.), Holy Spirit (Apr.).

Gleanings: "She was born to impulses that rode her before she could ride them."[12]

DAY 6

Bad News

"I don't like to spread bad news, but . . ."[13]

Wilbur panics with the sheep's announcement of his planned Christmas demise as the dinner ham. Then his last hope of getting a reprise through receiving a blue ribbon fades with news of the blue ribbon being given to the thug hog at the fair. Wilbur learns his truest friend will no longer live in the barn with him. But when Templeton spouts his discouraging words near the end of the fair, Wilbur shows surprising maturity and grace when he changes the course of conversation.[14]

When Charlotte lets Wilbur know of her impending death, he's terrified and grieves wretchedly. Of course, considering the deep love he feels for his friend, we can understand his initial reaction. But then Wilbur has an idea. Thinking of the precious egg sac and how he'll need Templeton to save it, his use of reason propels him into productive action. Charlotte's mentoring kicks in at the moment of greatest consequence."[15] Wilbur acts decisively and courageously.

When we get bad news, what happens? Panic? Or if the source of bad news is unreliable (i.e., Templeton) and the news is unfounded, do we change the subject and refuse to let the tactless bearer of the bad news take the foreground of our emotional well-being?

But if the news is real, life-threatening, or life-changing for the worse, we can respond well by *lamenting*, kneeling, crying out to God with tears, and *praying* for God's guidance for a clear, stable plan of action. This may involve dealing with a disinterested, unhelpful, selfish but necessary agent like Templeton.

Prayer: God, carry my bad news. What should I do?

Radiant Action: Journal Entry: My own lament based on the Psalms (for examples Ps. 3, 4, 5, 7, 9-10, 13, 14, 17, 22, 25, 26, 27, 28, 31, 36, 39, 40:12-17, 41, 42-43, 52, 53, 54, 55, 56, 57, 59, 61, 64, 70, 71, 77, 86, 89, 120, 139, 141, 142). I will cultivate a strong prayer life and positive friendships (find a prayer partner) before I receive bad news so I will find support at the time most needed.

Webs: Finding the Good in the Bad (Feb.), Faith (Apr.), Disappointment (Mar.)

Gleanings: "I have said these things to you, that in me you may have peace. In the world you will have tribulation. But take heart; I have overcome the world" (John 16:33).

DAY 7

Disappointment

"It's a dud."[16]

The goose has one bad egg out of eight. It's a dud, but it's that one egg that protects Charlotte.

The psalmist wrote, "Blessed are those whose strength is in you ... As they go through the Valley of Baca [weeping], they make it a place of springs" (Ps. 84:5-6). What has been the place of disappointment, the Baca, in your life? Could it be that God is going to use the loss of that "egg," that unhatched potential buried in the depth of your heart, to bring grace to you and someone else?

In the book of Revelation, we read that the martyrs of this earth crowd around the Father's throne and ask, "How long, O Lord, ... until You judge and avenge our blood?" (Rev. 6:10 NKJV). As for you, the timing of your justification, restoration, and repayment for wrongs done is unknown. What is known is that the heavenly Father cares for you and will not let you go, will not forget your pain, and will bring you through it in this life and into victory.

God heals and restores, while the enemy comes to steal, kill, and destroy. But the enemy doesn't have the last word. Consider the anguish of the Jews as they watched the ravaging of Jerusalem in 70 AD. Ten years later, John wrote his gospel as a beam of light to show that there is something and Someone much better and greater than the earthly Jerusalem.

The things that crush and disappoint us are tombs with resurrection nearing. We wait for the Lord to make our enemies a footstool for our feet—a resting place. Judas was the "bad egg" among the disciples, but his evil brought about good as did the evil done to Joseph.

> *"As for you, you meant evil against me, but God meant it for good, to bring it about that many people should be kept alive"* (Gen. 50:20).

Prayer: Dear Lord, we give to You our "rotten goose eggs" for Your use.

Radiant Action: Journal Entry: What are the opportunities for me to see God bring good out this? I will remember Joseph's life and Jesus's death and resurrection as I read Romans 8 and Psalm 23. My attitude will be: "Weeping may stay for the night, but rejoicing comes in the morning" (Ps. 30:5 NIV).

Webs: Uninvited (Mar.), Tears (Sept.)

DAY 8

Fear

He would dream that men were coming to get him.[17]

E. B. White himself had "fear of the dark, fear of the future, fear of the return to school after a summer on a lake in Maine, fear of making an appearance on a platform, . . . fear that I was unknowing about things I should know about."[18] The reality is that there is stark terror in living. How will we manage our own terror with its myriad shades from faint red to charcoal black? Will we sob and panic like Wilbur? Or will we find backbone to cope like Esther? Coping and hoping always spring from trusting the character of the unchanging, all-wise God.

Fear can cause us to withdraw from God and community right when we need Him and them the most. Fear is food for the enemy. Take your rightful place in authority over the fear. As someone said, "Make progress in its presence and don't wait for its absence." Don't focus on what you fear. Remember Job's words, "For the thing that I fear comes upon me" (Job 3:25). There's release from the control of this disabling emotion when we fix our eyes on the Lord and reflect on who He says He is and who He says we are. If we resist, the devil will flee.

"The LORD is the stronghold of my life; of whom shall I be afraid?" (Ps. 27:1).

Prayer: Lord, when I'm afraid, sometimes I can hardly utter a squeal. All I can do at such times is fall on my face and wait for You, the Creator. We are Yours. Strengthen me so I don't faint. Let Your will be done in my life and the lives of my loved ones. Your mighty presence drives away fear. Rebuke the Evil One for harassing me with a spirit of fear.

Radiant Action: Journal Entry: What am I facing today that's scary? What Scriptures address it? I will research the 366 verses on fear, one for every day of the year, even leap year. I will not trust in outer appearances.

Webs: Dreams (Mar.), Blood (Apr.), Courage and Risk (June)

Gleanings: "You came near when I called on you; you said, 'Do not fear!'" (Lam. 3:57).

DAY 9

Mud and Manure

Wilbur . . . went to live in a manure pile.[19]

Manure can be helpful and even, in the nose of some, poetic. E. B. White certainly thought so, as Scott Elledge in his biography of the writer, points out in quoting White: "There is no doubt about it, the basic *satisfaction* in farming is manure, which always suggests that life can be cyclic and chemically perfect and aromatic and continuous."[20]

But for most of us, manure is an appropriate metaphor for when we're in the pits, the absolute worst and most depressing state. Suffering, like manure properly pitchforked and worked to add nutrients to the soil, can improve and enrich us. But manure can suggest another meaning too, as when someone exploits a problem to garner attention. Sadly, some people enjoy rolling around in the dung of their problems to gain the sympathy of others. While we all have woe-is-me parties from time to time, habitual wallowing in self-pity signifies an unhealthy and selfish focus. The essay "Bye Low Baby" by E. B. White illustrates this perfectly. In the essay, the bird named "Baby" is going to throw a pity party for himself. But to his dismay, his girlfriend intervenes with kindly intended advice. Baby grumbles, "I was just getting into the doldrums when Justa came over and said: 'Hop down and take a drink of water, you'll feel better.' I could have wrung her little yellow neck!"[21]

If you want to be whole, you must get out of the manure and find solid ground. There is only one Person who can help, He who "lifted me out of the slimy pit" (Ps. 40:2 NIV).

Prayer: Help me get out of the manure of self-pity and complaining to get attention.

Radiant Action: Journal Entries: 1. Have I been habitually indulging in self-pity? Seeking the attention of others by magnifying my problems? I will ask a trusted friend for observations. 2. I will name any self-centered, self-pitying thoughts and declare them conquered by Christ.

Webs: Emotional Self-Control (Mar.), Energy and Hope (May), Rain (June)

Gleanings: The name "Dung Gate" is found in four passages in the book of Nehemiah and refers to one of the gates of Jerusalem in Nehemiah's day. Some have called it the gate of deliverance.

DAY 10

Smelling

"I'd really like to be . . . sniffing along the ground, smelling, smelling . . ."[22]

Wilbur's snout is his treasured possession. He rejoices in it, wishing to use this gift of snout to root in the forest. Elledge explains White's special use of the sense of smell: "In all White's writings, the smell of manure (or of such other rich organic matter as leaf mold) is always exciting, promising, or reassuring."[23]

It's true of life that a sweet aroma is pleasant. Think of the tempting smell of cookies baking or the fragrance of fresh-cut grass. The Scripture compares its blessing to that of good counsel. "Oil and perfume make the heart glad, and a person's advice is sweet to his friend" (Prov. 27:9 NASB). Charlotte's counsel is sweet to Wilbur.

The Bible also relates the sense of smell to faith. "For we are a fragrance of Christ to God among those who are being saved and among those who are perishing; to the one an aroma from death to death, to the other an aroma from life to life" (2 Cor. 2:15–16 NASB). No doubt that a life consecrated to God has a sweet aroma like the Old Testament sacrifices.

On the other hand, a smell can be foul. Wilbur hasn't a clue as to how he stinks to others as the lamb lambasts him for his reeking odor.[24] Could what we consider our greatest strengths be weaknesses that smell bad in community? For example, administrative gifts to organize and equip may irritate others and come across as overbearing and superior. Someone may think they're doing another a favor by rearranging another's closet, but it might be overstepping. Or could it be that it's not the ability or gifting that makes us stink, but the pride or other attitudes behind its use?

Prayer: God, I don't know how others look at me. What I consider an ability, others may think stinks. Please help me clearly evaluate my gifts and abilities. Make me fragrant in a way that attracts, not repels, others.

Radiant Action: Journal Entry: What are my strengths (often the flip side of weaknesses)? What is the best use of my gifts? How should I get training to develop them?

Webs: Humble (Feb.), Equipping and Design (May), Purpose Series (May)

Gleanings: "Why do you look at the speck of sawdust in your brother's eye and pay no attention to the plank in your own eye?" (Matt. 7:3 NIV).

DAY 11

Uninvited

Wilbur was taken from his home under the apple tree.[25]

Mr. Arable uninvites the little pig from the farmhouse. Wilbur then lives under the apple tree in a large, straw-filled wooden box. But not long after, he's uninvited from this happy home too. He is sold out from under his apple tree to live in a manure pile. To be uninvited is to be rejected and unwanted.

Joseph's brothers tried to kill him and then sold him as a slave. Falsely accused, Joseph was cast into prison, but in each case, he rose up. The more degrading the situation, the more he rose up. Jesus followed this same pattern. "He was in the world, and the world was made through Him, and the world did not know Him. He came to His own, and His own did not receive Him" (John 1:10–11 NKJV).

For every person who uninvites you as a child of God from their circle, many more will arise to invite you in. When you're invited into God's circle, you will come to "Mount Zion, to the city of the living God, the heavenly Jerusalem. You have come to thousands upon thousands of angels in joyful assembly, to the church of the firstborn, whose names are written in heaven" (Heb. 12:22–23 NIV). God is always calling us.

> "The Spirit and the Bride say, 'Come.' And let the one who hears say, 'Come.' And let the one who is thirsty come; let the one who desires take the water of life without price" (Rev. 22:17).

Prayer: Lord, if I am rejected or "uninvited" by others when I share my faith, or for any other reason, please let it not be because of any insensitivity on my part. When I'm rejected by those who refuse or misunderstand me, grant me a gracious, forgiving spirit. God, show me if there is a reason for the uninvite and help me humbly address it.

Radiant Action: Journal Entry: Have I been uninvited from a place or someone's life for a good reason? Maybe not. I will give my rejection over to the One who knows, and express confidence that He has a good plan for me despite what others might think or do.

Webs: Insignificance (Feb.), Weakness (Feb.)

Gleanings: "Come and see" (John 1:46).

DAY 12

Waiting

"If they'd . . . wait quietly, maybe something good would come along."[26]

"Life is always a rich and steady time when you are waiting for something to happen or to hatch."[27] Charlotte's philosophy is to learn to wait quietly. The super charger may miss much good by rushing around. The goose waits well as she sits on her eggs. Wilbur, too, waits, but not patiently. He waits for the dawn, for Charlotte to come up with a plan to save him, for the judging at the fair, for Charlotte's offspring to hatch. But sometimes the waiting has a cast of doom. Wilbur's reaction to the old sheep's warning of certain doom to come was panic; he didn't know his savior sat confidently above him.

As we wait on things we hope and long for, sometimes sensing a darker tide about to sweep toward us, we, too, can find assurance in knowing that our Savior is seated victoriously at the right hand of the Father and that He is watching over us. We cry out to Him, but usually we must wait patiently for His timing.

Joseph the patriarch waited seventeen years for his vindication and promotion. A lame man waited over forty years for healing. The disciples watched Jesus ascend to heaven and waited obediently forty days for the outpouring of the Holy Spirit. The martyrs are crying out around God's throne even now, "How long before you judge?" (Rev. 6:10). We wait because we live in a broken world that will one day be redeemed completely, but the time is not yet.

When we go to God for any situation, we know that we are wrestling "against the rulers, against the authorities, against the cosmic powers over this present darkness, against the spiritual forces of evil in the heavenly places" (Eph. 6:12). Daniel fasted three weeks before the angel answered because of spiritual warfare. Our comfort lays in knowing that God loves us, that He is in control.

"Our soul waits for the Lord; he is our help and our shield" (Ps. 33:20).

Prayer: Dear God, teach me how to wait on You, how to fight and fast, how to confess, and persevere. Teach me how to wrestle as I wait.

Radiant Action: Journal Entry: I will make a spiritual, moral, and economic inventory to see where I need to change. I won't give God a deadline for removing sources of irritation, inconvenience, or pain.

Webs: Relationship Series (Jan.), Waiting for the Dawn (Feb.), Passion (May)

Gleanings: "It is good that one should wait quietly for the salvation of the Lord" (Lam. 3:26).

DAY 13

Enemies

"There's a regular conspiracy around here to kill you."[28]

Wilbur was living with his enemies who fed him well but with an ulterior motive. Like the witch in Hansel and Gretel, they were fattening him up to be eaten!

The Bible has a lot to say about enemies:

- **Be realistic.** They are *present*. "Look! Evil people . . . are planning to shoot from the shadows at those who have honest hearts" (Ps. 11:2 NIrV).
- **They can be powerful.** "For the enemy . . . has crushed my life to the ground" (Ps. 143:3).
- **"Do not be afraid of them**; remember well what the LORD your God did to Pharaoh and to all Egypt" (Deut. 7:18 NIV).
- **Stand for what is right.** (Eph. 6:13)
- **Use your weapons.** (Eph. 6:11-18)
- **Wait on His timing.** "Sit at my right hand until I make your enemies a footstool for your feet" (Ps. 110:1 NIV).
- **Let God take revenge.** "Beloved, never avenge yourselves, but leave it to the wrath of God, for it is written, 'Vengeance is mine, I will repay, says the Lord'" (Rom. 12:19; see also Matt. 5:39).
- **Believe the enemies of the servant of God will be overcome.** "You will destroy all the adversaries of my soul, for I am your servant" (Ps. 143:12).
- **Believe Jesus conquered all evil** through His death on the cross and His resurrection. He will put all things under His feet, including death: "For he must reign until he has put all enemies under his feet" (1 Cor. 15:25).
- **Remember sometimes our enemies are *not who we think they are.*** Sometimes there is a Judas on our team. The Jews thought the Romans were the enemy, but in fact, the real enemy was (and is) sin (Rom 3:23).

Prayer: Father, I have enemies within and without. Grant me victory over my inner wolves, addictions, and all causes of darkness, including the devil and the world. Help me to love and pray for those people who oppose me. Thank You that Jesus conquered and that You will make all things new one day.

Radiant Action: Today is the day for me to pray for my enemy, to do him good and to forgive, knowing that as I forgive, I will be forgiven. I will stand strong in the strength God gives.

Webs: Suffering (Mar.), Murder and Betrayal (Apr.), Weapons (Apr.)

Gleanings: "No wisdom, no understanding, no counsel can avail against the LORD" (Prov. 21:30).

DAY 14

Dreams

Avery lay dreaming that the Ferris wheel had stopped and that he was in the top car.[29]

Stuart Little, the mouse in E. B. White's beloved book by that title, asks a classroom of children as their substitute teacher, "What is important?" The answers are "a shaft of sunlight at the end of a dark afternoon, a note in music, and the way the back of a baby's neck smells if its mother keeps it tidy, . . . ice cream with chocolate sauce."[30] These answers reflect what the students dream about.

Charlotte dreams of keeping Wilbur alive. Wilbur's dream is to keep living past Christmas. (He also has a passion to be "in a forest looking for beechnuts.")[31] Mr. Zuckerman dreams of having the first prize pig. Mrs. Zuckerman wishes for a deep freeze. Lurvy hopes to play the games at the fair and win an Indian blanket.

But the human heart is not satisfied with the substances of our fast-melting present, the new wing on the house, new cars, or a vacation fling. The soul longs for something that is beyond music and poetry and the smell of a baby's neck, for God has put eternity into the heart of every person (see Eccl. 3:11).

Jesus sounded the depths of a rich young man's heart by telling him, "'If you would be perfect, go, sell what you possess and give to the poor, and you will have treasure in heaven; and come, follow me.' When the young man heard this he went away sorrowful, for he had great possessions" (Matt. 19:21–22). This young man broke the first commandment—to love God with all his heart. Money and position stood in the way of his acquiring the most precious possession of all and finding lasting joy.

Prayer: Dear Father, help me long for what You desire. You said that if I delight in You, You will give me the desires of my heart. May my joy and pleasure be in knowing You more intimately.

Radiant Action: Journal Entry: What is the dream underneath my desires? What gives me hope? Are my dreams big enough? Just opening my freezer—what Mrs. Zuckerman dreams of owning—can remind me to pray for God to give me the right desires.

Webs: Purpose Series (May), More Dreams (May), Singing (June), Longings (Oct.)

Gleanings: "But seek first the kingdom of God and his righteousness, and all these things will be added to you" (Matt. 6:33).

DAY 15

Barnyard Disciples

Fern liked to sit nearby and watch.[32]

A disciple is a student. Wilbur is Charlotte's disciple. He watches and listens to her carefully and admiringly. She tutors him in logic, self-control, vocabulary, common sense, faithfulness, strategic thinking, thinking ahead, and friendship. When crisis comes, he is prepared. Wilbur becomes like Charlotte in heart and mind.

The diverse animals in the barnyard are reminiscent of the diversity of the original twelve disciples and the diversity of people Jesus came to save. Just as the ark held all the different kinds of creatures, so God's kingdom will embrace all kinds of believers. To bring all nations, tribes, and tongues into the kingdom, Jesus tells us that our first calling is to make disciples—to bring people to know Him, grow in Him, and share His love with others (see Matt. 28:19–20). Though the calling comes with a promise of hard work and even persecution, it also comes with a future of hope, joy, peace, and God's presence.

By the power of the Spirit, we can imitate Jesus and overcome our selfishness, apathy, and reluctance to obey. We can learn from Him how to negotiate the world's spiritual darkness with logic, love, and power. Generations of Charlotte's progeny thrive in the barnyard and beyond because of Wilbur's loving actions. Future generations of people will live to know Him because we've obeyed His command to disciple.

Prayer: Help me to love disciples with all types of personalities, backgrounds, and giftings.

Lord Jesus, thank You for this prayer You prayed for me: "I am praying for them. I am not praying for the world but for those whom you have given me, for they are yours. All mine are yours, and yours are mine, and I am glorified in them" (John 17:9–10).

Radiant Action: I will ask God to send me someone to disciple. I will ask that I will walk in a way worthy of having a disciple. If I am in need of discipling, I will pray for a mature mentor. When I see a sheep, a donkey, a goat, or a goose, I will be reminded to pray about discipling or influencing others or to pray for others to help me grow.

Webs: Friendship (Feb.), Calling: "Here Pig" (Mar.), Changed (Apr.), Ethnic Barriers Broken (Dec.).

Gleanings: "Go therefore and make disciples of all nations, baptizing them in the name of the Father and of the Son and of the Holy Spirit" (Matt. 28:19).

DAY 16

Division of Responsibility

"Bring me back a word!"[33]

An unlikely team of a rat and a spider wins the day. The curmudgeon, the rodent, resentfully fetches words so the little spider can weave her magic. Together, despite imminent death for one and weakness of character in the other, they prevail.

Author Blake Snow explains the human situation in terms of interdependence: "Your success depends on others . . . Humans are social creatures and must rely on each other to thrive."[34] He goes on to quote a New York business entrepreneur, James Song, who wrote, "To succeed, you need other people to compensate for your personal shortcomings."[35]

Templeton has long ugly teeth and Charlotte has eight hairy legs. We each have something to offer God's team although they may not look so great. Combining lists of spiritual gifts found in different New Testament books reveals there are many: administration, pioneering, discernment, encouraging, evangelism, exercising faith, giving, hospitality, knowledge, leadership, shepherding, prophesying, teaching, serving, showing mercy, and wisdom. You have a gift!

"To each is given the manifestation of the Spirit for the common good" (1 Cor. 12:7).

Prayer: Dear Lord, You crafted all of us and lavished Your gifts upon us. Please grant me the power and wisdom to know how to best serve and be a good teammate for Your glory.

Radiant Action: I will take a spiritual gifts inventory and a personality test like the Enneagram[36] to see how I could be most effective in serving.

Webs: Teamwork (Feb.), Communication in Community (Mar.), Barnyard Disciples (Mar.), Surprising Deliverers (Apr.)

Gleanings: "For none of us lives to himself, and none of us dies to himself (Rom. 14:7).

DAY 17

Communication in Community

Then one of the cows told one of the sheep, and soon all the sheep knew.[37]

The barnyard animals telegraph news with lightning speed. They even debate which words are most effective in the war for Wilbur. Charlotte illustrates the power of refining words for success; the more adept one is at choosing and using the best words, the more that person's influence multiplies.

We can grow in our ability to use words and communicate clearly. The ability can be lifesaving. "Death and life are in the power of the tongue, and those who love it will eat its fruits" (Prov. 18:21). Wielded with the right heart, language can be a highway for the light of life. "Your word is a lamp to my feet and a light to my path" (Ps. 119:105).

Community and communication are integrated. Relationships depend on all parties communicating in such a way that each understands the other's message. Members of a community make progress because they communicate openly and convey the message they intend in a way the receivers can comprehend. Communication is fragile; what I think I said may not be what you understood because our backgrounds and perspectives differ. Imagine a gaggle of geese pondering the use of words. Add a sheep, a lamb, a pig, and a spider, and you have the challenge of communication in an ordinary office or church.

Speech can create worlds, good or bad. God destroyed the power of the prideful people of Babel by confusing language so no one understood one another. Their work on the tower of pride stopped. But God redeemed language at Pentecost for His purpose of saving the world. The disciples praised God that day in languages unknown to them and reached many foreigners visiting the city for celebration. Wielded with the right heart, language can be a highway for the light of life.

Prayer: God, help me use words skillfully. Make my heart humble so my words are productive.

Radiant Action: I will look up a word a day (subscribe to Merriam-Webster's Word of the Day) and write it in a section of my journal designed for New Words. I will aim to use my new words and to also develop a good reading plan.

Webs: Expectations of Others (Feb.), Teamwork (Feb.), Listening (Apr.), Words (Oct.)

DAY 18

Calling: "Here, Pig"

Fern, being a nurturing little girl, delivers Wilbur from his fate and cares for him with motherly love. But as she matures, her focus changes from devotion to Wilbur to finding joy in a boy. God calls us to undertake different roles and missions in life according to the seasons of our lives. These callings stem from our purpose planted in us by God. As David wrote in Psalm 57:2, "I cry out to God Most High, to God who fulfills his purpose for me."

Physician and Bible teacher Dr. Kenneth Acha explains "calling" in his blog. He cites Merriam-Webster's definition of calling as "a strong inner impulse toward a particular course of action, especially when accompanied by conviction of divine influence."[38] For the Christian, a calling is something that "carries the connotation that our lives were made for someone bigger than ourselves and that we are called by someone—a divine being—or by something bigger than ourselves to fulfill that service . . . Calling embodies both the *beckoning and the task* that is given when we answer" (emphasis mine).[39]

A calling can come as a surprise. Fern is meekly setting the table for breakfast before school one morning when her calling comes to save Wilbur. Saul, before becoming Paul the Apostle, was on his way to persecute disciples when he was struck blind on the road to Damascus and told, "Arise and go into the city, and you will be told what you must do" (Acts 9:6 NKJV). David was tending sheep when he was called to be king. Believers are admonished to "make every effort to confirm your calling" (2 Peter 1:10 NIV). Sometimes outsiders determine your purpose to be one thing, but that might not actually be your true purpose or calling. Wilbur is called to be a friend, but the farmers thought otherwise.

Prayer: Heavenly Father, give me discernment to understand times and circumstances, and to know what to do. Prepare me so I'll be ready whenever Your call may come, and may I never ignore whatever calling is right in front of me.

Radiant Action: Charles Spurgeon remarked that roses are symbols for open doors, so when I see a rose, I will ask God for an open door or for courage to go through the open doors He has already shown me.

Webs: Vision (Mar.), Mission: Specific Assignments (Mar.),Equipping and Design (May), Voices (June)

DAY 19

Mission: Specific Assignments

"One of the pigs is a runt."[40]

Fern was only eight when she received her calling to save Wilbur. She knew instinctively that it wasn't right to murder something small and helpless. Her specific mission at that moment was to save the runt pig from destruction. The tasks she performed on his behalf, what can be called assignments, missions, or callings, flowed out of her greater purpose of nurturing. Mission is a specific application of purpose.

Sometimes we need to experiment, try new things, crash through labels and limitations, swerve in a new direction as the Spirit guides. We usually have more than one gift, and sometimes it takes many seasons to use them. Charlotte calls herself "versatile," meaning, "I can turn with ease from one thing to another. It means I don't have to limit my activities to spinning and trapping and stunts like that."[41] She becomes a rescuer, planner, community public relations expert, and a friend. She wears all these hats but executes each part of the mission with the one purpose of saving Wilbur.

> "Many are the plans in the mind of a man, but it is the purpose of the Lord that will stand" (Prov. 19:21).

Prayer: God, please give me discernment about which mission I'm on now. Cleanse and heal me of any moral fracture that may be hindering my sensitivity to the Spirit's leading. I annoy myself with herding all the inner cats—and all the little squirrels of ideas and the connections with people that flood my orderly schedule. O Lord, order my chicks, herd my cats, give me love for people so that my heart, soul, and body would be one with You and bring You joy. Show me Your will and Your ways.

Radiant Action: Journal Entries: 1. What keeps me from my mission? Debt, unstable relationships, apathy, health concerns, fear, sin, lack of training for spiritual growth? 2. How can I develop a servant's heart? 3. How do I grow the desire to go to where God is calling? 4. What are strategies to overcome obstacles to progress?

Webs: Vision (Mar.), Calling: "Here Pig" (Mar.), Equipping and Design (May)

Gleanings: Brian Frost, senior pastor of Providence Baptist Church in Raleigh, North Carolina, said in a sermon he delivered on November 22, 2020, "What we adore becomes our mission because we want to share our delight in our adoration."

DAY 20
Quarterly Review

January–March

1. Have your kept your journal handy? It is your friend. It's your home for reflections, to record struggles, and victories. Reflection is the way to catch an updraft and get unstuck! You also have needed a Bible and probably a copy of *Charlotte's Web*.
2. Which Scriptures have spoken to you the most? How's the Bible reading going? Are you able to read at least five minutes a day?
3. Introduction: Do you ever wonder how and why someone would spend so long coming up with 240 devotions based on a children's book and the Bible? It all has to do with swimming in a pool on a sunny day and watching the refracted light dance in the depths. We humans inhabit of a fallen world and see only through a glass darkly. But consider how shafts of light streak into dark waters of a pool and shatter. If we peer into those waters to admire the glorious disarray, refracted radiance plays both downward and ricochets upward toward the surface. Light from a parable is like that display of light in a pool. Prisms of faith, imagination, and inspiration allow us to detect the brilliance of grace hidden in the barnyard. Who knows when and where you will be inspired?! Be open.
4. January: Do you identify more with Fern, Wilbur, Templeton, or Charlotte or all four at different times?
5. January: Which aspect of personality intrigues you the most and why? Emotions, thinking, identity with its purposes and preferences, relationships, or boundaries?
6. February (Relationships): Were there any entries that covered a topic that pierced you or brought you special satisfaction?
7. February: When have you, like Wilbur, felt runty, humble, insignificant, small, or uninvited? Do you have a place in your journal to write about those moments? (Don't bear grudges but remember that with humility comes more grace.) God "gives grace to the humble" (James 4:6 NET).
8. February: Wilbur had to wait for the dawn to meet Charlotte. What a long night! When have you had to "wait for the dawn," waiting on someone or for an issue to resolve?
9. March: Have you been tempted to wallow in the manure of self-pity?
10. March: What is your calling? What is your mission in this season of life?

Challenge: Keep a record of Scriptures that are special to you, answers to prayer, and songs that encourage. Make notes on God's timing, wisdom (understanding), grace, and provisions. Even note where you find God breaking through in the ordinary, sometimes with humor! You will build a strong story to help others.

APRIL
ROOTS OF FAITH

In *Romeo and Juliet*, Shakespeare describes spring as "well-appareled April" following "on the heel of limping winter."

As spring progresses, apple tree buds appear and mature. The buds are like our new hopes and songs. It's a time of renewal, as nourishing and vital to our heart as sap in a living tree. April is for planting. Unseen roots grip the soil to drink in nutrients. Our April devotions are based on the roots of faith: sin, deliverance, resurrection, and changed lives.

Enemy Territory, *p. 79*
Appearances: Perception, Deception, and Fraud, *p. 80*
Captured: Sin, *p. 81*
Boards, *p. 82*
Shadows of Death: God Gives Hope with New Life, *p. 83*
Murder and Betrayal, *p. 84*
Discipline, *p. 85*
Faith, *p. 86*
Surprising Deliverers, *p. 87*
Blood, *p. 88*
Baptism: The Buttermilk Bath and Baptism into New Life, *p. 89*
Death, *p. 90*
Scriptures about Death, *p. 92*
Easter: The Gospel in *Charlotte's Web*, *p. 93*
Holy Spirit: The Warm Breeze, *p. 95*
Mornings, *p. 97*
Listening: The Discarded Milking Stool, *p. 100*
Changed, *p. 101*
Unstuck with an Updraft: Out of the Deep Freeze, *p. 102*
Weapons, *p. 103*

DAY 1

Enemy Territory

"He'll take a knife to you, my boy."[1]

Wilbur dwells in enemy territory as do we. The farmers seemed so kind in feeding Wilbur, but they plotted to turn him into pork chops. Whispers of Hansel and Gretel! Satan's ministers may appear as benefactors or "angel[s] of light" (2 Cor. 11:14), but the enemy and his demons, seeking vengeance on the Creator, intend to kill, steal from, and destroy God's people. The devil is a real and evil being who denies the authority of God and plots with cold calculation the confusion and obliteration of positive personal identity and the ability to build community.

The apostle Paul explains we are in spiritual warfare. We don't struggle against flesh and blood, but against principalities—the malevolent spiritual rulers and powers that wreak havoc and destruction on the earth. To deal effectively with the enemy and his minions, Peter warns that we should "be sober-minded; be watchful. Your adversary the devil prowls around like a roaring lion, seeking someone to devour. Resist him, firm in your faith, knowing that the same kinds of suffering are being experienced by your brotherhood throughout the world (1 Peter 5:8–9).

Jesus came to destroy the works of darkness, and through Him, the enemy has already been defeated (see 1 John 3:8). Although a wily murderer, he has been unseated and *has no authority* over the believer. Ask God to rebuke him in the name of Jesus. He's a toothless old lion roaring at you with the aim of making you run the other way toward the "young lions" who devour you. But Satan is not our focus. God is our center, and we can keep our eyes on Him through praise, thanksgiving, fellowship, reading the Scriptures, community worship, prayer and fasting.

Prayer: Lord, rebuke the devil in whatever way he is trying to devour me or my family. In the powerful name of Jesus, enable me to resist him so he will flee from me (see James 4:7).

Radiant Action: Journal Entries: 1. I will praise God, quiet my heart before Him, confess my sins, ask Him to meet my needs, fast, pray, stay in community, and write regularly in my journal in a section labeled *struggles*. This will be a keen testimony to help others with similar struggles. 2. State resolve that with the help of God I won't be ignorant or deceived but rather self-controlled and alert. The devil is defeated. Jesus has won. I will resist the devil in the name of Jesus.

Webs: Enemies (Mar.), Holy Spirit (Apr.), Weapons (Apr.), Unseen (June)

DAY 2

Appearances: Perception, Deception, and Fraud

"I dare say my trick will work."[2]

Charlotte's web is a trick to save Wilbur's life. Based on the hypothesis that humans are gullible and desire fame, Charlotte weaves a deceptive plot and wins.

Unlike Charlotte's clever ruse to save her friend, the devil and his henchmen weave webs of deception to trick humans and destroy their very identities as made in the image of God. "Come, Eve. Did God say not to touch the fruit? Is he keeping something good from you?" (See Gen. 3:1.)

Like Eve, the adversary's followers are deceived, "blinded by the god of this world" (see 1 Cor. 2:14; 2 Cor. 4:4). The enemy can make people whose minds and motivations are controlled by him seem credible—he can beguile the most astute, and when the Antichrist appears at the end of time, he will deceive even believers. (Matt. 24:24). The devil plays on our human susceptibility to fear and our desire for glory, status, ease, and security, and uses these feelings to deceive us. We are so easily lured into deceptions that emotional insecurities manipulate us into believing.

Rascal is the true story of a pet raccoon saved by a motherless boy during World War I in the Great Lakes region of the United States. Rascal ends up in a trap because of his love of shiny objects. Are we gullible too, lured by shiny objects?

"The serpent deceived me, and I ate" (Gen. 3:13 NIV).

Prayer: Father, bring my heart and mind under the authority of Your Spirit so I may not be deceived by what *appears* to be true. Show me where I am believing empty lies and making false assumptions.

Radiant Action: Journal Entry: What hidden desires or incomplete knowledge might make me vulnerable to deception? I determine not to be deceived, even though the devil may appear as an angel of light. I will begin a Bible memory program like Fighter Verse.[3]

Webs: Dreams (Mar.), Enemy Territory (Apr.), Murder and Betrayal (Apr.), Captured: Sin (Apr.)

Gleanings: "Man looks on the outward appearance, but the Lord looks on the heart" (1 Sam. 16:7).

DAY 3

Captured: Sin

"A spider's life can't help being something of a mess."[4]

White describes Templeton's debauched, ratty nature with thorough blackness: "The rat had no morals, no conscience, no scruples."[5] To persuade him, the sheep appeals to "his baser instincts, of which he has plenty."[6] And although White asserts his animals are amoral,[7] Templeton exemplifies the sinner's nature.

Flannery O'Connor, stated that a "Christian novelist . . . sees [sin] not as sickness, an accident of environment, [or a 'mistake' as E. B. White's father viewed sin,[8]] but as a responsible choice of offense against God which involves his eternal future."[9] Augustine defined sin as the state of being "caved in on oneself."[10] Sin is disobedience to the One who made us, and it has consequences.

Charlotte wraps her prey round and round with a slender thread until it can't move. Sin begins with only a small thread, a seed of a thought, perhaps an attitude of discontentment, entitlement, or rebellion. Jesus explained "But I say to you that everyone who looks at a woman with lustful intent has already committed adultery" (Matt. 5:28). We may indulge our small sins, but like Charlotte's threads around her prey, daily sinful thoughts or habits wrap round and round us until we're trapped, and escape becomes tremendously difficult. How foolish for a fly to sidle up close to a spider web. How foolish for humans to be comfortably cozy with sin. "The cords of death entangled me; the torrents of destruction overwhelmed me" (Ps. 18:4 NIV).

"For the wages of sin is death, but the free gift of God is eternal life in Christ Jesus our Lord" (Rom. 6:23).

Prayer: "Almighty and most merciful Father, we have erred and strayed from Your ways like lost sheep. We have followed too much the devices and desires of our own hearts."[11]

Radiant Action: I will be accountable. "Exhort one another every day, . . . that none of you may be hardened by the deceitfulness of sin" (Heb. 3:13). Windshield wipers on a rainy day are reminders of sin wiped away.

Webs: Templeton Series (Jan.), Identity (Feb.), Easter (Apr.)

DAY 4

Boards

Lurvy . . . nailed the board in place.[12]

After Wilbur's wild escapade into freedom outside his pen because the goose told him a board was loose, Lurvy nailed the board back on the fence. Wilbur never escaped again.

We need to consider how to "nail up boards" as a defense against unleashed exploration of sin. Unlike the Romantic poets, Paul exhorts the believer to "put on the Lord Jesus Christ, and make no provision for the flesh, to gratify its desires" (Rom. 13:14). Nailing up a loose board means fleeing from temptation; it means making a serious change in your routine; it means associating with trustworthy people who will help you walk victoriously; it means not buying that stash of whatever you soothe your emotions with on a bad day.

Take stock of your emotions and motivations. For example, are you frustrated with a marriage partner? Put a "board" around your attitude and love your spouse. Get help; talk it out take a vacation together; invest in your spouse with a tangible gift and with a servant's heart. Are you inclined to manipulate through flattery, or inwardly pass judgment, or do you generally maintain an angry or vengeful attitude? These are but a few of the myriad ways we give into our weaknesses and temptations.

Nail these fleshly attitudes and actions to the cross; take them to the Savior. "For we do not have a high priest who is unable to sympathize with our weaknesses, but one who in every respect has been tempted as we are, yet without sin" (Heb. 4:15). The nails in Jesus's hands and feet won the victory over our transgressions. Those nails killed Him, and we identify our old selves as having died with Him. Likewise, we identify with His resurrection life.

> "I have been crucified with Christ. It is no longer I who live, but Christ who lives in me. And the life I now live in the flesh I live by faith in the Son of God, who loved me and gave himself for me" (Gal. 2:20).

> "No temptation has overtaken you that is not common to man. God is faithful, and he will not let you be tempted beyond your ability, but with the temptation he will also provide the way of escape, that you may be able to endure it" (1 Cor. 10:13).

Prayer: God, show me where I need to board up a hole in my "fence."

Radiant Action: Journal Entry: List tendencies to sin and triggers. I will board up or say no to the situations that contribute to my bent to sin. Prayer, the Word, fellowship, and counsel will be my fences. I will build habits and strategies based on my weaknesses. (See Celebrate Recovery.)[13] A pile of boards will remind me to tighten my defenses.

Webs: Emotional Self-Control (Mar.), Changed (Apr.), Weapons (Apr.), Captured: Sin (Apr.).

Gleanings: "Make straight paths for your feet" (Heb. 12:13).

DAY 5

Shadows of Death: God Gives Hope with New Life

"I'm languishing."[14]

The shadow of death falls over Charlotte. She feels the reality that she's passing from the earth and will be no more. Charlotte accepts death as part of life. She lives well, loyally, and fruitfully. She dies and her children live after her. Charlotte's shadow of death, however, is not like the shadow of death for believers. And the new life, her offspring, is not the new life of the believer.

Believers languish, growing weaker and feebler with the weight of years. But we aren't held hostage to thanatophobia— "fear of one's own death"— which grips Wilbur. Instead, Paul desires "that you may not grieve as others do who have no hope. For since we believe that Jesus died and rose again, even so, through Jesus, God will bring with him those who have fallen asleep" (1 Thess. 4:13–14). Paul's goodbye to the Ephesian Christians in Acts 20 was imbued with the sense that death awaited him. The people wept. In His earthly life, Jesus wept too, even knowing He would raise Lazarus from the grave. The shadow of death doesn't sweep over without leaving grief and loss.

When Christ returns, He will vanquish death, the last enemy. Meanwhile, we have assurance of eternal life now in our possession and physical resurrection after we die. As new creations, we have new life in our being while we are on earth. When we sense the shadow of death in our lives, we can take comfort knowing that the Lord is sovereign and that He is with us. "The LORD will keep your going out and your coming in from this time forth and forevermore" (Ps. 121:8). He will guard us coming and going for all our days and be with us in the final going out.

> "So we do not lose heart. Though our outer self is wasting away, our inner self is being renewed day by day" (2 Cor. 4:16).

> When Jesus returns, "Then we who are alive, who are left, will be caught up together with them in the clouds to meet the Lord in the air, and so we will always be with the Lord" (1 Thess. 4:17).

Prayer: Thank You, God, that Jesus is the resurrection and the life.

Radiant Action: Journal Entry: Affirmation of belief in the resurrection and find resource material with the evidence. "Whoever believes in me, though he die, yet shall he live, and everyone who lives and believes in me shall never die. Do you believe this?" (John 11:25–26).

Webs: Waiting for the Dawn (Feb.), Finding the Good in the Bad (Feb.), Vision (Mar.).

Gleanings: "Be gracious to me, O LORD, for I am languishing" (Ps. 6:2). God "turns the shadow of death into morning" (Amos 5:8 NKJV).

DAY 6

Murder and Betrayal

"Everybody is in the plot."[15]

E. B. White expresses indignation over the fate of farm pigs, to which he himself had been party:

> The scheme of buying a pig in blossom time, feeding it through summer and fall, and butchering it when the solid cold weather arrives . . . is a tragedy enacted on most farms with perfect fidelity to the original script. The murder, being premeditated, is in the first degree.[16]

White assuaged his guilt by writing *Charlotte's Web*. Betrayal, we assume, is a bad thing—treachery, selfishness, lying, double dealing. But if betrayal meets grace, it can spark the crisis that leads to a new beginning—a death leading to life. Judas led Jesus to the cross, fulfilling His mission to open the way of salvation. "Judas, would you betray the Son of Man with a kiss?" (Luke 22:48).

If we are the betrayer, the only way we can find comfort from guilt's torment is, ironically, through the Holy Spirit's conviction of our own betrayal of the Lord. Our sin killed the innocent Son of God. This leads to the cross and the forgiveness He offers, which in turn enables us to forgive the betrayals of others. But repentance and restitution for the hurt person is required.

If you are the betrayed, God will give you the grace and power to turn it into a new story like Joseph, like Jesus, like Paul.

"Father, forgive them, for they know not what they do" (Luke 23:34).

Prayer: God, the wound is deep, but I give You my betrayer and the betrayal. I forgive. Show me the new way You are making through this treachery. Thank you for sending your only Son, Jesus, to die on the cross as the target of Judas's betrayal. For my own moments of disloyalty to You or others, I ask You to forgive me and help me do what I need to for reconciliation.

Radiant Action: If I have been hurt by someone who betrayed my trust, I will seek counsel and take steps to forgive the offender. If I am the one who in some way has betrayed a trust, I will repent, seek the Lord's forgiveness, and do what I can for the one I hurt. Seeing a pig will make me ponder about forgiving others or seeking forgiveness.

Webs: Disappointment (Mar.), Waiting (Mar.), Enemies (Mar.).

Gleanings: "Be kind and compassionate to one another, forgiving each other, just as in Christ God forgave you" (Eph. 4:32 NIV).

DAY 7

Discipline

"Be quiet, Wilbur!"[17]

More than once, Charlotte reproves her young friend for his behavioral excesses. Reacting with uncontrollable sobbing, his carousel of emotions begs for discipline. She treats him like a loving parent, and to his credit, he responds graciously. He bears the fruit of her discipline when he exercises restraint and, under great duress, uses reason when Charlotte is dying.

Medicine and discipline are neither tasty nor pleasurable, but they usher in health of mind or body. "God disciplines us for our good, in order that we may share in his holiness. No discipline seems pleasant at the time, but painful. Later on, however, it produces a harvest of righteousness and peace for those who have been trained by it" (Heb. 12:10–11 NIV).

The Oxford dictionary defines self-discipline as "the ability to control one's feelings and overcome one's weaknesses; the ability to pursue what one thinks is right despite temptations to abandon it." The Google dictionary puts it simply: "Self-discipline is self-command and self-mastery."

Managing oneself is what Peter Drucker says is the first step in being an effective executive who manages others. "Executives who do not manage themselves for effectiveness cannot possibly expect to manage their associates and subordinates. Management is largely by example. Executives who do not know how to make themselves effective in their own job and work set the wrong example."[18] Charlotte certainly set a right example for self-discipline.

Prayer: Enable me to wisely discipline my children or others in my charge, and to receive discipline where I need it. There are lonely caverns in me, secret places of my heart that crave "crack" of some form while I resist acknowledging my real needs. Cleanse me of what draws me to indulgence instead of discipline. Make me rest, be rooted in your ways, and delight in Your ways as I remember that You watch over me (from Psalm 1).

Radiant Action: Journal Entry: How is God speaking to my heart through Proverbs? Proverbs 3:11–12; 6:23; 12:1; 17:10; 25:12; 29:1. Proverbs is an abundant source of guidance for balanced living and a demonstration of the vital role discipline plays in our attaining it.

Webs: Emotions and Motivations Series (Jan.), Identity (Feb.), Emotional Self-Control (Mar.), More Dreams (May)

Gleanings: "He disciplines us for our good, that we may share his holiness" (Heb. 12:10).

DAY 8

Faith

"We simply know that we are dealing with supernatural forces here."[19]

Wilbur does nothing to save himself. He's just a young pig with a corkscrew tail. Charlotte's the one who does all the planning and implementation. Neither are we saved by our own efforts. God had a plan and executed it without our help. "For by grace you have been saved through faith. And this is not your own doing; it is the gift of God" (Eph. 2:8).

Wilbur put his faith in Charlotte, and he's saved for another spring. We put our faith in God and are saved for eternity. "And without faith it is impossible to please him, for whoever would draw near to God must believe that he exists and that he rewards those who seek him" (Heb. 11:6).

Wilbur's belief in Charlotte is rewarded. She does the impossible and changes the course of destiny. We as believers can exercise our faith to break through insurmountable challenges in real living.

> God has redeemed us forever.
> He has given us His Holy Spirit.
> He is remaking us into His image.
> Whatever problems we have, He is bigger.

> *"But now the righteousness of God has been manifested apart from the law, although the Law and the Prophets bear witness to it—the righteousness of God through faith in Jesus Christ for all who believe"* (Rom. 3:21–22).

Prayer: "I believe; help my unbelief!" (Mark 9:24). Father, increase my faith. Hear my voice in the morning (see Ps. 5:3).

Radiant Action: I will stir up my faith by reading the Bible each day (see Rom. 10:17). I will show my faith is real by doing what God requires: to love Him and to help my neighbor (see Luke 10:27; James 2:14–16). I will step out in faith about what He calls me to do.

Webs: Mornings (Apr.), Purpose Series (May), Flight (May), Direction (May)

Gleanings: "Faith says it's not where you are, but where you're going that is important."[20]

> *"Faith is thanking God in advance."*[21] *"Now faith is the certainty of things hoped for, a proof of things not seen"* (Heb. 11:1 NASB).

> *"Your faith is growing abundantly"* (2 Thess. 1:3).

DAY 9

Surprising Deliverers

[Templeton] took Wilbur's tail in his mouth and bit it . . . The pain revived Wilbur.[22]

The deliverers in *Charlotte's Web* are not superheroes. Out of the smallness of childhood comes Fern. Out of the darkness comes Charlotte. Out of the manure comes Wilbur. Out of the dump comes Templeton, the accidental deliverer. (Templeton is only persuaded to help because the sheep lets him know he'll starve if Wilbur dies.)

And God also uses the unlikely to accomplish victory. "God chose what is low and despised in the world" (1 Cor. 1:28). Does it seem foolish that a certain Jew born into poverty in an oppressed country turns out to be the Savior of the world? Does it seem unlikely that Jesus would chose a person who was not only a despised Samaritan, but who was also a woman, to be the first evangelist? (See John 4:29.)

Once when John Wesley was preaching in England, a mob accosted him. Honest Munchin, a prizefighter from the attacking mob, suddenly declared, "Sir, I will spend my life for you!" and proceeded to break the arm of a man trying to throw Wesley off a bridge.[23] A surprising deliverer indeed!

Wilbur never could have concocted a plan to save his own life through a small gray spider and a rat accomplice. Neither could we have ever devised our own plan of salvation. As one disciple exclaimed, "Can anything good come out of Nazareth?" (John 1:46). Would we have ever imagined that God Himself would come to earth and die for us when we were still sinners or "in the manure"?

Prayer: Dear God, help me to be receptive to Your means of help, no matter how surprising. Help me be open to Your grace working in all sorts of ways and people, including letting me find spiritual inspiration in *Charlotte's Web*, a book about an unlikely pig and a spider.

Radiant Action: I won't reject help because it seems unlikely. (See 2 Kings 5:1–17; Isaiah 43:18–19; Acts 16:26; 1 Peter 1:18–19.

Webs: Finding the Good in the Bad (Feb.), Humble (Feb.), Uninvited (Mar.), Small Things (Mar.), Insignificance (Mar.),

DAY 10

Blood

"I love blood."[24]

Charlotte is bloodthirsty. That's her nature and the only way she can survive. It's a quirky trait, in Wilbur's opinion. The shadows of realities present in a simple children's story hint of the redemption story for mankind. Christians share something in common with Charlotte in a spiritual application.

We can survive only by the blood of Christ in eternity and the present. His blood alone defeats sin's darkness within and without. "Worthy are you to take the scroll and to open its seals, for you were slain, and by your blood you ransomed people for God from every tribe and language and people and nation" (Rev. 5:9). Jesus offers His life and His blood, so we can share in His life. Like Wilbur, who initially couldn't understand Charlotte's need for blood, the world too fails to grasp the spiritual value and necessity of the blood of Jesus.

In the Bible we read that God used the blood of bulls and goats to foreshadow the power of Jesus's blood. Wilbur declared, "I would gladly give my life for you—I really would."[25] Jesus gladly gave His life—for us. He really did.

The writer of Hebrews explains: "But when Christ appeared as a high priest . . . not by means of the blood of goats and calves but by means of his own blood, thus securing an eternal redemption . . . how much more will the blood of Christ, who through the eternal Spirit offered himself without blemish to God, purify our conscience from dead works to serve the living God" (Heb. 9:11–14).

Prayer: Lord Jesus, thank You for the blood. Your death brings me life. I pray that You would cover my loved ones and anyone else who comes to mind by the power of your blood. Help them understand the beauty and wonder and power of your blood. I acknowledge with gratitude that You have jurisdiction over all parts of my being and that You won the complete victory over the enemy by shedding Your precious blood on the cross.

Radiant Action: I will be thankful for Your sacrifice and marvel at the power of Your blood. I can look up and sing "There Is a Fountain Filled with Blood" by William Cowper. I will claim the power of Your blood in prayer.

Webs: Baptism (Apr.), Death (Apr.), Holy Spirit (Apr.)

DAY 11

Baptism: The Buttermilk Bath and Baptism into New Life

Avery slowly poured buttermilk on Wilbur's head and back.[26]

The buttermilk bath readies Wilbur for winning his special prize. It cleanses him and makes him like new, a kind of consecration for the life to come in his peaceable kingdom, the barn, where he would spend the rest of his days well cared for by Mr. Zuckerman. "It was the best place to be, thought Wilbur."[27]

Baptism for the believer readies us for a new life in God's kingdom, both here and in the kingdom to come. It represents a cleansing from our old life of sin and our resurrection in a redeemed state. It is not the means of salvation but rather the mark of the redeemed. It's an outward sign of an inward reality—that the believer is consecrated as a member of God's family:

> *And Peter said to them, "Repent and be baptized every one of you in the name of Jesus Christ for the forgiveness of your sins, and you will receive the gift of the Holy Spirit. For the promise is for you and for your children and for all who are far off, everyone whom the Lord our God calls to himself." And with many other words he bore witness and continued to exhort them, saying, "Save yourselves from this crooked generation. "So those who received his word were baptized, and there were added that day about three thousand souls* (Acts 2:38-41).

> *"Baptism, which corresponds to this, now saves you, not as a removal of dirt from the body but as an appeal to God for a good conscience, through the resurrection of Jesus Christ"* (1 Peter 3:21).

Prayer: Dear God, thank You for cleansing me and for baptism that marks me as Yours forever. Help me not to wallow in my old ways like Wilbur in the manure pile, but to embrace the future. Help me to be consecrated or set apart as redeemed for Your purposes as Your dearly loved child.

Radiant Action: When I see buttermilk (or even plain milk or almond milk), I'll remember that God has washed me clean and baptized me into a new life.

Webs: Marriage (Feb.), Dreams (Mar.), Changed (Apr.), Look Up! (June)

Gleanings: "Therefore, if anyone is in Christ, he is a new creation. The old has passed away; behold, the new has come" (2 Cor. 5:17).

DAY 12

Death

"In a day or two I'll be dead."[28]

Death is an inescapable part of all our lives. Death comes in varying degrees: the departure of loved ones to faraway places, loss of health and vitality through serious illness, personal failure, loss of a job, of money, of hope. And there is the crushing sadness of permanent loss of a life.

But the death of anything and anyone can open a passageway for the new. Charlotte dies after spinning her egg sac, but all 514 of her children hatch, and life begins again. Author Christy Wright asserts that "endings make new beginnings possible."[29] She admonishes her readers to stop regretting and lamenting past seasons.

For the believer in Christ, His death gives us new life. Our death here is the entrance to glory. "For to me to live is Christ, and to die is gain" (Phil. 1:21). Madeleine L'Engle recounts sitting in her grandmother's lap after a funeral. "That evening we sat out on the porch and listened to the ocean rolling into shore and I sat in my grandmother's lap, and she sang to me 'Jesus Tender Shepherd,' and I knew that despite the nearness of death I was loved, and that love was stronger than death."[30]

> "He will wipe away every tear from their eyes, and death shall be no more" (Rev. 21:4).

Prayer: "Lord Jesus Christ, by your death you took away the sting of death: Grant to us your servants so to follow in faith where you have led the way, that we may at length fall asleep peacefully in you and wake up in your likeness for your tender mercies' sake. Amen." (*The Book of Common Prayer*)

Radiant Action: I will look for new life after the death of a dream, or a job, when children leave home, when a relationship ends, or when a loved one dies. I will plant bulbs or even plan and plant a garden (or even just a pot).

Webs: Mornings (Apr.), Passion (May), Seed Life (May)

Gleanings: "Life gives us time to reckon with eternity."[31]

The Gardener

I haven't talked to you about
a dark space I dug up.
Clods and rocks I can pick out of soil,
blue-veined clay I can nourish;
weeds, yank up; shade, cut back.
But this

hollow where no seed is meant to grow
astounds. I go back to basics,
trusting my hands to find the dirt
as it always was, humid and maternal,
easily worked to hatch seeds,
but this

breach of earth voids every breathing
speck so that the spade of my hand
weighs more than death and the leaves
I touch are stillborn. Tell me,
must I keep tending, must I
turn this

blank into myself and vanish,
or is the hole an entrance
into some new ground that is yet
familiar, tilled and fertile, vast
as my loss, tenderly sown with
this?

Suzanne U. Rhodes
(in *Weather of the House*)

DAY 13
Scriptures about Death

"But we do see Jesus, who was made lower than the angels for a little while, now crowned with glory and honor because he suffered death, so that by the grace of God he might taste death for everyone. In bringing many sons and daughters to glory, it was fitting that God, for whom and through whom everything exists, should make the pioneer of their salvation perfect through what he suffered" (Heb. 2:9–10 NIV).

"For you died, and your life is now hidden with Christ in God. When Christ, who is your life, appears, then you also will appear with him in glory" (Col. 3:3–4 NIV).

"My sheep hear my voice, and I know them, and they follow me: I give them eternal life, and they will never perish, and no one will snatch them out of my hand" (John 10:27–28).

"For God did not appoint us to suffer wrath but to receive salvation through our Lord Jesus Christ. He died for us so that, whether we are awake or asleep, we may live together with him" (1 Thess. 5:9–10 NIV).

"But in fact Christ has been raised from the dead, the first fruits of those who have fallen asleep. For as by a man came death, by a man has come also the resurrection of the dead. For as in Adam all die, so also in Christ shall all be made alive. But each in his own order: Christ the firstfruits, then at his coming those who belong to Christ. Then comes the end, when he delivers the kingdom to God the Father after destroying every rule and every authority and power. For he must reign until he has put all his enemies under his feet. The last enemy to be destroyed is death" (1 Cor 15:20–26).

"'There will be no more death' . . . or pain, for the old order of things has passed away" (Rev. 21:4 NIV).

"He will swallow up death forever" (Isa. 25:8 NIV).

"God raised him up, loosing the pangs of death, because it was not possible for him to be held by it" (Acts 2:24).

DAY 14

Easter: The Gospel in *Charlotte's Web*

The Lord Jesus Christ . . . will transform our lowly body to be like his glorious body, by the power that enables him even to subject all things to himself" (Phil. 3:20–21).

Charlotte dies alone after she finished her magnum opus.
Jesus dies as the Father turns away from Him on Calvary.

Charlotte saves others but couldn't save herself (had no choice).
Jesus came to save others but chose not to save Himself.

Charlotte eats blood for life.
Jesus gives His blood to bring new life and the new covenant.

Templeton is greedy and selfish.
Roman soldiers greedily gamble for Jesus's clothes. They represent all sinners.

Charlotte's egg sac is waterproof and sealed.
Jesus is laid in a tomb, and a stone seals it.

Charlotte goes the way of all earthly creatures.
Jesus rises again and is alive forever, making eternal life available to all who believe.

Charlotte's old web is torn and empty.
Jesus's tomb is empty. He is not there.

Lurvy, the humble farmhand, is the first to see the wonder of the web.
Mary Magdalene, a humble woman, is the first to encounter the risen Lord.

Wilbur's medal hangs on a nail. He is no longer under a death sentence.
The piercing of Jesus's hands and feet with nails undoes the death sentence of the sinner.

The geese had one bad egg out of seven but has nine the next year, making up for the lost one—plus one.
God promises to restore all the years the "locusts" have eaten.

Prayer: We rejoice in Your victory, O Lord!

Radiant Action: I will celebrate Easter every day. New clothes remind me of my new life based on the resurrection. My soul is made new; I am clothed in newness (2 Cor. 5:17).

Webs: Shadows of Death (Apr.), Energy and Hope (May), Eggs and the Art of Hatching (May)

Gleanings: "…the sun of righteousness shall rise with healing in its wings." (Mal. 4:2).

Easter Wings[32]

Lord, who createdst man in wealth and store,
Though foolishly he lost the same,
Decaying more and more,
Till he became
Most poore:
With thee
O let me rise
As larks, harmoniously,
And sing this day thy victories:
Then shall the fall further the flight in me.

My tender age in sorrow did beginne
And still with sicknesses and shame.
Thou didst so punish sinne,
That I became
Most thinne.
With thee
Let me combine,
And feel thy victorie:
For, if I imp my wing on thine,
Affliction shall advance the flight in me.

George Herbert (1593–1633)

DAY 15

Holy Spirit: The Warm Breeze

A warm draft of rising air blew softly through the barn cellar.[33]

As the warm spring air blows softly through the barn cellar, change is coming. The baby spiders are about to launch. Jesus said that He would send the Holy Spirit, unseen like the wind, to empower His disciples to launch as well. The Spirit remains in us and with us always. "And I will ask the Father, and He will give you another Helper (Comforter, Advocate, Intercessor—Counselor, Strengthener, Standby), to be with you forever—the Spirit of Truth" (John 14:16–17 AMP).

The Holy Spirit works within us as believers to carry us through life and make us like Jesus. The Spirit adjusts our focus to be on Jesus, and this focus transforms us. "We all, who with unveiled faces contemplate the Lord's glory, are being transformed into his image with ever-increasing glory, which comes from the Lord, who is the Spirit" (2 Cor. 3:18 NIV).

The Holy Spirit grows us up. We will no longer mind the things of childhood. We'll change the way we spend our time, as Fern did. We'll change our priorities like Wilbur did when he yielded his favorite things to gain something much more precious.

"Do not quench the Spirit" (1 Thess. 5:19 NIV).

Prayer: God, grow me up through the Spirit.

Radiant Action: Journal Entry: I will read a chapter from the book of Acts and then John 14 each day for a month, and record my reactions and applications, prayers, and surprises. I will practice listening to the Holy Spirit (He always aligns with Scripture).

Webs: Unseen (June), Listening (Apr.), Anointing (May), Passion (May), Eggs and the Art of Hatching (May)

Gleanings: "And I will ask the Father, and he will give you another Helper, to be with you forever, even the Spirit of truth, whom the world cannot receive, because it neither sees him nor knows him. You know him, for he dwells with you and will be in you" (John 14:16–17).

God's Grandeur[34]

The world is charged with the grandeur of God.
It will flame out, like shining from shook foil;
It gathers to a greatness, like the ooze of oil
Crushed. Why do men then now not reck his rod?
Generations have trod, have trod, have trod;
And all is seared with trade; bleared, smeared with toil;
And wears man's smudge and shares man's smell: the soil
Is bare now, nor can foot feel, being shod.

And for all this, nature is never spent;
There lives the dearest freshness deep down things;
And though the last lights off the black West went
Oh, morning, at the brown brink eastward, springs—
Because the Holy Ghost over the bent
World broods with warm breast and with ah! bright wings.

Gerard Manley Hopkins (1844–1889)

"We feel the breath of the wind upon our cheeks, we see the dust and the leaves blowing before the wind, we see the vessels at sea driven swiftly toward their port; but the wind itself remains invisible. Just so with the Spirit; we feel His breath upon our souls, we see the mighty things He does, but Himself we do not see. He is invisible, but He is real and perceptible."
—R. A. Torrey

DAY 16

Mornings

"You'll see me in the morning."[35]

Wilbur meets his friend on that joyful morning after having heard only a small voice the night before, a night that surrounded the pig with both physical and emotional darkness. How often the morning chases away the weeping of the night. One day there will be a morning when our Friend appears. The new day will break, as expressed in lines from a beautiful hymn:

> "The King will come when morning dawns
> And light triumphant breaks;
> When beauty gilds the eastern hills
> And life to joy awakes."[36]

"[His mercies] are new every morning" (Lam. 3:23).

Prayer: "Lord God, almighty and everlasting Father, you have brought us safely to this new day: Preserve us with your mighty power, that we may not fall into sin, nor be overcome by adversity; and in all we do, direct us to the fulfilling of your purpose through Jesus Christ our Lord. Amen." (*The Book of Common Prayer*)

Radiant Action: I will greet each new day with, "This is the day the LORD has made. We will rejoice and be glad in it" (Ps. 118:24 NLT).

Webs: Waiting for the Dawn (Feb.), Shadows of Death (Apr.), Look Up! (June)

Gleanings: "The term is over; the holidays have begun. The dream is ended: this is the morning."[37]

Suggested hymns:
- "Break forth, O beauteous heavenly light / and usher in the morning" ("Break Forth, O Beauteous Heavenly Light")
- "Yea, Lord, we greet thee / Born this happy morning" ("Adeste Fideles")
- "Sing, O sing, this blessed morn, Jesus Christ today is born" ("Sing, O Sing, This Blessed Morn")
- "Awake, awake to love and work! / The lark is in the sky / The fields are wet with diamond dew / The worlds awake to cry / Their blessings on the Lord of life / as he goes meekly by" ("Awake, Awake, to Love and Work")

What hopeful, tender words Peter Marshall spoke to his wife, Catherine, after a heart attack that would claim his life: "Darling, I'll see you in the morning."[38]

(Photo by James PT/Unsplash)

Prayer at Sunrise[39]

O mighty, powerful, dark-dispelling sun,
Now thou art risen, and thy day begun.
How shrink the shrouding mists before thy face,
As up thou spring'st to thy diurnal race!
How darkness chases darkness to the west,
As shades of light on light rise radiant from thy crest!
For thee, great source of strength, emblem of might,
In hours of darkest gloom there is no night.
Thou shinest on though clouds hide thee from sight,
And through each break thou sendest down thy light.

O greater Maker of this Thy great sun,
Give me the strength this one day's race to run,
Fill me with light, fill me with sun-like strength,
Fill me with joy to rob the day its length.
Light from within, light that will outward shine,
Strength to make strong some weaker heart than mine,
Joy to make glad each soul that feels its touch;
Great Father of the sun, I ask this much.

James Weldon Johnson (1871–1938)

DAY 17

Listening: The Discarded Milking Stool

She placed the stool in the sheepfold next to Wilbur's pen. Here she sat quietly . . . thinking and listening.[40]

Fern's milking stool is the ideal place to take in the conversation of the barnyard animals. She is "milking" the opportunity to listen. Priest and theologian Henri Nouwen wrote, "Somewhere we know that, without silence, words lose their meaning, that, without listening, speaking no longer heals."[41] Philosopher and theologian Paul Tillich's words echo this idea: "The first duty of love is to listen."[42]

One of the most urgent but elegant things we can do today is take time to be quiet and *listen* to God. If we are to know our purpose, our calling, our mission, our vision, and how to make a lasting impact, we need to slow down. Like Fern, find some quiet. Listen to the Holy Spirit with Scripture guiding the way. If we don't, we may miss a turn or a miracle.

Lydia was a businesswoman in the New Testament who took time to listen. "One of those listening was a woman from the city of Thyatira named Lydia, a dealer in purple cloth. She was a worshiper of God. The Lord opened her heart to respond to Paul's message" (Acts 16:14 NIV). "Faith comes from hearing, and hearing through the word of Christ" (Rom. 10:17). We are His sheep and we listen to Him: "The sheep listen to his voice. He calls his own sheep by name and leads them out" (John 10:3 NIV).

God Himself is a listener. Pour your heart out to Him.

> *"He has not hidden his face from him, but has heard, when he cried to him"* (Ps. 22:24).

Prayer: Dear Lord, who is present with me, please quiet my heart to listen to You. Help me to listen as Fern did, with joy and anticipation. You listen better than Dr. Dorian. "In the morning, Lord, you hear my voice; in the morning I lay my requests before you and wait expectantly" (Ps. 5:3 NIV). Open my ears to hear (see Job 36:10).

Radiant Action: When I pour a glass of water or pour from a pitcher, I will remember to pour out my heart to You and take time to listen for Your response.

Webs: Waiting (Mar.), Holy Spirit (Apr.), Singing (June), Voices (June)

Gleanings: "Blessed is the one who listens to me, watching daily at my gates" (Prov. 8:34).

DAY 18

Changed

Wilbur rushed to the front of his pen. He put his front feet up on the top board and gazed around . . . He knew he would have to act quickly.[43]

Charlotte's Web seems to be a book of seemingly static characters. But, on careful reading, we perceive change. Wilbur loses his standard mode of operation of fainting and stands up to Templeton. He changes because he knows Charlotte loves him. At the end, he is no longer helpless but is a Wilbur Force, empowered by love. Mr. Arable becomes Fern's advocate instead of a practical killer. Avery becomes a helper instead of causing catastrophe. Fern loses her interest in Wilbur but refocuses on Henry Fussy.

When we come to Christ we are changed because we have a completely new identity in Jesus. We are to "put on the new self, which is being renewed in knowledge after the image of its creator" (Col. 3:10).

Paul went from persecutor to apostle by the power and calling of the Holy Spirit. Augustine went from profligate to apologist after his mother persevered in prayer for years. Peter went from betrayer to kingdom preacher. The church is built on the same grace that changed these men. None of us are saved by our own efforts. We all go the same path: conviction of sin, repentance, restoration, cleansing through the blood of Christ, gifted with the God's grace, and powered by the Holy Spirit.

God loves us first; we love Him back. His love changes us. No longer settling for toys, we find real life in God. He expects us to change and become what He has designed us to be. We grow up "so that we may no longer be children, tossed to and fro . . . and carried about by every wind of doctrine, by human cunning, by craftiness in deceitful schemes . . . We are to grow up in every way into him who is the head" (Eph 4:14–15).

Prayer: Dear Father, first, I ask that You change my heart and make me new. And I bring to You those who remain stuck in sin and paralyzed by fear, bitterness, or addiction.

Radiant Action: Journal Entry: I will ask the Lord to show me where I need to change, and I will ask a friend or family member if they see any change in me.

Webs: Easter (Apr.), A Warm Breeze (Apr.), Energy and Hope (May), Flight (May)

Gleanings: "When I was a child, I spoke like a child, I thought like a child, I reasoned like a child. When I became a man, I gave up childish ways" (1 Cor. 13:11).

DAY 19

Unstuck with an Updraft: Out of the Deep Freeze

"This is our moment for setting forth."[44]

The spiderlings launch with their balloons, no longer stuck in the egg sac or merely wandering around aimlessly. They're propelled forward by a warm spring updraft to leave the place of birth. Sounds like graduation!

God may be calling you to graduate too—to leave old things and take up new. But life can be heavy. Losses and traumas can cement the feet. Negative attitudes within and without lock down forward motion, and time rolls past you. You may wonder, *Where's* my *updraft?*

Wilbur experienced grief, and he appreciated the time he had with Charlotte. He never had another friend like her, but he was delighted with his new friends every spring. He found contentment in a new normal. His sorrows did not keep him from new joys.

Maybe your updraft is waiting for you, and you have to decide to place yourself where you can catch it. In other words, you need to move out of the barn and stand on the fence. Challenge your boundaries. Has the Holy Spirit been nudging you to make a kind of change, but you're resisting? Maybe you are in the "barn," and what you have always done feels safe and secure.

Sometimes, it is false expectations we have of ourselves or others, or perspectives that are old, rusty, or tattered that keep us in the deep freeze. As Christian psychologists Cloud and Townsend explain: "Guilt will keep you from doing what is right and will keep you stuck."[45] They give in-depth instructions for dealing with guilt and a multitude of other emotions and misunderstandings that keep us from moving forward.

Prayer: Guide me to the place and state of soul where I can receive Your updrafts. Help me move by grace into a new season. Open my eyes to see today's mercies and joys. Help me to lay aside the weights that keep me stuck.

Radiant Action: I will journal answers to these questions: Am I stuck in a barn of status quo? What weight do I need to lay down in order to fly? When I feel a breeze on my face, I'll think of the Holy Spirit changing me.

Webs: Expectations of Others: Do What? (Feb.), Holy Spirit (Apr.), Flight (May)

Gleanings: "Lay aside every weight, and the sin which doth so easily beset us, and let us run" (Heb. 12:1 KJV).

The Celebrate Recovery program offers successful help for addiction.[46]

DAY 20

Weapons

He was heavily armed.[47]

Battles abound in *Charlotte's Web*. Charlotte tells the story of her cousin who won a fight with a fish in "a never-to-be-forgotten battle." Charlotte and Zuckerman are in a fight with life-or-death consequences. Avery was ready for battle before breakfast.

Every day, the believer battles the world, the flesh, and the devil, and with life-and-death consequences. We must be heavily armed before breakfast just to stand our ground. It's not easy. Daniel prayed for three weeks, and it was only after that extended amount of time that the angel Michael was able to break through and answer his prayer.

Paul warns that we live in wartime and will be until we die. "For our struggle is not against flesh and blood, but against the rulers, against the authorities, against the powers of this dark world and against the spiritual forces of evil in the heavenly realms" (Eph. 6:12 NIV).

He lists our wardrobe for warfare: the belt of truth, the breastplate of righteousness, sandals of readiness with the gospel, the shield of faith, the helmet of salvation, the sword of the Spirit and mental alertness for praying. Singing is a powerful weapon against the enemy. As Paul and Silas sang and praised God despite their circumstances, the jail broke open.

When battles arise, will we be heavily armed? Will we be ready?

Prayer: One day at a time, Lord, help me fight the good fight with all my might, empowered by Your might (see Eph. 6:10–18).

Radiant Action: I won't be complacent; I will have to fight, die to self, engage in prayer, and be patient. I will "nail up my boards." I will forgive others and be forgiven so the enemy does not have a stronghold. I will practice singing or listening to spiritual songs.

Webs: Enemy Territory (Apr.), Boards (April), Music (June), Puddle Jumping (June)

Gleanings: "No weapon forged against you will prevail" (Isa. 54:17 NIV).

> "I broke the fangs of the unrighteous and made him drop his prey from his teeth" (Job 29:17).

MAY

BRANCHING OUT, BUDDING, AND BLOOMING

An apple tree usually blossoms in May. The tree shoves off dormancy and bursts into a spectacle of pink petals that dance in dew and rain and sunlight. This is a season of new life, exploring direction, dreams, purpose, calling, and gifts—a time to celebrate the God of life's delight in life.

Passion: Fire in the Tennis Shoes, *p. 105*
Anointing: Dew, *p. 106*
Power of One, *p. 107*
Direction, *p. 108*
Life Goals, *p. 109*
More Dreams, *p. 110*
Purpose I: Why Are You Alive?, *p. 111*
Purpose II: You Have Been My Friend, *p. 112*
Purpose III: Working It Out, *p. 113*
Purpose IV: Oops, *p. 114*
Purpose V: It Could Be Right in Front of You, *p. 115*
Equipping and Design, *p. 116*
Energy and Hope, *p. 117*
Eggs and the Art of Hatching, *p. 118*
Seed Life, *p. 119*
Motherhood, *p. 120*
Names, *p. 121*
Lament to Creativity: From the "Dung and the Dark", *p. 122*
Balance, *p. 123*
Flight, *p. 124*

DAY 1

Passion: Fire in the Tennis Shoes

"Please don't kill it!"[1]

Fern risks her relationship with her father to chase justice. Her rewards are a pig, a story to tell, a barnyard community, and her family's influence extended into a story bigger than themselves. She has fire in her tennis shoes to meet the challenge. She has passion.

The Lord loves justice (see Ps. 33:5), and Jesus calls us to risk all for it, to work to right the wrongs we see around us, to advocate for the weak, the oppressed, the powerless members of the human family. Jesus left heaven to mediate the justice of God on the cross. He who was without sin suffered an excruciating death for the love of us who are sinners, taking our guilt upon Himself so we could be reconciled to the holy, perfect God.

Jesus expects His followers to blaze with Holy Spirit passion and lay down everything that keeps us from pursuing justice and reconciliation. He will reward us with more than we can imagine, blessing us individually and in our relationships with others as we walk in step with Him to live out the story that is bigger than ourselves.

"Do not be slothful in zeal, be fervent in spirit, serve the Lord" (Rom. 12:11).

Prayer: I ask You, dear God, to cleanse me of double-minded living and give me Your passion for leading others from death to life. Help me run to do what You call me to do.

Radiant Action: When I put on my tennis shoes, I will ask for more passion after God's heart—for fire in the soles for souls—to pursue the lost and wandering with love and prayer.

Webs: Love (Feb.), Equipping and Design (May), Life Goals (May), Goodness (June)

Gleanings: "Serve wholeheartedly, as if you were serving the Lord, not people" (Eph. 6:7 NIV). "As *shoes for your feet, . . . put on the readiness* given by the gospel of peace" (Eph. 6:15, emphasis mine).

> "Come down, O Love divine, seek thou this soul of mine, and visit it with thine own ardor glowing; O Comforter, draw near, within my heart appear, and kindle it, thy holy flame bestowing."[2]

DAY 2

Anointing: Dew

Charlotte's web never looked more beautiful . . .
*Each strand held dozens of bright drops of early morning dew.*³

As Fern runs to intervene and prevent Wilbur's untimely death, her tennis shoes are sopping wet with early morning spring dew. Dew can be a reminder of the anointing we need from God to work out our purpose. Anointing is the empowering by the Holy Spirit that enables us to follow through effectively on a mission. Jesus was anointed to finish His work. Whether we are bricklayers, artists, pastors, or nurses—whatever our vocation—we need God's anointing to finish the job. He has promised His power: "But you have been anointed by the Holy One" (1 John 2:20).

"The Spirit of the LORD is upon Me, because He has anointed Me to preach the gospel to the poor; He has sent Me to heal the brokenhearted, to proclaim liberty to the captives and recovery of sight to the blind, to set at liberty those who are oppressed; to proclaim the acceptable year of the LORD" (Luke 4:18–19 NKJV).

Prayer: Lord, fill me with Your Spirit, anoint me with Your power, to fulfill the work you call me to do. May You give me of the dew of heaven (see Gen. 27:28). I plead for the power of the Spirit—the anointing.

Radiant Action: The morning dew reminds me to ask for a renewed empowering to do the work of God. I will "dew" my part to keep the unity of the Spirit since peace fuels anointing.

Webs: Holy Spirit (Apr.), Passion (May), Energy and Hope (May)

Gleanings: "The central problem of our age is not liberalism or modernism . . . nor the threat of communism, nor even the threat of rationalism and the monolithic consensus which surrounds us. All these are dangerous but not the primary threat. The real problem is this: the church of the Lord Jesus Christ, individually, corporately, tending to do the Lord's work in the power of the flesh rather than of the Spirit." —Francis A. Schaeffer, *No Little People*⁴

> "Behold, how good and pleasant it is when brothers dwell in unity! It is like the precious oil on the head, running down on the beard, on the beard of Aaron, running down on the collar of his robes! It is like the dew of Hermon, which falls on the mountains of Zion! For there the LORD has commanded the blessing, life forevermore" (Ps. 133).

DAY 3

Power of One

Nobody . . . knew that a grey spider had played the most important part of all.[5]

One gray spider, endowed with wit and equipped with hairy legs and spinnerets, saves a pig. She brings glory to the farmers and creates her magnum opus, her egg sac. Unsung, she carries through despite obstacles (wobblestacles), true to her promise to Wilbur.

Consider the roll call of Old Testament heroes who stayed true and carried through. God used the power of each one of these men and women to execute His plan of salvation through time and circumstance, heroic figures like Abel, Noah, Enoch, Abraham, Moses, Joshua, Rahab, David, Nehemiah, Esther, Job, and Amos.

In the New Testament, we encounter the courage and obedience of Mary, mother of Jesus, as well as Peter, Paul, Stephen, Lydia, Phoebe, and many others. The apostles Peter and John, who had been performing signs and wonders and causing multitudes to believe, provoked the jealousy of the religious leaders and were thrown into jail. After an angel orchestrated a jailbreak, the apostles began teaching and confronting the Jews for the murder of Jesus. Enraged, the religious rulers conspired to put them to death. But Gamaliel stood up. In the book of Acts we read that the Pharisee Gamaliel, "a teacher of the law held in honor by all the people" (Acts 5:34), defended the apostles and persuaded the religious leaders not to kill Peter and John; otherwise, Gamaliel said, they might be fighting against God Himself!

Jesus is the Son of God. One person. The one person who completely submitted Himself to the Father's dangerous mission to save fallen humanity. He took the sins of the whole world and smashed the power of the devil, sealing his doom when He cried, "It is finished!" (John 19:30). The risen Christ's very Spirit lives within each believer. We are not grasshoppers as the shy Israelites thought of themselves when they refused to go into their promised land. We are anointed, empowered, and equipped to stand for God and against evil.

Prayer: I give You all that I am to do whatever You want me to do, in Your power and for Your glory alone. Refresh and empower my vision of what Your will.

Radiant Action: Journal Entry: Record my refreshed vision of how I can make a difference in my sphere of influence.

Webs: Vision (Mar.), Mission (Mar.), Purpose Series (May)

Gleanings: "For the eyes of the LORD run to and fro throughout the whole earth, to give strong support to those whose heart is blameless toward him" (2 Chron. 16:9).

DAY 4

Direction

"Don't just stand there, Wilbur! Dodge about!"[6]

Wilbur listens to the goose's confusing advice. He hears a clamor of myriad of barnyard voices telling him to move every which way. He has no clear direction but to frantically run. Overwhelmed, he starts to cry. Direction can come from voices with either good intent or bad. But God has promised to be our faithful and steadfast guide. He will confirm your purpose, calling, missions, and vision.

> *"And your ears shall hear a word behind you, saying, 'This is the way, walk in it,' when you turn to the right or when you turn to the left"* (Isa. 30:21).
> *"I am the LORD your God, who teaches you to profit, who leads you in the way you should go"* (Isa. 48:17).

Prayer: "Teach me to do your will, for you are my God! Let your good Spirit lead me on level ground!" (Ps. 143:10). "Make me know the way I should go, for to you I lift up my soul" (Ps. 143:8).

Radiant Action: I will set time aside to listen to God and realize I must practice discerning between God's voice, the flesh, the devil, and the world. I will search Scriptures for wisdom to make decisions.

Webs: Identity (Feb.), Holy Spirit (Apr.), Listening (June)

Gleanings: "In their hearts humans plan their course, but the LORD establishes their steps" (Prov. 16:9 NIV).

> *"He gave him the plans of all that the Spirit had put in his mind"* (1 Chron. 28:12 NIV).

> *"All this he made clear to me in writing from the hand of the Lord, all the work to be done according to the plan."* (1 Chron. 28:19)

> *"Behold, I am doing a new thing: now it springs forth, do you not perceive it? I will make a way in the wilderness and rivers in the desert"* (Isa. 43:19).

DAY 5

Life Goals

"Who's going to save me?"
"I am," said Charlotte.[7]

Charlotte knew what she had to do. Her life goals were to produce her magnum opus, and by writing in her web, to prevent Wilbur from becoming the Christmas fatted porkchops. She was single-minded in her tasks and keenly aware of her gifts.

The book of Proverbs admonishes us to be focused on God's will and plans for our lives. Jesus is the ideal goal maker and keeper. He knew His earthly life goals:

"The Spirit of the Lord is upon me,
because he has anointed me
to proclaim good news to the poor.
He has sent me to proclaim liberty to the captives
and recovering of sight to the blind,
to set at liberty those who are oppressed,
to proclaim the year of the Lord's favor" (Luke 4:18–19).

He didn't heal everyone or save all, but through daily prayer He discerned the Father's will. He did just that—no more or less. He *accomplished all His Father asked him to do* (see John 17:4).

Paul also was single-minded about his life goals: "Not that I have already obtained all this, or have already arrived at my goal, but I press on to take hold of that for which Christ Jesus took hold of me. Brothers and sisters, I do not consider myself yet to have taken hold of it. But one thing I do: Forgetting what is behind and straining toward what is ahead, I press on toward the goal to win the prize for which God has called me heavenward in Christ Jesus (Phil. 3:12–14 NIV).

He declared, "However, I consider my life worth nothing to me; my only aim is to finish the race and complete the task the Lord Jesus has given me—the task of testifying to the good news of God's grace" (Acts 20:24 NIV).

Prayer: Show me Your will for my life.

Radiant Action: Journal Entry: I will clarify my passions and my priorities, Then, I will write down specific, measurable, attainable, realistic, time-bound goals for two of my most important priorities.

Webs: Emotions and Motivations Series (Jan.), Vision (Mar.), Dreams (Mar.), Wobblestacles (June)

Gleanings: "Let your eyes look straight ahead; fix your gaze directly before you. Give careful thought to the paths for your feet and be steadfast in all your ways" (Prov. 4:25–26 NIV).

DAY 6

More Dreams

"In a forest looking for beechnuts and truffles and delectable roots."[8]

Wilbur dreams of rooting around a forest looking for woodsy treats. Mr. Zuckerman dreams of having the first-prize pig at the fair. Mrs. Zuckerman dreams of a deep freeze. Lurvy wants to play the games at the fair and win an Indian blanket. The material things we desire in this life are impermanent. Chocolate melts; moths attack blankets; freezers break. What is a worthy desire or dream? Do we dream of something more?

C. S. Lewis found that in chasing God's dreams, we find our own. "Glory, as Christianity teaches me to hope for it, turns out to satisfy my original desire and indeed to reveal an element in that desire which I had not noticed. By ceasing for a moment to consider my own wants I have begun to learn better what I really wanted."[9]

Madeleine L'Engle expresses the concept this way: "Fulfill yourself, that's what the world says is important. But the people I know, in literature and in life, whose chief concern is fulfilling themselves, are always empty."[10]

> *"If then you have been raised with Christ, seek the things that are above, where Christ is, seated at the right hand of God"* (Col. 3:1).

Prayer: God, inspire me to dream what is on Your heart.

Radiant Action: Journal Entry: I will take time to look at what I am running after and write down my dreams and see how they align with Scripture, counsel, giftings, and open doors.

Webs: Expectations of Others (Feb.), Passion (May), Courage and Risk (June)

Gleanings: "Do not work for food that spoils, but for food that endures to eternal life, which the Son of Man will give you. For on him God the Father has placed his seal of approval" (John 6:27 NIV).

DAY 7

Purpose I: Why Are You Alive?

He planned to stand perfectly still and think of what it was like to be alive.[11]

Wilbur schedules time to contemplate life. Sometimes, around four o'clock, on a gray and windy day a month past Christmas, with sleet spitting at the window, you may find questions bubbling up from your innermost self. What is my purpose? What *is* purpose anyway? Why do I exist? Am I fulfilling God's purpose for my life? What about the future?

Purpose means believing in something; it is not about doing. It is trusting in Someone or something because whatever you trust in or delight in becomes your focus. God's purpose for us is to trust and delight in Him. Our purpose lays not in the seen but the unseen.

Jesus knew His purpose. "For the Son of Man came to seek and to save the lost" (Luke 19:10). Paul knew his purpose—to "know Him and the power of His resurrection, and the fellowship of His sufferings . . . [that] I may attain to the resurrection from the dead" (Phil. 3:10–11 NASB). In his *Confessions*, Augustine of Hippo summed up mankind's purpose, "Thou hast made us for thyself, O Lord, and our heart is restless until it finds its rest in thee."

Holding a right perspective on purpose will affect our work, marriage, and communities.

If our purpose is rooted in God, we won't be looking to the temporal to fill the heart's eternal longing. We won't trust in what we can feel and see and touch, because satisfaction comes from God.

"I cry out to God Most High, to God who fulfills his purpose for me" (Ps. 57:2).

Prayer: You have put me in this world for something, Lord; show me what that is, and help me to work out the purpose of my life. "I am all Yours. Take me and enable me to glorify You now in all that I say, in all that I do, and with all that I have."[12]

Radiant Action: I will memorize this: "Love the Lord your God with all your heart and with all your soul and with all your mind and with all your strength" (Mark 12:30 NIV).

Webs: Belonging and Adoption (Feb.), Unstuck (Apr.), Holy Spirit (Apr.)

Gleanings: "He has also planted eternity [a sense of divine purpose] in the human heart" (Eccl. 3:11 AMP).

DAY 8

Purpose II: You Have Been My Friend

"Why did you do all this for me?"[13]

Charlotte did "all this" (planning, weaving, risking her egg sac, coordinating team meetings) because she loves Wilbur. She wants to secure his future. As the book begins, breakfast is cooking, with the smell of bacon heavy in the air. Mr. Arable plops Wilbur onto the table. The scene hints at what could be Wilbur's future—breakfast.

The tender love between Charlotte and Wilbur is the centerpiece and driving force of the story. God's love for us is the centerpiece of human history. Our primary purpose is to be in relationship with God and others, and to preach and teach the good news.

God loves us and commands us to love one another, honor one another, and live peaceably together. Being in community is central to Christian purpose and heritage. God's plan for individuals often can only be lived out with others. Jesus calls us His friend and prays that all those who follow Him will be one.

He expects us to live in community, even though it's much harder to be "nice" when dealing with other humans. The virtual world can be powerful, but it's a shadow of the vibrant full life God has for us. Jesus shows us how to live with one another.

> *"For the whole law is fulfilled in one word: 'You shall love your neighbor as yourself'"* (Gal. 5:14).

Prayer: Lord, give me a willing heart to cast out my preeminent self and let your Spirit love my neighbor through me.

Radiant Action: To whom will I reach out to today?

Webs: Friendship (Feb.), Teamwork (Feb.), Home (June)

Gleanings: "The second [command] is this: 'You shall love your neighbor as yourself'" (Mark 12:30–31).

DAY 9

Purpose III: Working It Out

He planned to scratch itchy places.[14]

Wilbur plans out his schedule for his day in the barnyard: breakfast, chat with a rat, nap, dig, watch. Charlotte plans too. She weaves words, chairs meetings, chooses to go with Wilbur to the fair, directs assistants, finds words, secures Wilbur's special standing, and spawns an egg sac.

There are concrete and practical steps, callings, or goals to walk out the "being" of purpose. Purpose of being must translate into doing. As James teaches, "Faith without works is dead" (James 2:26 KJV).

What is our place in the forward march of God's kingdom? What are the specific plans His Spirit is nudging us to do to accomplish His greater purpose?

Jesus stated, "For the Son of Man came to seek and to save the lost" (Luke 19:10).

Paul the apostle's purpose statement from God was, "I am sending you to [the gentiles]" (Acts 26:17 NIV).

Jesus tells us to "go therefore and make disciples of all nations, baptizing them in the name of the Father and of the Son and of the Holy Spirit" (Matt. 28:19).

> *"For we are His workmanship, created in Christ Jesus for good works, which God prepared beforehand so that we would walk in them"* (Eph. 2:10 NASB).

Prayer: God, sing Your song through me for Your good pleasure, that I would do Your will and Your work (see Phil. 2:13). You have called me to go and proclaim the kingdom of God (see Luke 9:60).

Radiant Action: Journal Entry: I will block some time to "scratch the itchy places" inside my soul and hear the Spirit's leading. I will pray, read, listen, and write down my own purpose statement with Scriptures.

Webs: Life Goals (May), Eggs and the Art of Hatching (May), Equipping and Design (May), Specific Goals (Aug.)

Gleanings: "Most of us go to our graves with our music still inside us, unplayed" —Oliver Wendell Holmes.

See Kevin McCarthy at On-Purpose Partners for more help on Purpose.[15]

DAY 10

Purpose IV: Oops

Rain upset Wilbur's plans.[16]

Lamenting the rain and feeling desperately lonely, Wilbur tries to ignite fellowship with even Templeton. All his glorious plans for the day—most of them involving food but also things like watching flies on the boards and bees in the clover—got rained on. In despair, he begins crying "for the second time in two days."[17]

We may hear God's voice, we may make plans, but rain comes. Lacking provision, battling health problems, hurting from relationship fractures—did I hear Him correctly? The woeful "wobblestacles" to the doing, the working out of the purpose, may send you crying—again. Just because you face trouble does not mean you are not in God's will (see Mark 4:35–41).

God can give you a plan, but it has to work out in His time. Noah waited for the rain to stop and then for the waters to subside—an entire year and ten days. Joseph languished in bondage for thirteen years as his character ripened and equipped him to be a godly prime minister. David was anointed king for thirteen years before he was crowned. If you are a writer, you have to wade through seemingly endless edits. Waiting has always been a part of walking with God.

Apart from God's timing, emotional scars are briars that keep the individual in "grasshopper" mode and wandering (see Num. 13:33). The enemy schemes to stop and destroy us (see Eph. 6:12). As Nehemiah sought to rebuild the walls of Jerusalem, enemies arose to stop the work. If Jesus was tempted by Satan to seek provision, position, and power as He began His ministry, then we will be as well.

You might think you have already messed up too much and missed God's plan completely. Rick Warren speaks to this self-condemnation: "Jonah thanked God by returning to his mission. Jonah knew he messed up. We've all been there, yet that doesn't stop God's mission for you. Jonah's life mission remained the same."[18] Job testifies, "I know that you can do all things; no purpose of yours can be thwarted" (Job 42:2 NIV). God's purpose for you remains. Love Him, love others.

Prayer: Heavenly Father, may all Your counsel and purpose stand in my life (Prov. 19:21; Isa. 46:10).

Radiant Action: Journal Entries: 1. What obstacles are distracting me from living a purposeful life? 2. What plans of my making have been dashed? What mess-ups have I made? I will reread and meditate on the Scriptures above and write how I can clear the way, discover God's higher plan, receive His forgiveness for failures and His peace for trials that reroute me.

Webs: Waiting (Mar.), Wilbur's Wobblestacles (June), Puddle Jumping (June)

DAY 11

Purpose V: It Could Be Right in Front of You (A Different Perspective)

He carefully took the little bundle in his mouth.[19]

Wilbur doesn't have a plan for the final crisis, but acting out of love, he thinks of an idea. He persuades Templeton to cooperate, sacrifices his dearest possession, and carries the egg sac safely home in his mouth. His purpose is to do the job in front of him. Sometimes you can't discern or plan a next stage of doing, but it's certain that God gives out handfuls of purpose. So, you do the next thing He opens up, thus fulfilling the duty set before you. Sometimes the doing means good stewarding of time and capabilities.

An article on the notion of purpose offers helpful insight:

> Finding your life's purpose can often feel just out of reach. A "maybe someday" revelation you hope to discover. But what if your purpose is already circling your feet—and the very things you're meant to breathe life into are actually, remarkably, within reach? What if your purpose comes from entirely unplanned circumstances, and suddenly, what you are meant to do is simply to respond with a full heart? These stories [in the article] aren't about purpose-chasers. They're about people who thought, *"This is where I am, and this is what I will do now."* People who chose to bend their life toward what was suddenly—or long present—at their feet.[20]

Jesus said, "As the Father has sent Me, I also send you" (John 20:21 NKJV).

Prayer: Lord, lead me to understand how my daily tasks contribute to the larger purpose of my life. Help me experience deep satisfaction as I discover and carry out my unique role.[21] Give me discernment to know the difference between distraction and loving duty. And also grant me perseverance.

Radiant Action: I will do the next thing God puts in front of me.

Webs: Self-Sacrifice (Feb.), Shadows of Death (Feb.), Surprising Deliverers (Apr.)

DAY 12

Equipping and Design

"I can make a web in a single evening."[22]

Wilbur's every attempt to spin a web is an utter failure, but he keeps trying, thinking that some string knotted onto his tail will be the key to success. Charlotte tells him a story about the Queensboro Bridge that illustrates the vital component of success in a project—being equipped for the undertaking. Unlike Wilbur, Charlotte has the right equipment—spinnerets, eight hairy legs—and she knows they are what's needed for making a web. Even Templeton has gifts—rat's teeth to snip the strings from Charlotte's magnum opus, her egg sac.

We *all* have God-given potential. Bezalel, chief artisan of the Old Testament tabernacle, was filled with wisdom, understanding, knowledge, and all kinds of skills.[23] Likewise, God has equipped each of His children for service with different callings in the church. "To each is given the manifestation of the Spirit for the common good" (1 Cor. 12:7).

We may admire someone and want to follow their example, as Wilbur admired and imitated Charlotte. We need to know who we are *not* to know what we're supposed to do. Jewish religious leaders asked John the Baptist who he was, and he adamantly denied he was the Christ. But he knew very clearly what his purpose was. He declared, "I am the voice of one crying out in the wilderness, 'Make straight the way of the Lord,' as the prophet Isaiah said" (John 1:23). He remained a faithful servant who acted according to his true identity and God's unique equipping of him for that service.

> "For as in one body we have many members, and the members do not all have the same function, so we, though many, are one body in Christ, and individually members one of another. Having gifts that differ according to the grace given to us, let us use them: if prophecy, in proportion to our faith" (Rom. 12:4–6).

Prayer: As Spurgeon prayed, "I have talents; help me to extol You by spending them for You."[24]

Radiant Action: I will take a spiritual gifts inventory to know my gifts and confirm my calling. I will also ask someone to confirm my findings and will take steps to develop my gifts and my children's gifts.

Webs: Identity (Feb.), Division of Responsibility (Mar.), Flight (May), The Honey of Wisdom (June)

DAY 13

Energy and Hope

Wilbur jumped to his feet.[25]

As Wilbur anticipates meeting his long-awaited friend, he jumps to his feet. When we feel excited, it's natural to want to spring to our feet. When Mary visited Elizabeth, John the Baptist perceived the presence of the Lord and leapt in his mother's womb for joy. Indeed, all of creation emanates jubilation, as we read in this poetic passage: "For you shall go out in joy and be led forth in peace; the mountains and the hills before you shall break forth into singing, and all the trees of the field shall clap their hands" (Isa. 55:12).

Not only do joyful events bring vibrant energy to life, so does hope. Despair, however, destroys verve. We are always looking for hope—for someone or something to lift us from doubt to trust. If we put hope in someone or something, we will experience despair. If we put our hope in Jesus, it's true that we may not always understand the path He's leading us on, but we can be confident that He will always be with us. As He promised, "For I know the plans I have for you, declares the Lord, plans . . . to give you a future and a hope" (Jer. 29:11). By His grace, we receive fresh hope and energy.

"And when Elizabeth heard the greeting of Mary, the baby leaped in her womb" (Luke 1:41).

Prayer: "Yes, my soul, find rest in God; my hope comes from him. Truly he is my rock and my salvation; he is my fortress, I will not be shaken. My salvation and my honor depend on God; he is my mighty rock, my refuge" (Ps. 62:5–7 NIV).

Radiant Action: Journal Entries: 1. In Whom or what do I hope? 2. What delights and refreshes me? I will meditate on Ephesians 1 since it reveals the great future my God of hope has planned for me and all who trust in Him.

Webs: Passion (May), Seed Life (May), Power of One (May), Flight (May)

Gleanings: In his biography of Lincoln, Carl Sandburg describes the president's mouth as "shaped with depths of hope that its fixed resolves would be kept and held."[26]

"For this I toil, struggling with all his energy that he powerfully works within me" (Col. 1:29).

"Do not be slothful in zeal, be fervent in spirit, serve the Lord" (Rom. 12:11).

"When Simon Peter heard that it was the Lord, he put on his outer garment, for he was stripped for work, and threw himself into the sea" (John 21:7).

DAY 14

Eggs and the Art of Hatching

They were in a desperately cramped position inside the shell and were most anxious to break through and get out.[27]

The goslings are frantic to gain freedom. Mama goose might have been recollecting her own claustrophobia from pre-hatched days when she urges Wilbur to break out of his pen. She wants to know, "How does it feel to be free?"[28] Isn't that the question for Christians?

Eggs fascinated E. B. White. He described an egg as "a morning jewel, a perfect little thing."[29] He "began to think of eggs as the symbol of life and versatility, the almost divine source of mystery."[30] Eggs play a central role in *Charlotte's Web*: goose eggs, Charlotte's eggs, orange potato-bug eggs. They are symbols of the future and tokens of potential. They require attention, time, and patience in the interim before their power is loosed.

White considered it one of "the most beautiful and miraculous things in the world."[31]

God thinks eggs are good things, too: "What father among you, if his son asks for . . . an egg, will give him a scorpion?" (Luke 11:11–12).

A person who needs nurture might be considered an "egg." Our dreams and ideas can be eggs that hatch into realization. Goals large or small are eggs. Which eggs (dreams, goals, talents) do you prize most?

Some eggs are better left unhatched. The rotten one in *Charlotte's Web* turned out to save the day and serve a greater purpose than the goose imagined. Letting go can be as much an art as hatching an egg.

Prayer: Creator, what are good eggs (people, goals) that I need to pursue, and what are the ones I need to leave alone? Would you bring the right eggs of opportunity? Help me to let go of dud eggs and other disappointments.

Radiant Action: The next time I eat an egg, I'll ponder its symbolism and potential and wonder about what new eggs could hatch in my life?

Webs: Small Things (Feb.), Waiting for the Dawn (Feb.), Life Goals (May), Flight (May)

DAY 15

Seed Life

Lurvy brought the squashes and pumpkins.[32]

Somehow, the farmers managed at least to sow some squash seeds despite the turbulent events and distractions of farm and fair. They forgot to do other things like putting up blackberry jam or hoeing the corn. Nonetheless, they had a harvest of squashes to show for their work, a crop that survived the heat of furor surrounding the miraculous words Charlotte wove on her web.

Jesus compares faith to a mustard seed, saying we only need a mustard seed-size faith to be fruitful. "What is the kingdom of God like? What shall I compare it to? It is like a mustard seed, which a man took and planted in his garden. It grew and became a tree, and the birds perched in its branches" (Luke 13:18–19 NIV).

The life of a seed is miraculous—parables bursting with vibrant truth. It's a wonder how God puts His instructions in a tiny seed and from it a mighty tree like a sequoia rises to boast its preeminence as an arbiter between earth and sky. Somehow in a similar way, He gives us His Spirit, the "DNA" of Jesus, and it can grow us for eternity. He gives His servants the message of salvation, and we plant seeds that last forever "that they may be called oaks of righteousness, the planting of the LORD, that he may be glorified" (Isa. 61:3).

Some seeds thrive on heat as their fuel for breakthrough. Fiery trials in our lives can change outer and inner characteristics, and lament can lead to creativity. To be fruitful, a seed must fall into the ground and lose its original outer shell for release of its inner potential.

> "Unless a kernel of wheat falls to the ground and dies, it remains only a single seed. But if it dies, it produces many seeds. Anyone who loves their life will lose it, while anyone who hates their life in this world will keep it for eternal life" (John 12:24–25 NIV).

Prayer: "Tonight as you pray, consider what seems to be too small and insignificant to be of value. Take a moment and pray for eyes to see a small evidence that God is present in this broken world and in the challenges you are facing. Hold that 'mustard seed' up to your Father and thank him for it." —Anglican priest, Rev. Nathan Baxter

Radiant Action: Journal Entries: 1. After observing a large tree, like an oak, I will describe it using specific details. 2. What thoughts about the tree come to mind? 3. The tree was once a small acorn. What seeds of good are growing in my life? What small seeds of resentment, unforgiveness, and past hurts that may be growing into large weeds with roots of bitterness? I will buy a packet of small seeds and plant them, then tend the plants that spring up.

Webs: Small Things (Feb.), Humble (Feb.), Insignificance (Feb.), Lament to Creativity (May)

DAY 16

Motherhood

"I'm in this thing pretty deep now—I might as well go the limit."[33]

Charlotte expresses the reality of motherhood. The commitment doesn't end—a mother's calling is to "go the limit." Until she passes away, Charlotte mothers Wilbur and her own progeny with loyalty and commitment. She gives Wilbur acceptance, belonging, and confidence. As Charlotte is for Wilbur, so God is in it for us, and for the long haul too: "I will never leave you nor forsake you" (Heb. 13:5). We are His family.

The mama goose nurtures her eggs, sitting on them patiently (except on warm days when she "cheats" with a little straw). The scene reminds us of Jesus lamenting for Jerusalem, longing to cover His chicks: "O Jerusalem, Jerusalem . . . How often would I have gathered your children together as a hen gathers her brood under her wings, and you were not willing!" (Luke 13:34). How tenderly He valued His mother by making certain she would be cared for after His death, a responsibility He gave to John as one of His last acts on the cross.

Fern also works hard at mothering, carrying Wilbur gently in her baby carriage. God carries us like a mother: "The LORD your God carried you . . . all the way that you went" (Deut. 1:31). The way Fern cherishes Wilbur as a young piglet reflects how God cherishes us too. You and I are His own possession, His special treasure.[34]

Prayer: Lord, show me how I may best honor my mother and father, and help me to be a good mother (or father)—(or if childless: help me to nurture others who need care). Scriptures to pray for children: Ephesians 1:7-9; 3:14-21; Colossians 1:9-12; and 3 John 4.

Radiant Action: I will keep a prayer journal for each child in my life and pray for them daily, blessing them. I will be careful not to pray amiss for my children (James 4) or to impress on them, even wordlessly, my own unfulfilled ambitions. I will plan a visit with my mother or an adopted one—or call or write a thank you note. I will focus on something good to remember.

Webs: Self-Sacrifice (Feb.), Belonging and Adoption (Feb.), Radiant (Feb.), Purpose Series (May)

Gleanings: "Honor your father and your mother, that your days may be long upon the land which the LORD your God is giving you" (Ex. 20:12 NKJV).

DAY 17

Names

Fern had named her pet.[35]

White delighted in finding the right names for his characters. Was he thinking of a fern, a plant that blows back and forth, when he named Fern, who moves this way and that so she can act as the need demands? Wilbur comes from a name that means resolute, which he indeed becomes. Perhaps White named her for the famous writer Charlotte Bronte. Wilbur himself composes names with meaning for Charlotte's spiderlings: Joy, Aranea, and Nellie.

Naming can be a means of protection. Fern gives Wilbur a name and we can understand from the beginning of the story that he is a personality worth saving. One actual farmer stated that her family made it a policy never to name their livestock because that would make it harder to kill them. Writer Robin Bates makes this astute observation about the importance of names and descriptions given to the Wilbur by the poet spider: "Through the aid of Charlotte's poetry, Wilbur can now be seen as a family pet and therefore [is] safe."[36]

Naming is also an indication of ownership. God gave Adam the authority to name all the animals in Eden. In doing so, he took dominion over them. God calls us by name too, a reminder that He is our Lord who loves us: "I have called you by name, you are mine" (Isa. 43:1).

When Jesus appears to the disciples after His resurrection, He and Peter have a private discussion where the Lord restores Peter following his betrayal. Jesus calls him Simon, his old name, a reminder of his old life and nature. He reminds him of what he *has* been and what he *is becoming*—Peter, the rock on which Christ builds His church.[37] One day, believers will each receive a new name a sign of victory and entering into the promised land of eternal life (Rev. 2:17).

Prayer: Lord, I will call on Your name, knowing that "everyone who calls upon the name of the Lord shall be saved" (Acts 2:21).

Radiant Action: Ann Spangler's excellent book *Praying the Names of God* (or any similar ones) will aid me in incorporating His names into daily prayers. I will remember He calls me by new names: Redeemed, Forgiven, Chosen, Worthy of Love.

Webs: Identity (Feb.), Mission (Mar.), Calling: "Here Pig" (Mar.)

Gleanings: "He determines the number of the stars; he gives to all of them their names" (Ps. 147:4).

DAY 18

Lament to Creativity: From the Dung and the Dark

"I will make you a solemn promise."[38]

Out of Wilbur's deepest sorrows comes his most creative strategy. He bribes Templeton with his best offer, his slops. Author Andy Crouch shows a profound understanding of this concept when he writes, "Lament is the seed of creativity."[39] Indeed, suffering can be the womb of new beginnings. The Jews in Babylon are told to do good to the city where they're held in exile. Even the great tribulation, the greatest suffering of the end times, is supposed to usher in the second coming of Christ.

Grace unlocks our ability to forge through wrongs and painful feelings and do something constructive. We're to comfort others with the comfort God gives us. The key is to first own the sorrow, reaffirm trust in God, and listen to His still, small voice intimating of how He can use you to love others. Healing comes with acts of obedience.

This transition from deep distress to expressions of trust in God is the litany in many psalms. "Why are you cast down, O my soul, and why are you in turmoil within me? Hope in God; for I shall again praise him, my salvation and my God" (Ps. 42:11).

Believe that in the crisis of deepest darkness, there are seeds of new beginnings, of fresh living and creating from those tears, life arising from the ashes. As the staff of the More House in Bridgeport, Connecticut, maintain: "Your misery is your ministry."

> "Blessed be the God and Father of our Lord Jesus Christ, the Father of mercies and God of all comfort, who comforts us in all our affliction, so that we may be able to comfort those who are in any affliction, with the comfort with which we ourselves are comforted by God. For as we share abundantly in Christ's sufferings, so through Christ we share abundantly in comfort too" (2 Cor. 1:3–5).

Prayer: Lord, redeem my "deep-in-the-mud-pit" situation and through this hurt bring something good into the world.

Radiant Action: Journal Entry: How is God comforting me, and how can I creatively and compassionately share this comfort with others? Let the dark of night remind me to ask God for the light of holy creativity. I will explore Kintsugi art where the broken vessel is more valuable after it is restored with gold than in its original state.

Webs: Suffering (Mar.), Mud and Manure (Mar.), Look Up! (June)

Gleanings: "When the righteous cry for help, the LORD hears and delivers them out of all their troubles. The LORD is near to the brokenhearted and saves the crushed in spirit" (Ps. 34:17–18).

DAY 19

Balance

"You're going with me, aren't you, Charlotte?"[40]

As the fair nears, Charlotte is pressed between purposes, but her friendship with Wilbur dictates her priorities. While laying her egg sac doesn't require her to be in the barn, Wilbur's future does require her to be with him ensuring there's someone present who knows how to write.

As conflict mounts between the two purposes, Charlotte's perseverance and loyalty enable her to accomplish both. Each purpose enriches the other. Sometimes, like Charlotte, God calls a person to more than one purpose and each, by God's grace, will benefit the other. When a person's life is complex in purpose, God's grace makes balance and victory possible.

Human life is filled with tensions between priorities. What is the most critical thing to do, and when? God can help. He will guide the whens, wheres, and whats if we take time to listen. Jesus spent much time in prayer asking God for wisdom and direction. His life was the most fruitful it could be, and He makes His children fruitful as well. The Lord, perfect in wisdom, gives grace for every work.

Think of the apostle Paul who felt the pull of competing goods: "For to me to live is Christ, and to die is gain. If I am to live in the flesh, that means fruitful labor for me. Yet which I shall choose I cannot tell. I am hard pressed between the two. My desire is to depart and be with Christ, for that is far better. But to remain in the flesh is more necessary on your account" (Phil. 1:21–24).

Think of Jesus, who proclaimed from the cross, "It is finished," although many people were left unhealed and untaught. Jesus knew what to do or not do because of the intimacy He had with His Father.

> *"I glorified you on earth, having accomplished the work that you gave me to do"* (John 17:4).

Prayer: My Father, You who created everything and continue to run the universe, clarify my thinking about what You want me to be and do. Make me a Mary soaking in Your presence; make me a balanced Martha when there is practical work to be done.

Radiant Action: I will endeavor to "line up my body under my soul, my soul under my spirit, and my spirit under the Holy Spirit."[41] When considering a commitment, I will ask, "Is it disobedient *not* to do it?" And "Would I feel *regret* if I do not do it?"

Webs: Division of Responsibility (Mar.), Fear (Mar.), Enemy Territory (Apr.)

Gleanings: "Look carefully then how you walk, not as unwise but as wise" (Eph. 5:15).

DAY 20

Flight

The spider let go of the fence and rose into the air.[42]

The baby spiders sail onward to their destinies on the warm wind. Their launch is a wonder of nature. A real-life, man-made wonder occurred in 1903 when Wilbur and Orville Wright made their first flight; at the time, E. B. White was about four years old. Talk of the marvel must have charged his family's imagination and planted seeds of wonder in the young boy's heart. Perhaps Wilbur was a name that to White signified overcoming impossibilities.

A bird's flight may have inspired David when he wrote, "If I take the wings of the morning . . . even there your hand shall lead me" (Ps. 139:9–10). With images of soaring, Isaiah writes this well-loved promise: "They that wait upon the Lord shall renew their strength; they shall mount up with wings as eagles" (Isa. 40:31 KJV).

Flight is a word of power, of perspective and overcoming what I call "wobblestacles," but I know how deadly serious those trials and deterrents can be. God can help us fly, not only in situations with enemies, distresses, and obstacles, but also over fences of time and space: "Then we who are alive, who are left, will be caught up together with them in the clouds to meet the Lord in the air, and so we will always be with the Lord (1 Thess. 4:17). What a glorious thought that we, too, will fly!

Prayer: Lift me, Lord, to soar on wings like eagles, to take the wings of the morning. Help me uplift others as I learn to fly.

Radiant Action: Journal Entry: What does it means to launch in my life and to help launch others? I will keep a model airplane on my desk as a reminder. When I see anything fly, animal or machine, it will remind me of the Lord's uplifting power.

Webs: Mornings (Apr.), Unstuck (Apr.), Easter (Apr.)

Gleanings: "I bore you on eagles' wings and brought you to myself" (Ex. 19:4).

The arctic bird, the dovekie, cannot launch from land. It must have water to fly. Think about what this might mean in terms of leaving security to launch.

(Photo by Noah Bostrom)

JUNE
PREPARING TO LAUNCH

As apple blossoms blush pink, the gardener watches for pests and disease. June's devotions include themes of listening to God, finding courage, playing, rain, and preparation for launching out.

Lend Your Ear

The Honey of Wisdom: Accepting God's Point of View, *p. 127*
Voices, *p. 128*
Music, *p. 129*
Singing, *p. 130*

Inward Preparation

Courage and Risk, *p. 131*
The Ferris Wheel, *p. 132*
Rain, *p. 133*

Launch Pad

Place, *p. 134*
Home, *p. 135*

Headwinds

Goodness, *p. 136*
Unseen, *p. 137*
Frogs, *p. 138*
Fern's Puddles, *p. 139*
Puddle Jumping, *p. 140*
Wilbur's Wobblestacles, *p. 141*
Templeton's Obstacles: TemPest Stations, *p. 142*
Charlotte's Entanglements, *p. 143*
Look Up!, *p. 144*
Glory!, *p. 145*
Quarterly Review: April–June, *p. 146*

DAY 1

The Honey of Wisdom: Accepting God's Point of View

"But I don't understand everything."[1]

Many characters in *Charlotte's Web* demonstrate wisdom: Fern, the old sheep, the minister, Mrs. Zuckerman, Charlotte, and Dr. Dorian. The old sheep speaks truth about Wilbur's future and Templeton's gluttony. The minister says people must always be on the lookout for wonders. Mrs. Zuckerman wisely recognizes Charlotte as the true talent. Charlotte uses wisdom to catch people with the writings in her web. Dr. Dorian has wisdom to counsel Mrs. Arable. He also possesses humility, the essential attitude for gaining wisdom.

Ken Boa defines wisdom as "the application of knowledge in very specific ways. Wisdom is skill in the art of living life with each component under the dominion of God."[2] God's words reveal His delightful wisdom: "How sweet are your words to my taste, sweeter than honey to my mouth!" (Ps. 119:103). Truly, His wisdom is sweeter than honey. Or doughnuts. Or cookies. Or chocolate bars. Living in the light of God's wisdom leads to the abundant (not carefree) life that Jesus promises His followers.

God says, "Trust in the LORD with all your heart and do not lean on your own understanding. In all your ways acknowledge Him, and He will make your paths straight" (Prov. 3:5–6 NASB). His wisdom is far superior to what we can come up with on our own and is all we need for the situations facing us each day.

The good news is that God's wisdom is readily available: "If any of you lacks wisdom, let him ask God, who gives generously to all without reproach, and it will be given him" (James 1:5). As Pastor Stephen Davey of Shepherd's Church, Cary, NC said, "God gives wisdom to all; he has unlimited stock to make it through today."

Prayer: "Teach us to number our days, that we may gain a heart of wisdom" (Ps. 90:12 NIV).

Radiant Action: Journal Entry: When I see sweets, I will think of God's wisdom and ask for some. "Doughnut" lean on your own understanding (see Prov. 3:5–6). I will read a chapter of Proverbs each day of each month and record any insights that encourage or admonish me.

Webs: Humble (Feb.), Listening (Apr.), Crisis: God Gives Wisdom (Mar.)

Gleanings: My goal is . . . that they may know "Christ, in whom" are hidden all the treasures of wisdom and knowledge" (Col. 2:2-3).

DAY 2

Voices

Her pleasant . . . voice grew even . . . more pleasant.[3]

Wilbur and Charlotte connect through their voices, and in this way communicate heart to heart. Likewise, we humans relate to each other through speech. The voice can make the heart transparent to others, although it's sometimes used to deceive and manipulate. With our voices we educate, inspire, discipline, prevent accidents, lead surgeries, make deals, problem solve. We communicate intensity by the volume of our voices.

In Scripture, we hear diverse voices, like John the Baptist's: "I am the voice of one crying out in the wilderness 'Make straight the way of the Lord'" (John 1:23). And then there's Peter yelling, "Lord, save me," when he was sinking in the waves after walking on water (Matt. 14:30). One of the most powerful moments was when Mary Magdalene heard the voice of Jesus after His resurrection calling her by name: "Mary" (John 20:16).

We all want to have a voice, meaning *we want to be heard*. This can mean utilizing other forms of nonvocal expression. Social media provides platforms for everyone to have a say in the events around them. But there's a better audience, and we don't have to go online to be heard. There's Someone who hears and cherishes our voices. God wants to know what is on our hearts, and desires that we seek Him in prayer. He hears our silent pleas too. "In my distress I called to the LORD; I cried to my God for help. From his temple he heard my voice" (Ps. 18:6 NIV).

Are we listening to His voice calling us by name?

"My sheep hear my voice, and I know them, and they follow me" (John 10:27).

Prayer: Lord, give me ears to hear Your voice and follow You. Hear me as I call to You. Hear me as I praise. Use my voice to share Your glory clearly with others. Please consecrate my voice for Your purposes and not for unhealthy venting or gossip.

Radiant Action: I will make time to listen to God's voice. I will use my voice, spoken or written, to tell others of His goodness. Whether I am a writer or a painter or have other gifts, I will employ my gifts and profession as a *voice* in the world to reveal something of the great God (see Psalm 19).

Webs: Friendship (Feb.), Listening (Apr.), Equipping and Design (May), Singing (June)

DAY 3

Music

"Yes," she replied in her sweet, musical voice.[4]

Life for the characters in *Charlotte's Web* runs on the current of music. The farm rejoices with the chorus of hundreds of little frogs in spring. The sad song of the crickets resounds throughout the community in the fall.

On any sky-blue afternoon in June, you can hear a robin sing out, "Cheery, cheery, cheery," and another answer, "Cheery, cheery, cheery." Frogs sing. Crickets croon. Birds warble. Brooks gurgle. And evidently, pigs like music too, according to researchers.[5]

God Himself sings over His children with rejoicing and quiets them with His love (see Zeph. 3:17). Worship leader Kim McNeal feels God invites His people to "listen for the songs that I will sing over you in the nighttime."[6] We can respond to God with a song like the psalmist: "You have been my help, and in the shadow of your wings I will sing for joy" (Ps. 63:7).

Prayer: Enable me by Your Spirit to let go of dark and demeaning music. Instead, help me be still and listen to You sing Your love song over me. Lead me to music that pleases You and brings life.

Radiant Action: Journal Entry: Applications of this verse: "To you, O LORD, I will make music" (Ps. 101:1). I can make a playlist of praise songs and let the power and energy of music inspire me. I will praise you in song (by voice or by recording) ten minutes a day.

Webs: Weapons (Apr.), Flight (May), Voices (June)

Gleanings: C. S. Lewis wrote these insightful words:

> As to . . . old composers like Schubert or Beethoven, I imagine that, while modern music expresses both feeling, thought and imagination, they expressed pure feeling. And you know all day sitting at work, eating, walking etc., you have hundreds of feelings that can't be put into words. And that is why I think that in a sense music is the highest of the arts, because it really begins where the others leave off.[7]

DAY 4

Singing

"Sing something!" begged Wilbur.[8]

Wilbur loves the lullaby that flows from Charlotte's tender heart for him.[9] It's clear that E. B. White delighted in the natural world, and his book rings with praises for natural joys. As the story closes, White pens a beautiful ode about the farm and its enchantments. "It was the best place to be, . . . this warm delicious cellar, with the garrulous geese, the changing seasons, the heat of the sun."[10]

God says there will be a new song for God's people, a song free from the dung and the dark. As the history of the old earth closes, the apostle John writes, "They were singing a new song before the throne" (Rev. 14:3). This song drowns out the evil dragon, tunes our hearts, and sets our lives on key.

But we don't have to wait for the grand new song. God gives each believer a new tune now.

> *"He put a new song in my mouth, a song of praise to our God. Many will see and fear and put their trust in the Lord"* (Ps. 40:3).

Prayer: Quiet me with Your stillness to receive the new song You desire to give me.

Radiant Action: I will memorize this verse: "The Lord your God is in your midst, a mighty one who will save; he will rejoice over you with gladness; he will quiet you by his love; he will exult over you with loud singing" (Zeph. 3:17).

Webs: Communication in Community (Mar.), Weapons (Apr.), Life Goals (May)

Gleanings: "Make a joyful noise to the Lord, all the earth! Serve the Lord with gladness! Come into his presence with singing!" (Ps. 100:1–2).

DAY 5

Courage and Risk

Wilbur was trembling again, but Charlotte was cool and collected.[11]

Courage flows from the core of one's being and beliefs. Courage means choosing to do the right thing even when there is risk of failure, injury, or loss. It is far different from showing off as Avery does before a crowd. It sizes up the situation at hand: What is the cost to oneself and what will it mean to others if no action is taken? For the believer, courage is anchored in God and His wise purpose, and in the welfare of others.

Charlotte, ever devoted to Wilbur, encouraged him when he needed it most and wanted to die. "'You shall not die,' said Charlotte, briskly."[12] And when Wilbur asked, "Who's going to save me?" she stated emphatically, "I am."[13]

Likewise, God gave courage to His people as they left what they knew. When the Israelites were coming out of Egypt and into the promised land, He said, "Have I not commanded you? Be strong and courageous. Do not be frightened, and do not be dismayed, for the LORD your God is with you wherever you go" (Josh. 1:9). For a people with God at the center of their communal life and radically different from the pagan countries surrounding them, God's words were mobilizing.

The Israelites were coming into a new season where a new kind of life awaited them. Freed from the bondage of slavery from a nation that had treated them as nothing, they anticipated a glorious future. So it is that new chapters in our lives can be exciting but also hold uncertainty and risk. God commands us to have courage to walk with Him in our new season and to believe He goes before and behind and protects us as we go. Grieve for the old for a time but embrace the new.

> "But Caleb quieted the people before Moses and said, 'Let us go up at once and occupy it, for we are well able to overcome it'" (Num. 13:30).

Prayer: Dear Father, examine my heart to see what beliefs I hold dear, hidden where no one sees but You. Give me strong confidence in who You say You are so I can face the future with courage.

Radiant Action: I will place all I have on the altar and trust You.

Webs: Identity (Feb.), Terrific (Feb.), Fear (Mar.), Faith (Apr.), Ferris Wheel (June), Uncertainty (Aug.).

DAY 6

The Ferris Wheel

"The most fun there is," retorted Fern, "is when the Ferris wheel stops...."[14]

Fern loves being stopped at the top of the Ferris wheel with Henry where she can see all around the countryside for miles. The top of the Ferris wheel is the place for perspective. When God is present with us, not only does His presence make life worthwhile, but He also gives us the perspective we need and can in no way gain apart from Him.

When the Israelites were leaving Egypt, they received divine assurance: "The LORD will fight for you, and you have only to be silent" (Ex. 14:14). Knowing that the Rock of Ages is your center, that God guards and guides you, allows you to be silent and confident in the storms and schemes of crisis threatening your peace.

The Ferris wheel's axis where the spokes are joined is like the still point in time that we access with praise. The Ferris wheel's body resembles a clock. Time, cycles, and seasons of earthly life are like spokes in the wheel. It is a symbol of time progressing, a crossroads of time. But God is ageless, outside of time, ever present. Use your imagination to see the center axis of a Ferris wheel as a symbol of the eternal, inextinguishable Life in the center of your being that gives foundation, direction, and energy to *your* seasons.

Prayer: Possibly, praise is the still point of our souls. Thanksgiving looks back. Supplication looks forward. Praise is the focus on the eternal God—His unchanging character that is the axis of all time. Lord, I will praise you often and relish extended times of steeping and soaking praise.

Radiant Action: Journal Entries: 1.What is the still point of my life, the never changing hub or axis from which all my movement, my dance, comes forth? 2. Am I connecting with the timeless One who weaves the web of my life, who stands alone in time, and invites me to join with Him in the eternal? I will let a Ferris wheel (or even a ceiling fan) remind me of the only Some God! I will kneel to make an axis with my body to remind myself of You being my center in the changing seasons of my life.

Webs: The Honey of Wisdom (June), Home (June), Death (Apr.), Purpose Series (May), Energy and Hope (May).

Gleanings: In *Four Quartets II,* "Burnt Norton," T. S. Eliot writes about the still point of the turning world:

> At the still point of the turning world. Neither flesh nor fleshless;
> Neither from nor towards; at the still point, there the dance is,
> But neither arrest nor movement. And do not call it fixity,
> Where past and future are gathered. Neither movement from nor towards,
> Neither ascent nor decline. Except for the point, the still point,
> There would be no dance, and there is only the dance.[15]

DAY 7

Rain

Rain fell in the barnyard and ran in crooked courses.[16]

Rain on this day in the barnyard is a drippy downpour of discouragement. Wilbur's plans are demolished. He is bereft of companionship. But amid his misery, he hears a voice. He has hope of a friend in the coming day.

There are times we all experience rain pouring down on us—our plans are crushed, and our friends are far away. But in the discouragement, if we listen for the Lord's voice over the rain and seek comfort through His Word, we will hear His invitation to be with Him and realize that His friendship is forever, and His plans for us are far greater than any we could devise. "Let us know; let us press on to know the Lord; his going out is sure as the dawn; he will come to us as the showers, as the spring rains that water the earth" (Hos. 6:3).

The rain that washes away our personal ambitions and brings us close to the Lord is the same rain that brings renewal and growth: "Then he prayed again, and heaven gave rain, and the earth bore its fruit" (James 5:18).

Prayer: Thank You for the rain that brings me back to You, refreshing me with the reign of Your Spirit (see Job 5:10).

Radiant Action: I will receive the Holy Spirit's refreshing. When it rains, I will look up and believe God is anointing me for greater purpose and deeper communion with Himself.

Webs: Suffering (Mar.), Bad News (Mar.), Anointing (May), Purpose IV: Oops (May)

Gleanings: "Then I will give you your rains in their season, and the land shall yield its increase, and the trees of the field shall yield their fruit" (Lev. 26:4).

> *"The Lord will open the heavens, the storehouse of his bounty, to send rain on your land in season and to bless all the work of your hands. You will lend to many nations but will borrow from none"* (Deut. 28:12 NIV).

DAY 8

Place

"Where's Papa going with that ax?"[17]

Wilbur's story starts with the word "Where." Place is a living character in Wilbur's life. His apple tree, his pen, his barn are the wheres or nests of his life. Mr. Arable delivers the runt pig to the breakfast table inside a carton on Fern's chair. He's seated with the family and not *on* the table. Instead of being a temporary, material source of food, he is a friend. His place at the table signals that he is not a commodity but a member of the community and representative of much greater things unseen and priceless.

For Christians, the ultimate place is not a physical spot on earth but a place found *in* God. Paul's purpose is to go to the gentiles "that they may receive forgiveness of sins and a *place among those who are sanctified by faith in me*" (Acts 26:18, emphasis mine). Where God wants the gentiles to be is a place in His family, and He invites everyone to a seat at His table.

> Jesus promised that He would go and prepare a place for us where we would be with Him forever. "If it were not so, would I have told you that I go to prepare a place for you?" (John 14:2).

Prayer: God, thank You for making a place for me at Your table (see Ps. 23:5). I accept Your kind invitation and thank You for Your love and hospitality.

Radiant Action: Journal Entries: 1. What places have shaped me? 2. How do I feel when I think of these earthly places? Do memories of them need redeeming or restructuring to bring healing? When I sit at a table, I will think of my place at God's table.

Webs: Belonging and Adoption (Feb.), Uninvited (Mar.), Purpose Series (May), Home (June)

Gleanings: "In my Father's house are many rooms. If it were not so, would I have told you that I go to prepare a place for you? And if I go and prepare a place for you, I will come again and will take you to myself, that where I am you may be also" (John 14:2–3).

DAY 9

Home

Wilbur was taken from his home under the apple tree and went to live in a manure pile.[18]

Wilbur's first home was in a carton set in Fern's chair at the breakfast table. His next home was outdoors under a blossoming apple tree, and after that, a barn with a manure pile.

Steve West, an attorney, writer, and blogger, fondly remembers his childhood home in North Carolina:

> Particular sights and sounds: the low voices of my parents around the kitchen table drinking coffee and reviewing the day, the lights of passing cars on my bedroom walls, the cicadas trill as the day ebbs, the smell of newly cut grass . . . Gray painted siding was peeling . . . There's the window over the kitchen sink where my mother prepared our breakfast and dinner every day . . . There's the double window in the dining room, the table where I wrestled with my homework.

Observing his childhood home forty years later, owned by a stranger, West writes, "I looked up at the windows. Gray painted siding was peeling. An old car was parked in the driveway, hoisted on blocks. Patchy and weedy grass licked the brick foundation."[19]

Editor and author Elizabeth Banks points out that like Wilbur moving from a lovely environment to a manure pile, God expelled humans from Eden into the fallen world. And, like Wilbur who preferred the manure pile, many humans prefer living in rot and darkness.

As believers in Christ, we will be restored to dwell in a forever home in heaven that will not change. Our bodies, the earthly homes for our souls, will wear out. The siding will "peel," the floors collapse. But "we know that if the tent that is our earthly home is destroyed, we have a building from God, a house not made with hands, eternal in the heavens" (2 Cor 5:1). The longing for home in the human heart is ultimately a longing for heaven, our true and perfect home.

"Even the sparrow finds a home, and the swallow a nest for herself" (Ps 84:3).

Prayer: "Lord, get me home before dark."[20]

Radiant Action: I will give to a food pantry or serve in a soup kitchen. I will keep bottled water and fruit, packaged crackers, and other simple foods available in the car and by giving those, along with a tract, to those in need, I will tell others of the joy of my heavenly home. I will make my home a place of love for others to come to know Him.

Webs: Uninvited (Mar.), Boards (Apr.), Place (June)

Gleanings: God Himself is our home: "Lord, you have been our dwelling place in all generations" (Ps. 90:1).

DAY 10

Goodness

"You are a good pig."[21]

Wilbur sees goodness all around: in the goodness of the barnyard, in Charlotte, in the joys of slops and friendship. All these are good things. During the fair, Wilbur starts worrying again about his fate after cold weather comes. Charlotte reassures him that because he's both famous and good, he has nothing to fear.

But what is goodness? It could be an outdoor paradise, a reunion with friends, or more importantly, a description of character. But real goodness, that which is inherent in God, is beyond our imagining. He is perfect in every way—perfect in character, purpose, and action. No one is good but God (see Mark 10:18).

People, however, tend to conceive of goodness in terms of material and relational security. C. S. Lewis explains in *The Problem of Pain* that our fallen state has complicated our perspective on goodness. Many want to see God as a benevolent and indulgent grandfather who wants everyone just to have a good time.[22]

But God, being a good Father, will not leave His children in this state. He shapes us for our good so we can become who we were meant to be. "We are . . . a Divine work of art, something that God is making, and therefore something with which He will not be satisfied until it has a certain character."[23] God wants to recreate goodness in us that befits a creature made in His image.

As Lewis explains, "A God who did not regard this [sin] with unappeasable dictate would not be a good being. We cannot even wish for such a God—it is like wishing that every nose in the universe were abolished, that smell of hay or roses or the sea should never again delight any creature, because our own breath happens to stink."[24]

"Oh, how abundant is your goodness" (Ps. 31:19).

Prayer: Lord, help me believe in Your abundant goodness. Help me to live out Psalm 37:3: "Trust in the Lord and do good; dwell in the land and befriend faithfulness."

Radiant Action: "I believe that I shall look upon the goodness of the Lord in the land of the living!" (Ps. 27:13).

Webs: Aloneness (Feb.), Appearances (Apr.), Anointing (May)

Gleanings: Look up "The Goodness of God" on YouTube.

DAY 11

The Unseen

They did not know that under the straw was a rat,
and inside a knothole was a big grey spider.[25]

The spider and the rat are hideaways in the crate to the fair. Unseen and despised, the duo is yet a force behind Wilbur's winning the special award. Also hidden is Wilbur's real purpose. The farmers think of him as a food source while his ultimate purpose, being a friend, is initially unseen and unforeseen. It's the eternal, not the temporary, the unseen, not the seen, that lasts.

Jesus taught in parables—stories with a point hidden in meaning to the self-righteous but revealed to those seeking to know what He intended. Connections between things can be unseen until someone points them out in a way that can be understood. One of the most famous parables of the Old Testament, found in 2 Samuel 12:1-7, relates how Nathan the prophet told a story to King David that corresponded to his sins of adultery and murder. Through the power of the parable, David's eyes were opened to his sin, leading him to deep repentance and a return to the Lord. In this way, parables can convict, enlighten, make the unseen visible.

Those who work behind the scenes in the spiritual realm (and very often in the physical realm too) are unsung but make things happen. Our Advocate is invisible, yet by faith we believe He is the Creator and Savior of the world. Unseen cheerleaders surround us as clouds of witnesses, as we read in Hebrews 12:1. (Note: the adversary, Satan, is likewise unseen. We do well to watch and keep our guard up.)

> "'O LORD, please open his eyes that he may see.' So the LORD opened the eyes of the young man, and he saw, and behold, the mountain was full of horses and chariots of fire all around Elisha" (2 Kings. 6:17).

Prayer: Open my eyes to see as Elisha did.

Radiant Action: I affirm the truths spoken in the Nicene Creed, "We believe in one God, the Father Almighty, Maker of all things visible and invisible." I will have faith to believe that things unseen are more real than what I can touch, smell, feel, or see. I will not make decisions based solely on what I can see now. Breezes will remind me of the reality of the unseen.

Webs: Small Things (Feb.), Insignificance (Feb.), Appearances (Apr.), Purposes (May)

Gleanings: "So we fix our eyes not on what is seen, but on what is unseen, since what is seen is temporary, but what is unseen is eternal" (2 Cor. 4:18 NIV).

DAY 12

Frogs

"I heard the frogs today."[26]

Avery has his very own pet frog friend. It swims in bubbly dishwater; it swings in Avery's pocket from the barn loft. When a preschooler, my youngest son also had a frog friend one Sunday. The frog was a passenger on his toy truck; he was a competitor in a race. Alas, that morning sent him into a world beyond puddles and gnats.

The chorus of frogs in *Charlotte's Web* heralds a new spring and new beginnings. And frogs give us good examples. They can jump over and into mud puddles. Just watching them can inspire us to jump over obstacles to reach goals. Or just to be fearless jump right in on a project with a splash of joy and confidence.

But frogs can also be symbols of problems. A flood of frogs comprised the second plague in Egypt, part of the barrage of ills to befall the tyrant, Pharaoh. They filled Egyptian beds, jumped on tables and into food, even into cooking pots, mixing bowls, and ovens. En masse they filled the Nile, a slimy, croaking horror. They were one of ten plagues God sent to show His power and glory. (By grace we can seek God's wisdom amid problems and not harden our hearts as did Pharaoh).

We might pray for our frogs (problems) to disappear. But all too often, when one set of problems goes away, new ones arise. After the frogs died, "the land stank" (Ex. 8:14). When asking God to remove "frogs" in your life, think of what other worse problems might take their place. You might even end up being thankful for the first frogs.

Prayer: Father, You who created frogs, enable me to jump, splash, and flex, and to depend on You for wisdom for handling problems. Thank You for rain and puddles.

Radiant Action: Journal Entry: What frog legs—that is abilities and strategies—do I have to jump over problems? God will give me grace and joy to make good progress despite them. A frog chorus announcing spring is a reminder that winters do end and new life plunges forward.

When I hear or see frogs, I will think about new ways for dealing with my problems and about possible new beginnings.

Webs: Marriage (Feb), Rain (June), Wilbur's Wobblestacles (June), Puddle Jumping (June)

Gleanings: FROGS = Fully Relying on God! We rely on Him to jump over the puddles.

DAY 13

Fern's Puddles

She took hold of the ax and tried to pull it out of her father's hand.[27]

Fern is quietly helping her mother set the table when suddenly, in the face of threat, she leaps up to prevent an injustice and stay an execution. She will not and cannot allow the little runty pig to be sacrificed. She literally "set the captives free," and it doesn't daunt her that the foremost one to dissuade is her father. Her observational skills and curiosity allow her to assess and act to save a small life while overcoming hurdles.

Notice all that she overcomes: compliance to her duty of setting the table, the physical obstacle of the chair, her familial responsibility of respecting her father's wishes, and even an attempt to overcome his strength by grasping the ax. Later, Fern overcomes her mother's skepticism.

Many things keep us from jumping over life's hurdles, like underestimating God's ability to help, not knowing His character or promises, not knowing who we are as well as whose we are, or expecting things to just happen. We're hampered by inner destructive thoughts and ensuing habits, feelings of hopelessness, lack of perseverance, lack of practical knowledge or knowledge of God's Word and our tendency to often ignore it.

As with Fern, having the engine of purpose within our God-given identity will see us through the nettles, marshes, and quagmires between our goals and us.

"Behold, I am the LORD, the God of all flesh. Is anything too hard for me?" (Jer. 32:27).

Prayer: Father, give me hope to overcome hurdles. Help me internalize the core beliefs about You and myself that are true and will lead me to victory. Make my heart believe these timeless words from the twenty-third Psalm: "The LORD is my shepherd; I shall not want" (v. 1). In You, I lack nothing that assures success as You conceive it. Grant me confidence to jump hurdles, and if I fail, to learn and persevere. I praise You as I think of who You are and how big You are, for in that knowledge I am assured You can handle anything.

Radiant Action: Journal Entry: What stands in the way of me fulfilling God's purpose for my life?

Webs: All of March, Wilbur's Wobblestacles (June), Charlotte's Entanglements (June), Frogs (June)

Gleanings: "Ah, Lord GOD! It is you who have made the heavens and the earth by your great power and by your outstretched arm! Nothing is too hard for you" (Jer. 32:17).

DAY 14

Puddle Jumping

Fern pushed a chair out of the way and ran outdoors.[28]

Obstacles have the potential to build a great story in our lives. Sometimes, like Fern and the chair, it's possible to push them out of the way. Sometimes it's impossible, and it's God's job to move the mountain. Our job is to be patient and do what we can. Sometimes all we can do is stand.

One of the biggest "puddle jumpings" in the Bible was over the Red Sea. God commanded Moses to lead the Israelites to freedom, but the Red Sea stood before the terrified multitude. However, it served as a barrier that gave God glory as He made a way for His people.

Modern stories of "puddle jumping," of overcoming obstacles, abound. In the movie *Woodlawn*, based on a true story, someone throws a brick through the window of the home of Tony Nathan, the African American football hero, demanding that he quit the game. Tony goes on to play for Alabama where he becomes a role model. Gladys Aylward was a determined English woman of the twentieth century. Though turned down by an official board for missionary service, she went to China, surviving the trip despite wars in Europe, and eventually leading one hundred orphans to safety in wartime.

What's the "puddle" or obstacle to your calling? There is no limit to God's grace, power, and provision through the Holy Spirit. One seminarian was deeply discouraged because he was nearly deaf and his hearing aids were faulty. His class prayed for him, and someone gave him four thousand dollars for new hearing aids![29] He was able to finish his classes.

> "For by you I can run against a troop, and by my God I can leap over a wall" (Ps. 18:29).

Prayer: Lord, would You move in a supernatural way to open an impossible gate in my life in a manner that brings You and You alone the glory? If the enemy is blocking the way, in the name of Jesus, remove him and accomplish Your plan.

Radiant Action: Journal Entry: I will record my findings as I search the Scriptures and listen to the Holy Spirit for creative wisdom in dealing with my "puddles." I will fill my mind with examples of those who overcame obstacles and won victory. (Movies: *The Hill*, *The Boys in the Boat*, *Lord of the Rings*, *Run the Race*)

Webs: Bad News (Mar.), Balance (May), Fern's Puddles (June), Provision (Nov.)

DAY 15

Wilbur's Wobblestacles

"I think I'm going to faint," he whispered.[30]

Wilbur has many challenges or "wobblestacles." Born a helpless runt without rank, dependent on a small girl and a spider, surrounded with unpleasant characters and murderous traditions of farmers who shoot and eat pigs, uneducated, subject to wobbly emotions, Wilbur has many "puddles to jump."

What can he do? How can he cope? How can he win? Once Fern frees him from his first death sentence, Wilbur's wise ally, Charlotte, helps him navigate some of these pitfalls. What can we humans do in our all too real and impossible situations?

We have an all-wise God on our side. Having God as our friend is key to breakthrough. He helps us know His will and to set and meet His goals. With God, nothing is impossible, as the Bible makes abundantly clear. He is with us through Christ, but He requires of us humility to accept His grace and His ways of doing things.

"I can do all things through [Christ] who strengthens me" (Phil. 4:13).

Prayer: Dear Mover of Mountains, thank You for watching over me. You saw my impossible obstacles to knowing You and struck my heart with Your Word as You did St. Augustine's. And now I love You. My future is secure in the risen Christ. Please grant me wisdom in my daily life to overcome wobblestacles. Give me spiritual strength to do warfare where necessary. Nothing is too hard for You. I submit my plans to You.

Radiant Action: Journal Entries: 1. What are some goals I have thought about for years but never pursued? 2. Am I convinced they are God's goals? 3. What could be strategies or advantages to following through? 4. What has kept me from meeting these goals? 5. What Scriptures apply and confirm their worthiness? I will aim for steadfastness as the Lord gives me grace to complete the race. The time for overcoming wobblestacles has come! 6. What or who is "under my trough" that makes my life harder?" I will turn it over to God because He cares for me and understands my troubles—whether they're like puddles or a raging open sea. He will steady me and turn wobblestacles to stepping stones. After the cross came the resurrection.

Webs: Belonging (Feb.), Waiting (Mar.), Barnyard Disciples (Mar.), Baptism (Apr.)

Gleanings: "For nothing will be impossible with God" (Luke 1:37).

DAY 16

Templeton's Temptations: TemPest Stations

"I came to this Fair to enjoy myself, not to deliver papers."[31]

Any critter who suggests something to Templeton that conflicts with his self-centered agenda is an irritating obstacle that provokes his ill temper. Ironically, he delivers the word "Humble" to Charlotte at the fair. Humble *he* is not. But then, he never gets a special award. Or a friend.

Only when he believes that helping someone else would serve his self-interest does the rat adjust his course and help. He goes to the fair because a fair is a rat's paradise.

Templeton's goals are simple: gain every pleasure. It might be a rotten egg or piece of dirty string; it isn't necessarily the nature of the possession. It's the pleasure and power of possessing the object that obsessed and possessed him.

But in aiding Wilbur, albeit with extreme reluctance, he actually forages the best scraps. In helping both Charlotte and Wilbur, he revels in rat treasures (of food) beyond his wildest dreams. He even gets to have the first dibs on Wilbur's trough after retrieving Charlotte's egg sac.

He would have lost those opportunities had he not engaged, bad attitude or not, in doing good. Perhaps the application to ourselves is found in the words of John Koessler: "Do not be too quick to judge your circumstances. What appears to us to be an obstacle or a setback may be God's way of strategically positioning you for the next stage in His plan."[32]

> "Fear not, for I am with you; be not dismayed, for I am your God; I will strengthen you, I will help you, I will uphold you with my righteous right hand" (Isa. 41:10).

Prayer: Grand Weaver, help me to not miss out on the glories of life because of any selfish intent on my part. Give me faith to believe You will work through the inconveniences that come when I help others, and You will bless me with the purposes You have woven into the inconsistencies of others.

Radiant Action: Journal Entries: 1. What or who am I holding off because it is inconvenient to reach out or is uncomfortable to do so? Am I supposed to reach out or quietly pray? 2. What am I missing out on by not being helpful or by sharing my resources? 3. What priorities do I need to change to find untold blessings?

Webs: Crisis (Mar.), Captured: Sin (Apr.), Surprising Deliverers (Apr.), Courage and Risk (June)

Gleanings: "But Jesus looked at them and said, "With man this is impossible, but with God all things are possible" (Matt. 19:26).

DAY 17

Charlotte's Entanglements

"I'm too tired."[33]

Charlotte has Goliath-size goals: to save a runty spring pig from becoming bacon, to be true to this pig who is her friend, and to deliver her magnum opus safely. But small and frail as she is, the hurdles she faces seem overwhelming. The farmers are bent on slaughter. She must depend on an unwilling rat with a giant ego. And then there is Avery. And her smallness. Her limited life span.

Obstacles can loom as large and terrifying to us as they are to Charlotte. But on examining them, we might ponder, what exactly is bigger than God? There is nothing too hard for Him! Consider "time," for example. God created time and exists outside it, yet he is sovereign over events in time. He can stretch time to make a small minute have an impact forever. In an instant, the thief on the cross was changed from a criminal to a citizen of paradise. The Old Testament book of Habakkuk describes when God even stopped time: "The sun and moon stood still in their place at the light of your arrows as they sped, at the flash of your glittering spear" (Hab. 3:11).

Our great God has divine purposes for us that no plan or scheme can thwart. He sees us with far greater value and potential than we can see. He sent Jesus to rescue us from feeble wanderings and unfocused endeavors for real purpose with eternal effects. "For we are his workmanship, created in Christ Jesus for good works, which God prepared beforehand, that we should walk in them" (Eph. 2:10).

No danger can stop us. Paul wrote, "Three times I was beaten with rods. Once I was stoned. Three times I was shipwrecked; a night and a day I was adrift at sea" (1 Cor. 11:25).

Prayer: Dear Heavenly Father, give me courage to take hold of what purposes You have for me. The devil cannot hold me; death cannot stop me. I come. I bow down. I surrender. Since You are with me, I will conquer.

Radiant Action: Journal Entry: Is there a lie about God or myself that keeps me from overcoming?

Webs: Fern's Puddles (June), Puddle Jumping (June), Frogs (June), Time and Seasons (Aug.)

Gleanings: "... Let us go up at once, and possess it; for we are well able to overcome it" (Num. 13:30 KJV).

DAY 18

Look Up!

"Look up here in the corner of the doorway!"[34]

Wilbur looks up out of despair. In the corner of the barn, up high, Charlotte's remaining offspring greet him. Wilbur finds hope, new friends, and the fruit of his sacrifice, Charlotte's children.

When we look up to Jesus, we find hope.

> "I lift up my eyes to the hills. From where does my help come? My help comes from the LORD, who made heaven and earth" (Ps. 121:1–2).

> "Therefore, since we are surrounded by so great a cloud of witnesses, let us also lay aside every weight, and sin which clings so closely, and let us run with endurance the race that is set before us, looking to Jesus, the founder and perfecter of our faith, who for the joy that was set before him endured the cross, despising the shame, and is seated at the right hand of the throne of God" (Heb. 12:1–2).

> "After this I looked, and behold, a door standing open in heaven!" (Rev. 4:1).

Prayer: Lord, nudge me to look up!

Radiant Action: I will go outside to look at the sky. (StarWalk is an app to help understand the stars and planets.)

Webs: Mornings (Apr.), Energy and Hope (May), Faith (May)

Gleanings: "Now when these things begin to take place, straighten up and raise your heads, because your redemption is drawing near" (Luke 21:28).

DAY 19

Glory!

. . . the glory of everything.[35]

The end of the story is filled with glory. Wilbur nearly swoons with ecstasy over the nearly inexpressible joys of his humble barnyard. He rejoices in the quintessential essences of its inhabitants and atmosphere: garrulousness, change, heat, passing birds, nearness of rats, sameness, even the smells.

If Wilbur, the humble pig of a children's story, can exult in the ordinary barnyard, how much more can the humble believer exalt in his future? Though Jesus promised us troubles in this life—hurricanes of woes, oppression, disappointment, grueling work, wobblestacles uncountable, persecution, deaths of all sorts—Christians have the hope of glory and the anointing of the Spirit to fuel the fire within.

Before His crucifixion, Jesus displayed His coming glory to Peter, James, and John on a mountain (see Matthew 17:1–13; Mark 9:2–13; Luke 9:28–36). They needed, before the time of anguish coming, to have a glimpse of who Jesus is and the eternal victory He will win.

> *"What no eye has seen, nor ear heard, nor the heart of man imagined, what God has prepared for those who love him these things God has revealed to us through the Spirit"* (1 Cor. 2:9–10).

Prayer: God, open our eyes, even through ordinary things like rats or everyday occurrences, to think about the glory that awaits us when we are with You forever. Do not allow our faith to dim because of trouble on this earth. Let us fix our eyes on You and trust You for the glory to come. Help us to know that that glory will all be worth the manure down here.

Radiant Action: I will look up to the skies and praise God for the unseen glory that awaits me. I will sing "For the beauty of the earth for the glory of the skies, for the love which from our birth, over and around us lies. Christ our God, to Thee we raise This our hymn of grateful praise."[36]

Webs: Easter (Apr.), Anointing: Dew (May), Apples (Sept.), Utopia (Dec.), Joy I and II (Dec.)

Gleanings: "Blessed assurance, Jesus is mine! O what a foretaste of glory divine!"[37] "Be exalted, O God, above the heavens! Let your glory be over all the earth!" (Ps. 57:11).

DAY 20
Quarterly Review

April—June

1. April: Templeton had a personality steeped in selfishness. What sin (inner or outer) is crouching at your door? Are you "nailing up boards" to keep temptations away or preparing to flee if necessary?
2. April: What weapons are you wielding to find victory? Are you learning to listen to the Holy Spirit and to depend on the blood of Christ?
3. April: How have you been changed or become unstuck?
4. May: Like Charlotte, do you have a plan? Do you have passion, purpose, and perseverance?
5. May: Do you understand the power of one? Jesus is the ultimate example here.
6. May: Unlike Wilbur, Charlotte had the right equipment to spin webs. Have you taken any inventories to discover more about your equipping and design of personality, spiritual gifts, what gives you joy? Application of this wisdom can lead to balance and flight.
7. May: Have you asked God for His anointing on your life? A fresh dew?
8. June: Are you accepting God's wisdom from the Bible, from the Holy Spirit, and from godly people? Are you finding it sweet like honey? Are you trusting the unseen God?
9. June: From the Ferris Wheel: Use your imagination to see the center axis of a Ferris wheel as a symbol of the eternal, inextinguishable Life in the center of your being that gives foundation, direction, and energy to *your* seasons. It does not move. It provides the power. Believe that at the still point of the Ferris wheel's axis "He will quiet you by his love" (Zeph. 3:17). Is this true for you?
10. June: What are your "wobblestacles" or your puddles? Remember, ironically, the dark character—the rat, Templeton—was key to fruitful outcomes.

Challenge: Keep a record of Scriptures that are special to you, answers to prayer, and songs that encourage. Make notes on God's timing, wisdom (understanding), grace, and provisions. Even note where you find God breaking through in the ordinary. You will build a strong story to help others.

JULY
FREEDOM AND THINKING

In July, the apple tree's fruit is now visible and will be round and ripe before long. Avery and Fern are in the height of their childhood summer of swinging and swimming. This is the month to ponder the meaning of real freedom in community, personal life, and the life of the mind.

What Is Freedom?

Liberty: Toward the Merry-Go-Round, *p. 148*
Clean and White: Moral Freedom, *p. 149*
Truth: Swinging, *p. 150*

Freedom of Eden (Innocence)

Childlike, *p. 151*
Imagination, *p. 152*
Play, *p. 153*
Humor, *p. 154*

Freedom of the Mind

Thinking, *p. 155*
The Dump, *p. 156*
Asking Questions, *p. 157*
Trapping: Rat Persuasion (Bribes), *p. 158*
Weaving, *p. 159*

Freedom to Choose

Life, *p. 160*
Life and Health, *p. 161*
Journeys, *p. 162*
Scatter, *p. 163*
Distractions, *p. 164*
Servanthood, *p. 165*
Justice, *p. 166*
Faithfulness, *p. 167*

DAY 1

Liberty: Toward the Merry-Go-Round

The children grabbed each other . . . and danced off in the direction of the merry-go-round . . . where they could be happy and free and do as they pleased.[1]

Avery and Fern are tipsy with joy from a sip of the wine of autonomy, the freedom from control of others. The siblings taste freedom, but within limits of parental oversight and as a healthy part of growing up and out into a broader world.

By contrast, the goose compels Wilbur to scoot through the loose board of his pen to a wild and purposeless liberty. Wilbur's freedom is autonomy for the sake of experiencing life without limits. He is a piggly-wiggly running in every direction not knowing how to leverage his liberty. Ill-advised, not knowing his own heart, Wilbur regrets his wild entre into unbounded liberty.

Our human nature most often seduces us into a wild, dissatisfying scurry for freedom. But, when we as believers stay securely tucked into the will and presence of the Lord, we can fully and freely explore life. God has our flourishing at heart and gives us boundaries for blessing. Real freedom lays in doing what the Lord says to do, when and how and where. In doing His will, we will experience wonderful music, adventure, excitement—all that represents the riches of life in Jesus.

> *"You make known to me the path of life; in your presence there is fullness of joy; at your right hand are pleasures forevermore"* (Ps. 16:11).

> *"Now the Lord is the Spirit, and where the Spirit of the Lord is, there is freedom"* (2 Cor. 3:17).

Prayer: Help me discern between autonomy (freedom from control of others) and liberty (freedom to conform to wholesome purposes).

Radiant Action: Journal Entries: 1. In what way does my heart cry for freedom? 2. Am I denying myself God-approved freedom by slipping into legalism? 3. Am I listening to other people, who, like the goose, may want to live vicariously through rebellion that poses as freedom? 4. How grounded is my sense of liberty in the eternal and the Scriptures?

Webs: Direction (May), Time and Seasons (Aug.), Clean and White: Moral Freedom (July), Fences (August)

Gleanings: "The Spirit of the Lord GOD is upon Me, because the LORD has anointed Me . . . to proclaim liberty to the captives, and the opening of the prison to those who are bound" (Isa. 61:1 NKJV).

DAY 2

Clean and White: Moral Freedom

He was pure white.[2]

Wilbur loves to roll around in the manure, but Mrs. Zuckerman's buttermilk baths clean him right up. The truth is that buttermilk doesn't change Wilbur's inner "pigginess." He'll wallow in the manure again as soon as he gets a chance. It's his nature.

We, like Wilbur, tend to enjoy a romp in our favorite form of "manure" as soon as our flesh gets loose from its outer restraints. Those restraints and laws won't change us. The only power that can set us free to make good choices is God's Holy Spirit: "And I will give you a new heart, and I will put a new spirit in you. I will take out your stony, stubborn heart and give you a tender, responsive heart" (Ezek. 36:26 NLT).

Fortunately, the Bible reveals the nature of redemption and moral freedom: Much as it hurts our pride, the truth is we are all "piggies" in need of a complete *inner* redemption: "All have sinned and come short of the glory of God" (Rom. 3:23 KJV).

The good news is that God can make piggies white on the inside and create a new nature within. He wants to draw us singly to Himself, with all the infinite varieties of personality that exist among us as human beings to make us new. Our inheritance is freedom. Our motivation is by love and awe of God, not fear.

> "For you were called to freedom, brothers. Only do not use your freedom as an opportunity for the flesh, but through love serve one another" (Gal. 5:13).

Prayer: Father, I praise You for freedom from sin, fear, loneliness, lack of purpose, hopelessness, and helplessness.

Radiant Action: Journal Entry: A prayer for deliverance. If I am entangled in a web of sin so hopelessly that I cannot break free, I will ask God for resurrection power instead of making deeper destructive patterns and seek counsel. God can; I can't. True freedom entails struggle.

Webs: Captured: Sin (Apr.), Baptism (April), Mud and Manure (Mar.), Childlike (July), Apples (Sept.), Choices (Sept.)

Gleanings: "Live as people who are free, not using your freedom as a cover-up for evil" (1 Peter 2:16).

"He rescued me from my strong enemy" (Ps. 18:17).

Flannery O'Connor notes, "Even if he [the author] writes about characters who are mostly unfree, it is the sudden free action, the open possibility, which he knows is the only thing capable of illuminating the picture and giving it life."[3]

DAY 3

Truth: Swinging

Mr. Zuckerman had the best swing in the county.[4]

The barn swing in Zuckerman's barn brings joy to Fern and Avery. For generations, swinging has been and still is a favorite pastime. But the swinging of today's culture is not between barn and sky but between facts and feelings. Abdu Murray says that now feeling and opinion hold the scepter although facts may get a nod.[5]

Culture's mantra "you do you" holds up not only in superficial preferences for pastimes like wallowing (Wilbur) or weaving (Charlotte), but in the basic moral bedrock determining right and wrong. Truth, if not objectively rooted in outside authority, swings. It's *every man for himself* as in ancient Israel (see Judges 21:25).

But this "freedom" from absolute truth and authority is not reality. Associate Supreme Court Justice Samuel Alito explains: "There are certain moral principles that are true and immutable . . . These principles of right and wrong are not relative or circumstantial. They are not of our making, and it is not within our power to change them, even though at times we might find that convenient."[6]

I wrote about the Ferris wheel as a metaphor: "Use your imagination to see the center axis of a Ferris wheel as a symbol of the eternal, inextinguishable Life in the center of your being that gives foundation, direction, and energy to *your* seasons."* Today we are like wheels without a still point, without an axis. In our centerless" culture, we are purposeless giant metal wheels swinging wildly about, clashing into each other, creating chaos and casualties.

There is only one way to come back to the still point to function as designed. Admit moral default and agree with Paul that "all have sinned and fall short of the glory of God" (Rom. 3:23). There is redemption. The still point is still available. Jesus taught "I am the way, and the truth, and the life. No one comes to the Father except through me" (John 14:6). If we want to know truth, then we need to know Jesus. He made a way for us if we will accept His love and the truth about our souls—but not if we are swinging around without axis.

Prayer: God, help me surrender to You and find Your purpose and perspective.

Radiant Action: A swing will remind me to no longer swing between feelings and opinions, but to decisively stand on truth.

Webs: *Ferris Wheel (June), Asking Questions (July), Decisiveness (Aug.)

DAY 4

Childlike

"Maybe our ears aren't as sharp as Fern's."[7]

Fern, as a child, can hear the talk of the barnyard critters. She perceives what adults cannot. Mr. Arable tells Mrs. Arable that she shouldn't "worry about Fern—she's just got a lively imagination. Kids think they hear all sort of things."[8] The child Fern is open to life adults can no longer discern.

Capacity for believing grows more easily in children than adults, for they are awake to wonders adults have left behind. As Fern grows older and is no longer fascinated by talking animals, she leaves the fellowship of the barn for the company of Henry Fussy.

Nurturing relationships remains her purpose, but justice is no longer her main concern. Perhaps this is a commentary on adults in general as they bend toward security and social positioning. They give up on dreams of changing the world. Like Wilbur, we choose the pen instead of exploring the vast wilderness of the outside world. We plod along in time and leave the things of childhood behind.

But, if we believe God's promises with childlikeness and trust God to meet our needs, Jesus says we are fit for the kingdom of heaven. Once adult cynicism peels away, childlike belief can flourish and be nourished in the revelations unveiled for believers but mystifying to doubters. A child trusts his father, believes his father, depends on his father. As we become more like little children in our faith, we put our hand into the heavenly Father's all-powerful one. We will find wonder and renewed vitality in our walk with Jesus.

> *"And calling to him a child, he put him in the midst of them and said, 'Truly, I say to you, unless you turn and become like children, you will never enter the kingdom of heaven. Whoever humbles himself like this child is the greatest in the kingdom of heaven'"* (Matt. 18:2–4).

Prayer: Heavenly Father, turn our skepticism into faith. Make me childlike and trusting.

Radiant Action: Journal Entry: What are some ways I can become more childlike? I'll make time to delight in dandelions, kites, and inchworms and watch the birds and children on a playground, talk to an old friend, and eat slowly.

Webs: Life Goals (May), Imagination (July), Humor (July), Time and Seasons (Aug.)

Gleanings: "A little child will lead them" (Isa. 11:6 NIV). Example: The boy who gave the Lord his lunch.

DAY 5

Imagination

"I could spin a web if I tried," said Wilbur.[9]

In childlike innocence, Wilbur imagines he can make a spider web like Charlotte's. Impossible, of course. Yet we can't help but smile at his exuberance in exercising "the faculty or action of forming new ideas, or images or concepts of external objects *not present to the senses.*"[10] Fern, too, possesses a large and vivid imagination. She could imagine potential in Wilbur whereas Mr. Arable could not. She hears things adults cannot fathom. Charlotte's imagination is at work when she makes Wilbur seem special, thus preserving his life, in spite of the old sheep's predictions.

Jesus could imagine potential in Peter when Peter was far from being a rock. After His resurrection, Jesus fixed breakfast by the shore for His disciples. Jesus took Peter aside and spoke new life, identity, and purpose to one who felt only shame. He could see beauty in Peter despite the betrayal because He loved him and affirmed his value. Imagination can be life-giving when we imagine as possible good things in and for others as well as in and for ourselves.

God imagined the universe and with His word, He brought forth worlds and declared them good. People, made in His image, also have the gift of powerful imagination, but apart from God it all too often leads to dark results. With the fall of man into depravity, and swept up by the desire to be God as described in the Babel account, the collective human imagination became a source of evil: "No evil thing they imagine they can do will be impossible for them" (Gen. 11:6 AMP).

Growth in faith reverses the bent toward evil imagination and harnesses creative power for good.

> "O Lord God of Abraham, . . . keep this forever in the imagination of the thoughts of the heart of thy people and prepare their heart unto thee" (1 Chron. 29:18 KJV).

Prayer: Grant me a redeemed imagination in which Your Word ignites my imagination and so it aligns with faith. But cast down any vain imaginations in me! Don't let me imagine goals You have not assigned for me.

Radiant Action: I will imagine Jesus with me wherever I go and practice being in His presence.

Webs: Identity (Feb.), Signs and Wonders (Dec.), Childlike (July), Presumption (July)

Gleanings: "The Christian is the one whose imagination should fly beyond the stars." —Francis Schaeffer

DAY 6

Play

"Skip and dance, Jump and prance!"[11]

There's lots of play in *Charlotte's Web*—swinging in the barn and putting frogs in pockets. Wilbur, all cleaned up and shiny, throws himself into his radiant new identity by galloping, jumping, and doing backflips. Avery has fun crawling in the pig pen and "hamming" it up.

According to author Randy Alcorn, the frolicking of animals displays the Creator's character. God likes to have fun: "Consider what's visible [of the attributes of God] in otters, dogs, and countless other animals: God's playfulness... I for one have praised God for and been drawn to him by the playfulness, exuberance, love, and devotion in the dogs I've had over the years. They communicate the beauty of their Maker."[12]

R. Paul Stephens, a professor at Regent College in Vancouver, agrees. "There is a playfulness and wastefulness built into God's creation: millions of seeds that will never germinate; leaves that turn into brilliant colors and die; and flowers that display their beauty even when no one is looking."[13] Jürgen Moltmann maintains, God was playing when He made the world: "The creation is God's play, a play of his groundless and inscrutable wisdom. It is the realm in which God displays his glory."[14]

Play offers evidence for eternity, that life is more than work. Stephens explains: "We were not created for the utilitarian purpose of getting work done on earth from God's perspective. Rather, we were created as the fruit of God's own love and for the delight of God. Similarly, the universe is the result of continuous covenant love between the Father, Son, and Holy Spirit."[15] Play is a sign of life and faith and fosters living. Even the Sabbath is given as a weekly reminder to rejoice in the art of playing.[16] If we play, we are reflecting His image.

Prayer: Lord, make me playful again by casting all my care on You.

Radiant Action: What is play to me? I'll cast my burdens on the Lord and enjoy some godly fun. A dog (or otter) will remind me to play.

Webs: Imagination (July), Routines and Rhythms (Aug.), Signs and Wonders (Dec.)

Gleanings: "And the streets of the city shall be full of boys and girls playing in its streets" (Zech. 8:5).

DAY 7

Humor

"Thith thtuff thticks in my mouth."[17]

We laugh at old Templeton trying to talk with a sticky mouth; his swollen size after a night of gorging at the fair; his comic grumpiness. We laugh at Wilbur in his clownish attempts to make a spider web. We laugh at the geese too, who repeat thrice everything they say. We laugh at Avery. "He liked being a clown in a ring, with everybody watching . . . He raised the pail high in the air and dumped the water on himself and made faces."[18]

Humor helps in tough times. Abraham Lincoln had a face written in humor, as described by his biographer, Carl Sandburg:

> Besides being tragedian, he was comedian. Across the mask of his dark gravity could come a light-ray of the quizzical, the puzzled. This could spread into the beginning of a smile and then spread farther into wrinkles and wreaths of laughter that lit the whole face into a glow; it was of the quality of his highest laughter that it traveled through his whole frame, currents of it vitalizing his toes.[19]

Author Mary Ann Shaffer wrote about the Doodlebug German bombs dropped on London in WWII. She notes:

> It seems impossible now that someone could have drawn a cartoon about Doodlebugs, and that everyone including me could have laughed at it. But we did. The old adage—humor is the best way to make the unbearable bearable—may be true . . . a light approach to the bad news would serve as an antidote and that humor would help to raise London's low morale.[20]

"A joyful heart is good medicine" (Prov. 17:22).

Prayer: Dianne Bundt prays this for her readers: "May you laugh long and often. May each day be filled with gladness so that even your sorrows turn into joy."[21] Help me to "go forth in the dance of the merrymakers" (Jer. 31:4).

Radiant Action: I'll try to find something funny every day: a comic strip, a funny movie, or share a humorous memory with a friend or family member. I'll try to see the humor in situations with grumpy or selfish people and especially aim to laugh at myself.

Webs: Play (July), Childlike (July), Imagination (July)

DAY 8

Thinking

"I'm hanging head-down at the top of my web. That's when I do my thinking."[22]

Charlotte is a thinker. She doesn't have hysterics like Wilbur or indulge in gluttony like Templeton. She keeps steady and analyzes situations, people, and animals. She refuses to write "Terrific" because she knows other bugs will come along and ruin her work. Wilbur is a thinker too. He thinks to ask questions. He thinks about Templeton being inconsiderate. And he thinks hard about the spiderling Nellie's name. He can't sleep because he has "too many things" on his mind."[23]

Thinking is one of our greatest capacities. However, popular trends focus on feelings and there is much pressure to conform to groupthink. The Bible identifies the helmet, the armor for the mind, as a critical piece of spiritual armor (Eph. 6:17). Memorizing Scripture adds steel to the helmet: "Keep this Book of the Law always on your lips; meditate on it day and night, so that you may be careful to do everything written in it. Then you will be prosperous and successful" (Josh. 1:8 NIV).

David exhorts us to relish God's Word. He describes the successful person this way: "His delight is in the law of the LORD, and on his law he meditates day and night. He is like a tree planted by streams of water that yields its fruit in its season and its leaf does not wither" (Ps. 1:2–3). Christians have the mind of Christ because we have the Holy Spirit (see 1 Cor. 2:10–12, 16). It's a mind of peaceful wisdom that thinks of God and others first.

The most wondrous truth is that God is thinking of us and knows our every thought.

> "How precious to me are your thoughts, O God! How vast is the sum of them! If I would count them, they are more than the sand" (Ps. 139:17–18).

Prayer: "Search me, O God, and know my heart! Try me and know my thoughts!" (Ps. 139:23–24).

Radiant Action: Journal Entries: 1. How well am I doing at reading Scripture consistently for at least five minutes each day? Scripture reading is putting on the "helmet" of salvation and the "belt" of truth to keep me from conforming to the world. 2. I will try a thinking-inking-inking plan—thinking things through, thinking ahead, thinking creatively and strategically, thinking with sound reasoning (see Acts 17:1–3), with curiosity, and by asking the right questions."

Webs: Thoughts and Beliefs: Thinking Upside Down with Charlotte (Jan.), Trapping (July), Truth (July)

Gleanings: "The mind governed by the Spirit is life and peace" (Rom. 8:6 NIV).

DAY 9

The Dump

Templeton knew the dump and liked it.[24]

Templeton, the quintessential self-interested, self-absorbed critter, crawled through the trash and sought to hide himself in the offscourings of life. The outcast reveled in the castoffs, the useless, the dirty—the stink thrown far away from the center of living.

Our minds too can run ratlike through a dump of negative thoughts and memories, and we can get stuck there. Dwelling on the past with all our misdeeds, regrets, and "if onlys" can lead to broken circuits mentally and physically. Paul urged the Philippians to positively set their minds on what is good: "Finally, brothers, whatever is true, whatever is honorable, whatever is just, whatever is pure, whatever is lovely, whatever is commendable, if there is any excellence, if there is anything worthy of praise, think about these things" (Phil. 4:8).

Sometimes we need counseling to clean and heal mindsets of oppression—to get rid of the rats and put up a "No Dumping" sign to the devil. God desires us to be free of any refuse of the past and to find new life in Him.

Community can help us clean out the dump and provide positive support. In Hebrews 10:25, believers are exhorted to stay in fellowship, "not neglecting to meet together, as is the habit of some, but encouraging one another, and all the more as you see the Day drawing near." Besides finding community in a biblically sound church, and especially meeting in small groups if your church has them, there are other support systems available like Celebrate Recovery and First Place for Health.

Meeting regularly with a trusted friend for encouragement and prayer can also help us get out of the snares of dark and unproductive thoughts that so often lead to wasted and hurtful actions. Our compassionate God is here for us. Healing can happen. There is no need to run with the rats into dumpish quagmires.

Prayer: Dear Father, sometimes I feel trapped in the dump of destructive thoughts and feelings. Please heal my mind and heart of any hurts that cause me to stumble. I know others who are struggling, and I pray for them. Please set their feet on a firm foundation and release them from the mental torments that keep them from fruitful thinking and a flourishing life.

Radiant Action: Journal Entries: 1. How does Hebrews 13:11–12 impact me? What thanks can I give Jesus for coming "outside the camp" to bring salvation to the world and to me? 2. List who I am called to reach. There's no one so lost in the dump that God can't reach him or her. The farthest anyone has been from God was Jesus on the cross when He became sin and was separated from the Father. There is hope for everyone.

Webs: Thinking (July), Asking Questions (July), Anxiety (Sept.)

DAY 10
Asking Questions

"How?"[25]

Wilbur asks Charlotte for definitions like versatile, untenable, sedentary, gullible, and others. But he asks one question that is weighty and with life-and-death consequences: "Who's going to save me?"[26]

God invites us to come to Him with our weighty and everyday questions. Moses inquired "If I come to the people of Israel and say to them, 'The God of your fathers has sent me to you,' and they ask me, 'What is his name?' what shall I say to them?" (Ex. 3:13). Jeremiah seeks to understand, "Why does the way of the wicked prosper?" (Jer. 12:1) The most intense question of anguish was the one Jesus cried out from the cross, "My God, my God, why have you forsaken me?" (Matt. 27:46).

God Himself asks probing questions to different individuals, all intended to open their eyes to spiritual truth. To Adam, in the garden of Eden, He asks, "Where are you?" (Gen. 3:9). To the prophet Ezekiel seeing a vision in the valley of dry bones: "Son of man, can these bones live?" (Ezek. 37:3). To Mary Magdalene at the site of the tomb, "Woman, why are you weeping?" (John 20:13).

Jesus used questions to disarm His opponents and expose their hypocrisy. "'And why do you break the commandment of God for the sake of your tradition?'" (Matt. 15:3). "Why do you question these things in your hearts? Which is easier, to say to the paralytic, 'Your sins are forgiven,' or to say, 'Rise, take up your bed and walk'?" (Mark 2:8–9).

Do I believe in God? How do I know the Bible is true? What is sin? What is *my* sin? What happens after death? Where will I go? What does the Scripture say about death and salvation? What are angels? Who is the Holy Spirit? How do I love my neighbor? What is right and wrong? What is my purpose? What sadness do I need to give to God? What healing do I need to ask Him for? How can I serve Him? What obstacles stand in the way of that service? What extra training do I need?

Prayer: God, help me to know how and when to ask critical questions. What are You asking of me?

Radiant Action: Journal Entry: 1. What do I need to ask God for today? 2. To whom do I need to ask hard questions (including myself)? 3. I will answer the quarterly and yearly reviews in this devotional.

Webs: Choices (Sept.), Words (Oct.), Reading, Education, and Vocabulary (Oct.)

DAY 11

Trapping: Rat Persuasion (Bribes)

"I bet I can get him to help." [27]

Persuasion can be defined as "putting a spin on things." According to Collins Online Dictionary, it is "to twist a report or story to one's advantage; to interpret an event to make it seem favorable or beneficial to oneself or one's cause." Charlotte puts in a lot of effort to spin things so Zuckerman will spare Wilbur.

In the barnyard council, the oldest sheep explains how she will use persuasion in the form of a bribe. At first, Templeton's response to being asked to be a word courier is cold and short: "Let him die."[28] But the sheep's threat of food deprivation brings the rat around. She later persuades Templeton to go to the fair by describing its food potential.

Making a heroic sacrifice, Wilbur persuades Templeton to retrieve Charlotte's egg sac with a reasoned promise. Wilbur bribes Templeton with the most effective way to motivate a self-centered, self-pitying bully—through his stomach. (Wilbur himself knows the power of persuasion through the stomach. His short-won loop of wild but unsatisfying freedom ended with a pail of slops leading him back into his pen.)

Hints of Eve and the forbidden fruit in Eden run through dark persuasions. In the garden, the ultimate trapper was spinning his webs of temptation and destruction as he has done throughout the ages. But the believer has persuasive power to employ for good goals: "We demolish arguments and every pretension that sets itself up against the knowledge of God, and we take captive every thought to make it obedient to Christ" (2 Cor. 10:5 NIV).

> *"A wise man scales the city of the mighty and brings down the stronghold in which they trust"* (Prov. 21:22).

Prayer: Heavenly Father, clarify my thinking and help me to reason well. Give me insight to understand the people I am trying to persuade, and may it always be for the right motives. Help me in my efforts to persuade people of the gospel.

Radiant Action: Journal Entry: 1. What is the best way to reason with or motivate an unprincipled person with whom I disagree but need to work with? What motivates them? 2. What are the ethics of persuasion? 3. How can I discern when someone is manipulating me?

Webs: Weaving (July), Naysayers (Aug.), Greed and Bribes (Nov.).

Gleanings: "Behold, you delight in truth in the inward being, and you teach me wisdom in the secret heart" (Ps. 51:6).

DAY 12

Weaving

Charlotte liked to do her weaving.[29]

Charlotte's love for Wilbur drove her to weave the first of several messages: "Some Pig." Her messages save his life. God's love wove a new message to save our lives with the threads of His own body, His back hanging in strips from scourging. He wrote "I love you" with His body as He hung on the cross.

The weaver of love formed us in the womb. Abdu Murray, cofounder and president of Embrace the Truth, a gospel ministry to Muslims, recalls his mother's weaving and relates it to God's love that wove us to life:

> When we read that word—knitted—the image appears of a maternal figure sitting in a chair, lovingly weaving together a blanket or sweater. When she was pregnant with me, my mother knitted a little purple sweater to bring me home from the hospital in. I've kept that sweater, and my wife and I have wrapped each of our kids in it for the journey home after their births. As my mother wove those threads together, I was on her mind. That kind of intimacy soaks God's description of how He created each one of us.[30]

> *"For you formed my inward parts; you knitted me together in my mother's womb"* (Ps. 139:13).

Prayer: God, thank You for weaving me as Your creation in my mother's womb. Thank You for Your great love that wove the message of salvation with the threads of Your body on the cross. Your back was ripped into strips for my healing. Give me a glimpse of how You are knitting my life events into a tapestry for Your glory.

Radiant Action: When I see a knitted blanket, I will remember that God has knitted me together, that He is able to reknit the broken pieces, and that He is knitting my future with skill and beauty.

Webs: Charlotte's Tips for Writing (Oct.), Coming Kingdom (Dec.), Established (Dec.)

DAY 13

Life

Everywhere you look is life; even the little ball of spit on the weed stalk.[31]

Life in this story thrives in abundance. Charlotte has 514 children. A newborn lamb is following the old sheep. The geese hatch two batches of goslings. There is an abundant harvest of squashes and pumpkins. Lilacs and apple trees blossom.

What is *life* to the characters in the story? Wilbur, Templeton, Charlotte, and Fern have varying views about it. Wilbur values life, for he screams that he doesn't want to die. Charlotte does all she can do to keep him alive but accepts the timing of her own death. Templeton cares nothing for Wilbur's life or any other's—unless food is in the bargain. Fern puts all her heart into saving a small life.

What if everyone felt the way Fern feels about life? And what if everyone acknowledged God as the giver of life? (See Ps. 36:9.) God loves the unborn, the weak, the elderly, the seemingly "nonproductive." Jesus said, "Whoever receives this child in my name receives me, and whoever receives me receives him who sent me" (Luke 9:48). "And the King will answer them, 'Truly, I say to you, as you did it to one of the least of these my brothers, you did it to me'" (Matt. 25:40).

The author of life came to give us life and fruitfulness: "In him was life, and the life was the light of men" (John 1:4). "My purpose is to give life in all its fullness" (John 10:10 TLB). He wants us to know Him so we will live with Him forever, so "... what is mortal may be swallowed up by life" (2 Cor. 5:4).

"*[His mercies] are* new *every morning*" (Lam. 3:22–23, emphasis mine).

Prayer: Lord, make my attitude about life reflect Yours. Help me respect others, even others who are very, very, small or very, very difficult, ill, or differ in philosophy. Help me see the fresh new life You offer every day. And show me what it means to help preserve life.

Radiant Action: In every instance, I will remember "Choose Life" and ask for wisdom. I will make life easier for others and look for the forever life You promise.

Webs: Cheerleaders (Sept.), Christmas (Dec.), Established (Dec.)

Gleanings: Another priest arises "... by the power of indestructible life" (Heb. 7:16).

DAY 14

Life and Health

"Keep fit, and don't lose your nerve."[32]

Templeton cares more about his autonomy—the freedom to do whatever he likes—and his rights to Wilbur's food than he cares for his health. The old sheep admonishes Templeton for his cavalier attitude toward his body.[33] Care and respect for the body is rooted in valuing life, but Templeton's concern is only for his own life and his ability to horde food or objects. He is like those people Paul described: "Their end is destruction, their god is their belly, and they glory in their shame, with minds set on earthly things" (Phil. 3:19).

Author and blogger Sarah Arthur writes about the importance of caring for our temples: "Setting yourself up for a bodily, emotional, and mental train wreck does violence to the image of God in you, to the purpose of God for you, and it helps no one, least of all those whom you claim to serve."[34]

In Philippians 3:8, the apostle Paul passionately affirms dying to sin and living for Christ: "Indeed, I count everything as loss because of the surpassing worth of knowing Christ Jesus my Lord. For his sake I have suffered the loss of all things and count them as rubbish, in order that I may gain Christ."

Prayer: Lord, help me to prize the treasures of eternity and be willing to give up worthless things for the certainty of invisible realities. Give me wisdom to be a good steward of this body, knowing I am just renting it from You who purchased it with Your life and precious blood.

Dianne Bundt voices this prayer, "May you and those you love remain strong in body and free from disease. May those who suffer from injury or illness recover quickly and completely. May you and those you love be kept from violence, calamity, and loss. May those who seek to hurt you physically, mentally, or emotionally fail so that you may live securely."[35]

Radiant Action: I repent of hardheaded piggy purposes. I will let my girth reflect my values that my body is the Temple of the Holy Spirit. I will try some form of fasting.

Webs: Life (July), Faithfulness (July), Harvest of Gluttony (Nov.)

Gleanings: "May God himself, the God who makes everything holy and whole, make you holy and whole, put you together—spirit, soul, and body—and keep you fit for the coming of our Master, Jesus Christ. The One who called you is completely dependable. If he said it, he'll do it!" (1 Thess. 5:23–24 MSG).

DAY 15

Journeys

Journey: to travel from one place to another

Some Journeys in *Charlotte's Web:*
Fern ran to the barn to grab the ax from her father.
Wilbur moved from the Arable's to the Zuckerman's barn.
People came from all around to see Wilbur.
Fern went to the Zuckerman's often.
Mrs. Arable drove to see Dr. Dorian.
Many took a trip to the fair.
Templeton reluctantly climbed up the shed wall to retrieve the egg sac.

Some Journeys in the Bible:
Abram began his faith journey not knowing where he was going.
Joseph went to Egypt without an idea of where he would end up.
Ruth left Moab and went to Bethlehem with Naomi.
David left his family and lived on the run from Saul.
Jesus left heaven and came to earth to face death to bring us to heaven.
Saul became Paul on the road to Damascus and went on
    many missionary journeys.
John was exiled to the island of Patmos, where he wrote Revelation.

We are pilgrims, sojourning toward our forever home, and hopefully, with the grace and indestructible life of the Holy Spirit inside us, we are changing the desert places into springs as we go through life.

"As they go through the Valley of Baca, they make it a place of springs" (Ps. 84:6).

Prayer: Lord, please keep me going step-by-step.

Radiant Action: I won't look at the whole trip all at once. I will concentrate on one day at a time.

Webs: Home (June), Place (June), Uncertainty (Aug.), Work and Diligence (Aug.), Coming Kingdom (Dec.)

Gleanings: One definition of *Metanoia* is "the journey of changing one's mind, heart, self, or way of life."[36]

    From "Little Gidding" by T. S. Eliot
    We shall not cease from exploration
    And the end of all our exploring
    Will be to arrive where we started
    And know the place for the first time.

DAY 16

Scatter

Charlotte's babies were disappearing.[37]

Wilbur is frantic and dismayed as he watches the baby spiders say goodbye. He thinks they are all leaving, and that he will be alone in the world again. He doesn't know that three will stay and be named friends, or that generations more of Charlotte's line will grace his life.

On the night Jesus most needed His friends, they scattered. While He sweated blood in agonizing prayer, they slept. When His accusers arrested Him, His friends ran away. Jesus was alone in the garden, but the Father was with Him. The young church also scattered, for fiery persecution peeled them away from Jerusalem and rocketed them out into the world with the gospel.

This scattering brought glory to God and great news to people.

Has someone you love left you alone and bereft of their fellowship? Abandonment takes many forms. Maybe it's a spouse who's consumed with their own activities or left you for someone else or left you by dying. Or it could be children living far away or friends who abandoned the faith? Encourage yourself by knowing that Jesus truly understands. He was deserted, yet He knew His Father was with Him.

Prayer: Lord, help me to know You are with me even though everyone else is somewhere else.

Radiant Action: Memorize John 16:32: "Yet I am not alone, for my Father is with me" (NIV).

Webs: Loneliness (Feb.), Journeys (July), Goodbyes (Sept.), Ethnic Barriers (Dec.)

Gleanings: "Then everyone deserted him and fled" (Mark 14:50 NIV).

DAY 17

Distractions

The Zuckermans were so busy with visitors they forgot about other things.[38]

Fame distracts the farmers. Mr. Zuckerman starts wearing his good clothes all the time. Mrs. Zuckerman forgets to make blackberry jam. Lurvy doesn't hoe the corn.

Jesus warns against distractions that keep the seed of faith from growing: "The cares of the world and the deceitfulness of riches choke the word, and it proves unfruitful" (Matt. 13:22). Pastor J. D. Greear contends that distraction sends more people to hell than doubt. He says distraction with good things keeps you from the eternal; it snatches away the Word and keeps us from thinking deeply. Distractions enslave an insecure heart and make it more worried, upset, drifting, and unsettled. Distraction "rules an unanchored heart," he writes, and warns, "Don't give up the irreplaceable for the important."[39]

Diversions like social media and cell phones lock us out from the real joys of the day and from sowing seeds for eternity as they prevent us from being present. On a larger scale are the distractions of wealth and fame. If we don't face each distraction with truth, we'll be sucked in and impoverished no matter how much money we make or fame we achieve.

> "Whoever loves money never has enough; whoever loves wealth is never satisfied with their income" (Eccl. 5:10 NIV).

Prayer: Father, open my eyes to see when I'm replacing the irreplaceable with just the important. Don't allow me to get distracted with moth-eaten things of earth like fame and money.

Radiant Action: Journal Entries: 1. It's not how can I do more, but how can I do *better* at what I am supposed to do? 2. How can I keep money, fame, my phone, and other distractions from dominating me and stealing the present?

Webs: Work and Diligence (Aug.), Decisiveness (Aug.), Evenings (Nov.)

Gleanings: "Seek first his kingdom and his righteousness, and all these things will be given to you as well" (Matt. 6:33 NIV).

DAY 18

Servanthood

"What do you think I am, anyway, a rat-of-all-work?"[40]

Templeton's life center is Templeton—Templeton's rewards, comforts, his possessions, his rights. He demands to be served as he prefers, immediately—and with due respect.

In contrast, Charlotte serves Wilbur, despite discomfort, to ensure *his* well-being. Going to the fair when she's ready to lay her eggs is a risky inconvenience. Unlike Wilbur, she is never publicly recognized. Jesus Himself, the exact image of God in human form, did everything necessary for our redemption, and He did it all without waiting to be served or praised. "For even the Son of Man came not to be served but to serve" (Mark 10:45). He promises, "Whoever would be great among you must be your servant" (Matt. 20:26).

We can serve with God's power and glory, and with our neighbor's greater good in mind, no matter if they are Templetonian or not. Jesus will say to those who do His will and serve well this commendation: "Well done, good and faithful servant! You have been faithful with a few things; I will put you in charge of many things. Come and share your master's happiness!" (Matt. 25:21 NIV).

Lurvy, the hired hand on the farm serving the Zuckermans, was the first to see the first miracle. In the Bible, Mary took a pound of expensive perfume to serve her Lord by anointing Him for His burial. She was the first person Jesus revealed Himself to after leaving the sepulcher and the first to hear His voice. Could it be that servanthood is related to our ability to sense His presence and the workings of the Holy Spirit?

Prayer: God, sift out of me self-pity and self-centeredness. Empower me with Your Spirit to be bold and selfless to do whatever furthers Your kingdom and helps my neighbor. Help me to be more like Charlotte and less like Templeton, more and more like Jesus and less and less like my natural self. When someone condescendingly treats me like a servant, grant me grace to consider it an honor, since You came to serve and not be served.

Radiant Action: Journal Entry: 1. How will I be remembered after I die? 2. How do I want to be remembered?

Webs: Insignificance (Feb.), Fences (Aug.), Legacy (Sept.), Fern: Apples (Sept.)

Gleanings: "Let each of you look not only to his own interests, but also to the interests of others. Have this mind . . . which is yours in Christ Jesus, who . . . emptied himself, by taking the form of a servant" (Phil. 2:4–7).

DAY 19

Justice

"This is the most terrible case of injustice."[41]

E. B. White was accused of failing to seek relief for the suffering of others through his anonymous editorials in *The New Yorker* during the Depression. Ralph Ingersoll, editor of *Fortune* magazine and who also had held key roles in *The New Yorker* and *Time*, labeled White's columns for *The New Yorker* as "gossamer writing."[42] Ingersoll concluded that White himself was responsible for *The New Yorker*'s avoidance of strong editorial stands on issues confronting the country during the ongoing Great Depression.

Perhaps Ingersoll's brutal words stuck with White. Justice is poignantly woven in as a major thread in *Charlotte's Web*, written decades later. Fern, at age eight, is small in a world of adults. She has high ideals and the strength to fight a giant of injustice—in this case, instigated by her father and the customs of the farmers.

A sense of right and wrong comes instinctively from the human heart. Just try to steal someone's money or hurt a family member or even eat their favorite snacks on a hiking trip. The belief that there even *is* a right and wrong, despite vastly differing interpretations in society of how these terms apply, originates from the moral nature of God, who made man in His own image and gave him a conscience.

God is the God of justice. Although He warns of judgment, He gives the most egregious offender opportunity to repent. The cross is the ultimate revelation of His justice because sin was dealt with for once and for all when Jesus became sin for us.

The sacrifice is profound, and in it is wrapped the heart of justice, which leads us to "speak up for those who cannot speak up for themselves" (Prov. 31:8 NIV). Israel and Judah, God's chosen people, were judged for their self-indulgence and their lack of concern for the poor.

> "Evil men do not understand justice, but those who seek the LORD understand it completely" (Prov. 28:5).

Prayer: Lord, move my heart and the hearts of my fellow believers to be far away from complacency, comfort, ease, and convenience. Move our hearts to something greater than ourselves.

Radiant Action: Journal Entries: 1. Do I comprehend the injustice of the cross and my part in it? 2. What is God calling me to do about different areas of injustice?

Webs: Faithfulness (July), Farmers (Aug.), Failure (Sept.)

Gleanings: "But let justice roll down like waters, and righteousness like an ever-flowing stream" (Amos 5:24).

DAY 20

Faithfulness

"I pledge my friendship, forever and ever."[43]

Wilbur welcomes Charlotte's daughters with his own declaration of faithfulness. He keeps his promises to Charlotte about taking care of her egg sac. Wilbur also keeps his promise to Templeton about having first dibs on his slops. And Charlotte keeps her promise to do all she can to save Wilbur, even in her time of greatest weakness with her greatest project.

God will honor the one "who swears to his own hurt and does not change" (Ps. 15:4). He has demonstrated His faithfulness through millennia as He led, protected, and redeemed His people and continues to do so. Charlotte promised to save Wilbur, a promise limited by finitude, but Jesus, at the most inconceivable inconvenience of His suffering, sealed His promise of salvation in time and eternity with His blood. Instead of living for the world, we are saved to love God, love each other, and bear witness of the true wonder. He was, is, and always will be the faithful One.

"Your faithfulness continues through all generations" (Ps. 119:90 NIV).

Prayer: Lord, You are my faithful friend. Mold me in faithfulness in all my relationships so I will be more and more like You.

Radiant Action: I will be faithful to keep my promises, even in the small things.

Webs: Servanthood (July), Perseverance (Aug.), Failure (Sept.)

Gleanings: "I gave my brother . . . charge over Jerusalem, for he was a more faithful and God-fearing man than many" (Neh. 7:2).

"Moreover, it is required of stewards that they be found faithful" (1 Cor. 4:2).

AUGUST
FARM AND WORK

The summer's green leaves and ripening fruit invite discussion about the aspects of a fruitful harvest. August is a collection of inspirations from farm life, including thoughts on time, management, work, and fatherhood.

Farming

Land: The Parable of the Arables, *p. 169*
Barns, *p. 170*
Fences: Boundaries, *p. 171*
Time and Seasons: God, *p. 172*
Time and Seasons: Man, *p. 173*
Routines and Rhythms of Life, *p. 174*
Patience, *p. 175*
Uncertainty, *p.176*

Practicalities

Management Tips from Charlotte, *p. 177*
Decisiveness, *p. 178*
Specific Goals, *p. 179*

Working Life

Work and Diligence, *p. 180*
Initiative, *p. 181*
Perseverance, *p. 182*
Rudeness, *p. 184*
Naysayers, *p. 185*
Farmers, *p. 186*
Hero: The Protector, *p. 187*
Transportation: The Farm Truck, *p. 188*
Grace, *p. 190*

DAY 1

Land: The Parable of the Arables

... they went down toward the pasture and picked wild raspberries. ....[1]

Arable land is land that's able to produce crops. Fern's family name, Arable, refers to fruitful soil. Soil and soul are words with similar sounds and, on the surface, they have very different meanings. But frequently the land and the community—that is, the souls that live on the land—are bound together.

In Israel's history, the identity of the Jewish people is integrated with the land God promised to them. In Numbers 13 we read of a dangerous mission where twelve spies, including a man of strong faith named Caleb, were sent into Canaan to check out land that God said He was giving to the people of Israel.

But the men who went with Caleb were gripped with doubt and fear, reporting to Moses on their return that they'd seen giants in the land. Caleb tries to rouse them out of their fear: "Then Caleb silenced the people before Moses and said, 'We should go up and take possession of the land, for we can certainly do it'" (Numbers 13:30 NIV).

The land God promises to us now as His children is not an earthly land but His own kingdom where we take possession of all the inheritance He plans for us. This means salvation, deliverance, the fruits of the Spirit, and fellowship with the family of God. He wants to give us abundant life pressed down and running over—life that lasts.

Jesus wants us to believe and follow Him into the abundant life of promise. In Mark's gospel, Jesus tells a story of soils and souls. The parable of the sower culminates with the good soil, the soul that cultivates His words. He describes the "good soil" as one that is "growing up and increasing and yielding thirtyfold and sixtyfold and a hundredfold" (Mark 4:8). In other words, Jesus is looking for arable hearts. He is teaching the *parable of the arables.*

Prayer: God, make my heart arable. Make it yield a hundredfold crop.

Radiant Action: I will give a packet of seeds, a pot, and some soil to a friend and select Scriptures to give them in a note to plant seeds of faith.

Webs: Seed Life (May), Home (June), Barns (Aug.), Harvest (Sept.), Coming Kingdom (Dec.)

Gleanings: "The wilderness and the dry land shall be glad." (Isa. 35:1).

> "But the meek shall inherit the land and delight themselves in abundant peace" (Ps. 37:11).

DAY 2

Barns

The barn was very large.[2]

Michael Sims, author of *The Story of Charlotte's Web: E. B. White's Eccentric Life in Nature and the Birth of an American Classic*, comments that Charlotte "embodied the spirit of the barn, which he [White] had once described as almost a sacred place, a stage for birth and death and the rhythms of life."[3] He proposes that "the barn is the most important character."[4]

A barn can be the place of small beginnings that lead to large results. It can be the most important "character" in a person's life. The prodigal son came to his senses in a pigsty. And Jesus, our Savior, was born in a barn. If you're in a "barn" place in life, be encouraged. Jesus delights in ministering in the humblest of places and hearts.

> *"And she gave birth to her firstborn son and wrapped him in swaddling cloths and laid him in a manger, because there was no place for them in the inn"* (Luke 2:7).

Prayer: Thank You, Lord, that You know where I am and how I came to be in this low place. Bring me revelation that I can receive only in the barn. What are You birthing in this humble place?

Radiant Action: "Lowest elevation, highest revelation." I will write these words on an index card and display it where I see it often. As asked in the introduction to this book, who will deny insight can come from a barn in a children's story?

Webs: Humble (Feb.), Insignificance (Feb.), Death of a Vision (Sept.), Generations (Dec.).

Gleanings: E. B. White's children's classic is often seen as a story of a spider and a pig. But White said, "This is a story of the barn. I wrote it for children, and to amuse myself."[5]

> *"The Lord will send a blessing on your barns and on everything you put your hand to. The Lord your God will bless you in the land"* (Deut. 28:8 NIV).

DAY 3

Fences: Boundaries

Then another baby spider crawled to the top of the fence.[6]

Fences mark cultivated fields and property lines and protect private land from pests. These barriers play different roles depending on their mission. Wilbur relished being *inside* his fence. It kept him safe from the wild uncertainty of Out There. But the fence that keeps him in and content is a launching pad for the baby spiders to go forth into Out There.

Like fences that protect physical property, good boundaries protect our emotional resources. Healthy emotional fences keep life focused and fruitful. These "fences" differ according to the individual and are part of healthy living. Boundaries get confused when one's sense of identity is confused. Good boundaries are critical in the church where sinners are in the process of being healed but are not yet perfected.

Good communication and loving relationships are virtues that can help us establish the boundaries best suited for us as individuals. God perfectly understands our emotions and thoughts. He communicates in a way that builds us up. We don't need to establish boundaries with God because He loves perfectly. But with human beings who struggle, as we do, in loving, we must consider what our emotional boundaries are—how we can best relate, what we can endure, what helps us and the other person to thrive, and what is healthy.

Words from a sermon by Rev. Claudia Greggs sheds light on the need for the church to maintain balance in establishing boundaries:

> The church's mission is to be a hospital for all sinners. So, . . . we will need to have in place good boundaries, so that the struggles of those suffering immensely from sin and its effects do not overwhelm us . . . Churches [that do well] understand that they cannot "fix" someone's brokenness, nor can they take away someone's pain; only Jesus can do that . . . And, they have learned how to encourage someone without doing . . . what he or she must do for themselves through the Holy Spirit.[7]

Prayer: Lord, help me be careful to respect other people's physical and emotional boundaries, and to understand my own.

Radiant Action: Journal Entries: What are healthy boundaries for those with whom I am having friction?

Webs: Boundaries Series (Jan.), Distractions (July), The Dump (July), Contentment (Nov.)

DAY 4

Time and Seasons: God

". . . winter and summer, spring and fall."[8]

Seasons are phrases of time, like measures of music alternating discord with harmony, quiet with crescendo. White depicts delight in every season: the maple that turns red; the apples the little foxes sniff; the warm sun and the life of spring; the joy of living in the summer with swings and frogs and fishing.

Time and seasons are central themes in Scripture. "For everything there is a season" (Eccl. 3:1–8). And in the book of Daniel we read about God's sovereignty, "He changes times and season; he removes kings and sets up kings" (Dan. 2:20–21).

Yet, He who created the tides of time submitted Himself to the limitations of time and space. As we read in Galatians 4:4, God sent His Son in "the fullness of time" for our salvation. The book of Hebrews affirms this sublime truth: "Long ago, at many times and in many ways, God spoke to our fathers by the prophets, but in these last days he has spoken to us by his Son, whom he appointed the heir of all things, through whom also he created the world" (1:1–2). Then, later in Hebrews, we find another truth: "Jesus Christ is the same yesterday and today and forever" (13:8). Before Abraham was born, Jesus exists. Jesus came in the perfect season for establishing salvation. He will come again in perfect timing. Maranatha! But Jesus does not change with the epochs but is the same "yesterday and today and forever." See the Ferris wheel in June.

Prayer: Help me honor You as the Eternal One.

Radiant Action: I will rejoice in each season, lingering and not rushing for the next. A turtle will remind me to slow down and linger. It can also remind me to be prepared to pivot for the next adventure since a turtle keeps its backpack ready.

Webs: Ferris wheel (June), Music (June), Coming Kingdom (Dec.), Generations (Dec.)

Gleanings: Henry David Thoreau, whom White considered his mentor through reading *Walden*, the classic work published a century before *Charlotte's Web*, wrote about time with profundity: "In any weather, at any hour of the day or night, I have been anxious to improve the nick of time, and notch it on my stick too; to stand on the meeting of two eternities, the past and the future, which is precisely the present moment; to toe that line."[9]

> "It is not for you to know times or seasons that the Father has fixed by his own authority" (Acts 1:7).

DAY 5

Time and Seasons: Man

She was growing up.[10]

Timing is everything in *Charlotte's Web*. The story begins in Fern's eighth spring as she becomes Wilbur's savior, nurse, companion, friend, and champion. By September, she's disinterested—Henry has turned her head. And then there's Charlotte who conceives a winning plan for Wilbur and weaves words *at precisely the right time*. Her final web secures Wilbur's future just before she expires.

A spider has a brief life. Human life also has an expiration date. From an eternal perspective, it's the time frame of a mist. As *The Message* puts it, "You're nothing but a wisp of fog, catching a brief bit of sun before disappearing" (James 4:14).

Knowing our lives are but a mist, that we are like grass that springs up in the morning to wither by evening, the most urgent consideration of time is this: *now* is the time to be reconciled with God. *Now* is the time to come to terms with who Jesus is and why He came, died, and was resurrected. See Ferris Wheel in June for a fuller explanation.

> "Behold, now is the favorable time; behold, now is the day of salvation" (2 Cor. 6:2).

Prayer: Lord, enable me to make the best use of my time (see Eph. 5:16).

Radiant Action: I will remember that "My times are in your hands" (Ps. 31:15 NIV).

Webs: Ferris Wheel (June). Music (June), Legacy That Lasts (Sept.), Coming Kingdom (Dec.), Generations (Dec.)

Gleanings: "For a thousand years in Your sight are like yesterday when it is past, and like a watch in the night. You carry them away like a flood; they are like a sleep. In the morning they are like grass which grows up: In the morning it flourishes and grows up; in the evening it is cut down and withers . . . So teach us to number our days, that we may gain a heart of wisdom." (Ps. 90:4–6, 12 NKJV).

> "Music is given to us with the sole purpose of establishing an order in things, including, and particularly, the coordination between man and time."
> —Igor Stravinsky

DAY 6

Routines and Rhythms of Life

They were setting the table for breakfast.[11]

The Zuckerman farm has good routines until fame sets in. Lurvy slops the pig twice a day. Charlotte weaves in the evening. Fern sets the table in the morning. Summer means mowing and stacking hay and having plenty of fun. Every September is the fair. Winter brings the cows into the barn and ham onto the table and the joy of snow and sledding.

The Lord Himself keeps the cycles of nature going and ensures that the stars and planets and their satellites have routine orbits. After the great flood of Noah's time, God made this promise: "While the earth remains, seedtime and harvest, cold and heat, winter and summer, and day and night, shall not cease" (Gen. 8:22). With knowledge this certain, we can plan on seasons.

Since God loves order, it is understandable that rhythm and routine nurture stability for us who are made in His image, and this is especially good to remember when we're in crisis. When routines and rhythms are disrupted, uncertainty gives rise to anxiety. God ministered to Elijah when he was submerged in a deep depression by providing a gentle rhythm of meals and rest (1 Kings 19:4–9).

One minister noted that rhythms of rest are important in fighting addiction, and that when we know what to expect, hope grows.[12] A passage from a children's book *Sunlight and Shadows* shows the wisdom of routine as an aid for grief:

> Right after Mama died, Josefina had thought that the world should end. How could life go on for the rest of them without Mama? It had seemed wrong, even cruel somehow, that nothing stopped . . . There were still chores to be done every day. There were clothes to be washed, weeds to pull, animals to be fed, socks to be mended. But as the year passed, Josefina began to see that the steady rhythm of life on the ranch was her best comfort. Mama seemed close by when Josefina and her sisters were together doing the laundry or mending or cooking or cleaning.[13]

Prayer: Guide me, Lord, to find my rhythm and routines.

Radiant Actions: I will go to bed and get up at the same time every day.

Webs: Work and Diligence (Aug.), Planning (Sept.), Last Day (Sept.), Grief (Nov.)

DAY 7

Patience

Charlotte was naturally patient.[14]

In the night of dire loneliness, Wilbur waits dark hours for the morning to meet his friend. He waits months for deliverance; he waits months for Charlotte's eggs to hatch. Charlotte spurs on Wilbur's hoping skills, so patience sprouts. Patience, the art of waiting, is time-based and rooted in hope and faith.

Patience, defined as "the capacity to accept or tolerate delay, trouble, or suffering without getting angry or upset," keeps one from rushing headlong into unnecessary pain and difficulty. Patience, or forbearance, is responding with grace to abrasive obstacles, people, or opposing spiritual forces. Willingness to wait patiently can even bring greater fulfillment than immediate gratification and revenge.

How patient is our all-powerful God, the Creator and Redeemer, as He waits for us to come to Him. Though as believers we flirt with the world, though we stumble, the Lord is patient with our weaknesses because He loves us. Patience defines love, as Scripture says, "Love is patient" (1 Cor. 13:4). He is patient with those who do not yet believe He exists or who prefer darkness and their cherished sin rather than His freedom. God's patience is toward the entire human race; His kindness is meant to lead to repentance.

Sometimes answers and progress are delayed, not because God is trying to teach us patience, but because of our disobedience. Think of the Israelites wandering in the desert for forty years. And sometimes spiritual warfare is behind the delayed answer, as was the case with the angel Michael (see Daniel 10).

Prayer: Dear Lord of time, You see from the beginning to the end, and You know all things. If spiritual warfare is what is preventing me from receiving an answer, teach me to wait on You. In the waiting teach me how to fight, fast, confess, persevere, and wrestle. Convict me of anything I need to change. "Help me to give You honor by being patient."[15]

Radiant Action: I will wait patiently for God to work things out, for my perfect heavenly home, and for my loved ones as I wait for them to become free to be who they are meant to be. Help me see them as they can be by Your grace.

Webs: Waiting (Mar.), Time: Man (Aug.), Perseverance (Aug.), The Last Day (Sept.)

Gleanings: "With patience a ruler may be persuaded, and a soft tongue will break a bone" (Prov. 25:15)

DAY 8

Uncertainty

He still worried some about the future.[16]

Wilbur's summer is full of troubling questions. Will he be allowed to live? Will Charlotte really be able to rescue him?

God hasn't promised us an easy road; rather, Jesus warned us, our earthly pilgrimage would be rough. We simply cannot know what will happen tomorrow, and James reminds us of this fact: "You do not know what tomorrow will bring. What is your life? For you are a mist that appears for a little time and then vanishes. Instead you ought to say, 'If the Lord wills, we will live and do this or that'" (James 4:14–15).

God called Abram out from his people, and Abram obeyed, not knowing where he was going. How opposite from the Israelite spies we read about in the first August devotion, "Land." All but two of them were paralyzed with uncertainty, fear, and unbelief, and they refused to obey the command to possess the land. Abram believed God; the spies did not.

What can we do in the face of uncertainty? Standing on faith, the habits below can help in uncertain times:

1. Review the names of God, praise His character, pray, and memorize Scripture.
2. Meet with others for encouragement or to encourage them.
3. Seek godly counsel.
4. Exercise.
5. Do the next productive thing.
6. Keep journals to remember answers to prayer.
7. Remember all your blessings as being founded in Christ (Eph. 1).
8. Refrain from comparisons with others via social media.
9. Take care of your health instead of seeking comfort in material pursuits. Rest and hydrate.
10. Support others in distress. Donate food. Check on elderly neighbors. Call someone you know who is depressed.
11. Keep journals of remembrance. Can you see Caleb's wife telling him, "Caleb, get that scroll out about the Red Sea swallowing the Egyptians!! That might help convince those guys to go on into the promised land!"
12. *Believe* God has a future for you and is *for* you (Rom. 8).

Prayer: Dear God, our refuge, some times are so confusing and overwhelming that it's hard to keep standing. Help me to do the next right thing; to take the step toward what You are calling me to do. I admit I can do nothing in my own strength.

Radiant Action: See list above

Webs: Asking Questions (July), Patience (Aug.), Death of a Vision (Sept.)

DAY 9

Management Tips from Charlotte

1. *Don't hurry.*
   "'Slowly, slowly!' said Charlotte. 'Never hurry and never worry.'"[17]

2. *Keep up your physical health and your confidence.*
   "Keep fit, and don't lose your nerve."[18]

3. *Don't listen to bad advice.*
   "'What kind of acrobat do you think I am?' said Charlotte in disgust [to the gander]. 'I would have to have the St. Vitus's Dance to weave a word like that into my web.'"[19]

4. *Know your materials.*
   "'If I write the word "Terrific" with sticky thread,' she thought, 'every bug that comes along will get stuck in it and spoil the effects.'"[20]

5. *Begin.*
   "Now let's see, the first letter is T."[21]

6. *Encourage yourself.*
   "I know a good thing when I see it, and my web is a good thing."[22]

7. *Be aware of the limitations of individuals involved in the project.*
   "'I'm not sure Templeton will be willing to help. You know how he is—always looking out for himself, never thinking of the other fellow.'"[23]

8. *Think of the other fellow.*
   "By helping you, perhaps I was trying to lift up my life a trifle."[24]

DAY 10

Decisiveness

"I am not going to let you die, Wilbur."[25]

Charlotte decided quickly that she would save Wilbur, and that was that. It took a little hanging upside down and a lot of thinking, but she created a web of a scheme, one that meant she had to make a decision and remain resolute in it.

What happens if we ask God for wisdom, but we're wishy-washy about it? James warns, "But let him ask in faith, with no doubting, for the one who doubts is like a wave of the sea that is driven and tossed by the wind. For that person must not suppose that he will receive anything from the Lord; he is a double-minded man, unstable in all his ways" (James 1:6–8). To receive from God, we have to repent of our indecisiveness. The Israelites who refused to go into the promised land were double minded at the root because they lacked faith.

Decisiveness is a trait based on wisdom and is necessary for acting on that wisdom. It is "the ability to finalize difficult decisions based on the will and ways of God."[26] We need to be ready to act decisively and wisely to answer someone asking for help to meet an urgent need. As God directs, we will say with Charlotte, "I'm here."

> *"God is not man, that he should lie, or a son of man, that he should change his mind. Has he said and will he not do it? Or has he spoken, and will he not fulfill it?"* (Num. 23:19).

Prayer: Dear God, make me wise and filled with faith. Make me decisive, and cleanse me of all my double-mindedness.

Radiant Action: Journal Entries: 1. In what areas am I double-minded? Am I trying to fit in with the world? 2. Where do I have trouble making decisions and why? 3. Am I letting the world meet my needs instead of God? 4. What choices do I have to make that are lingering unnecessarily?

Webs: Clean and White: Moral Freedom (July), Liberty (July), Choices (Sept.)

Gleanings: "May you have wisdom to determine the best course of action in every situation. May you receive sound advice from those you ask for counsel."[27]

DAY 11
Specific Goals

"I'm working on a plan."[28]

Seven things to help you stick to your goals:

1. Ask, why am I undertaking this project or pursuit? What are my gifts? What brings joy?
2. How is the Holy Spirit nudging?
3. Make a plan, a road map to where you are going, with adjustments as needed.
4. Start out small (don't despise the day of small beginnings). Just begin.
5. Stay in the moment. Progress takes time, so don't let unexpected challenges overwhelm you.
6. Replace negative self-talk with positive. You will make mistakes; get up and keep moving.
7. Manage your expectations as to how much you can realistically accomplish in a given amount of time. Seek help, plan more time, narrow priorities, take on fewer responsibilities, and set boundaries with other people and commitments.

Goals should be the following:

Specific-Measurable-Attainable-Relevant-Time bound (vision).

Life Principles

(These are from Charles Stanley's Life Principles Bible. Read Philippians 3:11–14):

- Believe and meditate on the promises of God.
- Have a consuming desire to achieve a precise goal.
- Have the courage to attempt, even at the risk of failure.
- Choose determination.
- Be persistent.
- Humble yourself.
- Let go of the past.[29]

Prayer: Help me make realistic and productive goals.

Radiant Action: Journal Entry: In what area do I need to make progress?

Webs: Naysayers (Aug.), Failure (Sept.), Planning (Sept.)

Gleanings: "And I am sure of this, that he who began a good work in you will bring it to completion at the day of Jesus Christ" (Phil. 1:6).

DAY 12

Work and Diligence

Around midnight, the spider was still at work.[30]

Charlotte takes joy in her work. She sees it as a good thing. Wilbur admires her for her intelligence and industry. Her craftsmanship and creativity, her purpose, calling, and equipping make her productive. Her life reflects somewhat 2 Peter 1:5–7: "For this very reason, make every effort to supplement your faith with virtue, and virtue with knowledge, and knowledge with self-control, and self-control with steadfastness, and steadfastness with godliness, and godliness with brotherly affection, and brotherly affection with love."

When believers commit work to God, life-giving results will ensue. "Commit your work to the LORD, and your plans will be established" (Prov. 16:3). "Let the beauty of the LORD our God be upon us: and establish thou the work of our hands upon us; yea, the work of our hands establish thou it" (Ps. 90:17 KJV).

As has been wisely said, "The awareness of God's presence energizes us for our work."[31] This is supported by the prophet Haggai's words, urging us to "take courage . . . and work; for I am with you" (Hag. 2:4 NASB)." Nehemiah encouraged the building of the walls of Jerusalem, saying, "The joy of the LORD is your strength" (Neh. 8:10). God alone is the solid foundation for any work and is the one who should receive the credit: "Unless the LORD builds the house, those who build it labor in vain" (Ps. 127:1).

God rewards those who diligently labor: "There is a reward for your work" (Jer. 31:16). The apostle Paul, writing to the Thessalonians, encouraged them with these words, "We always pray for you, that our God . . . may fulfill every resolve for good and every work of faith by his power" (2 Thess. 1:11). "Be steadfast, immovable, always abounding in the work of the Lord, knowing that in the Lord your labor is not in vain" (1 Cor. 15:58).

Prayer: Dear Lord, help us all get to work!

Radiant Action: "May you take pleasure in all your work. May every task you undertake succeed, and may you enjoy the good things your labor supplies."[32] I will understand work as holy, consecrated to God.

Webs: Energy and Hope (May), Decisiveness (Aug.), Magnum Opus (Sept.), Harvest (Sept.)

Gleanings: "Whatever you do, work heartily, as for the Lord and not for men" (Col. 3:23).

DAY 13

Initiative

"It just shows what can happen if a person gets out of bed promptly."[33]

Initiative, according to a Google search of the word, is "the ability to assess and initiate things independently; . . . the power or opportunity to act or take charge before others do; . . . an act or strategy intended to resolve a difficulty or improve a situation; a fresh approach to something."

Charlotte fulfills all three aspects of this worthy attribute. First, she sizes up Wilbur's perilous situation. Then she uses her spider powers to spin words into a web to attract everyone's notice and draw attention to Wilbur. She decisively acts to resolve the difficulty with a fresh approach. Wilbur, too, demonstrates initiative by seeking to learn words and ways from Charlotte, who is both friend and mentor.

Initiative is a necessary character trait for believers to possess in service to our Lord and others. We're called to love people, evangelize and disciple them, and stand for holiness in a fallen world bent on pursuing darkness and destruction. For Christ followers, it means leaving complacency and eagerly attending to the things of God's kingdom, asking Him to show us how we can accomplish His will in His ways and timing.

It's interesting to note that initiative is the opposite of despair. Madeleine L'Engle's insight here is illuminating: "For despair is perhaps the most terrible of all the monsters, leading to apathy, indifference, what the medieval theologians called 'accidie,' the sloth of the soul."[34]

The Lord wants to equip us for loving service. Jesus said, "Ask, and it will be given to you; seek, and you will find; knock, and it will be opened to you" (Matt. 7:7).

Prayer: Dear Father, enable me to take initiative in seeking Your kingdom. This may mean change and leaving some of my old ways and life behind.

Radiant Action: Journal Entries: 1. Why am I holding back? 2. What am I supposed to seek in my life? I know I always need to seek God more, but in my quest, could it be I need a different job, more education, or something else?

Webs: Faithfulness (July), Work and Diligence (Aug.), Farmers (Aug.), Finances (Nov.).

Gleanings: "So Abraham rose early in the morning, saddled his donkey" (Gen. 22:3).

DAY 14

Perseverance

"The fish lost the fight."[35]

Charlotte's cousin caught a fish in her web and fought valiantly with it. She persevered and won. When Wilbur tried to spin a web and kept on trying despite the impossibilities, Charlotte was pleased: "She was proud to see that he was not a quitter and was willing to try again to spin a web."[36] Wilbur's name suggests being "resolute" ("will"), and perseverance is a trait he develops. This character trait is related to persistence, determination, resolve, patience, and endurance.

Every morning when he shoveled out manure in his barn, E. B. White saw a spider in the stall. Every day, he would tear down its web. And every night the spider repaired her web, eventually spinning it outside the path of destruction. He jokingly said he would train it to spin "Some Book."

Robert the Bruce of Scotland supposedly watched a spider try six times to knit her web together before finally succeeding. The spider's perseverance may have encouraged Bruce, who'd already lost six battles against the English. He went on to win many other fights, including Bannockburn in 1314.

Examples of perseverance in the Bible abound and include both godly and ungodly figures, like Moses and Pharaoh, David and Goliath, Mordecai and Hamon, Elijah and Jezebel, Jesus and the religious leaders, and Saul before and after he was renamed Paul. Read their stories and others as they demonstrate the power of perseverance (for better or worse).

> *"May the Lord direct your hearts into God's love and Christ's perseverance"* (2 Thess. 3:5 NIV).

Prayer: May I not throw away my confidence; it will be richly rewarded. Let me persevere so that when I have done the will of God, I will receive what He has promised (see Heb 10:35–36).

Radiant Action: Journal Entries: 1. When do I feel like giving up? 2. Who encourages me? 3. Have I counted the cost for being a follower of Jesus? A spider's web (a reminder of the fish story) will encourage me to persevere.

Webs: Patience (Aug.), Generosity (Nov.), Plot and Providence (Nov.)

Gleanings: "I've worked much harder, been jailed more often, beaten up more times than I can count, and at death's door time after time" (2 Cor. 11:23 MSG).

(Photo by Ann K. Ayers)

DAY 15

Rudeness

"We were so rudely interrupted."[37]

Wilbur and Charlotte are having an intimate conversation about their inmost natures. Wilbur is joyfully revealing his heart's desire to be in a forest, searching and sniffing, when the lamb snidely remarks that Wilbur is "the smelliest creature in the place."[38] The lamb's cutting insult hurts Wilbur deeply and draws tears of shame.

It's pretty certain that you, like most people, have been around someone who doesn't appreciate you or your work, and who even disdains your inmost identity. What do you do with individuals whose words and attitude are hurtful and embarrassing?

These are clearly EGN situations (Extra Grace Needed). Charlotte proves how much she values Wilbur's thoughts by putting the lamb in her place with a sharp reprimand. This is what we must do too, when the devil or others tempt us or even when we denigrate ourselves. We can ask God to rebuke the source or in the right situation, stand up and command the source of insult to "cease and desist!" Or we may need to walk away, change the subject, or de-escalate, as Wilbur does with Templeton when he delightfully delivers terrible news to Wilbur.[39]

Another option is to ignore the comment or perhaps even express empathy toward the verbal attacker by probing into the reason for the offensive words. This approach, of course, depends on your relationship with the speaker and the situation as well as on your own emotional state.

> "Above all else, guard your heart, for everything you do flows from it. Keep your mouth free of perversity; keep corrupt talk far from your lips"
> (Prov. 4:23–24 NIV).

Prayer: Lord, in Your name, we take authority over every false, critical word spoken to us by ourselves, the devil, or others. We stand in our new identity in Christ.

Radiant Action: Journal Entries: 1. I will review what God says about me. 2. I will guard my heart from lies and negativity while being realistic and honest about weaknesses. 3. I will refuse to allow negativity to make me surrender. 4. I will practice saying, "Cease and desist!" to temptations or negative voices.

Webs: Identity Series (Jan.), Identity (Feb.), Some People (Feb.), Terrific (Feb.), Radiant (Feb.), Bad News (Mar.), Naysayers (Aug.), Fences (Aug.), Management Tips (Aug.).

Gleanings: "See to it that no one fails to obtain the grace of God; that no 'root of bitterness' springs up and causes trouble, and by it many become defiled" (Heb. 12:15).

DAY 16

Naysayers

"'Fern,' said her mother sternly, 'you must not invent things.'"[40]

Fern's mother, like many good parents, teaches her children the importance of honesty. When it comes to the barnyard and talking animals, in her mind such things are impossible, and she sternly rebukes Fern for making up "wild tales." Worried about her daughter, Mrs. Arable makes an appointment with Dr. Dorian, who gently corrects her and turns the situation on its head by explaining that the world is full of wonder and things we don't understand—things we take for granted like a spider's web.

If you've ever heard a chorus of summer frogs swimming in the unexpected windfall of a watershed pond, you might think it sounds like something a naysayer would say: *Nay-umph, nay-umph*—a lot of voices intoning the same negative opinion.

Sometimes God calls us into relationships with people who may sound like those frogs. Such naysayers might simply lack the ability to comprehend things outside their logic, things born of imagination. They might righteously consider themselves "warners" who are keeping you from going over the edge. And yes, sometimes we need to listen.

But sometimes we need to be like Fern and hold on to what we know, standing firm against skeptics. In such instances, it's best to pray for an intervention to mend the relationship. Dr. Dorian eased Mrs. Arable's mind by assuring her that Fern would grow up and be naturally interested in other things. He counseled her not to worry about the other world Fern sees. It is a world of wonder—of childlike imagination.

"But others mocking said, 'They are filled with new wine'" (Acts 2:13).

Prayer: God of wonders, help me hold on to my beliefs based on Your Word, despite the unbelief of others. If I'm misguided in my thinking and imagination, correct me and lead me in sure paths. Give me a humble heart and clear direction.

Radiant Action: If someone tries to impose their notion of what is "realistic" on me to divert my path, I will take it to God and His Word and talk with mature believers who can help sort out my calling. I will consider whether Jesus's words apply from Matthew 7:6: "Do not . . . cast your pearls before swine" (NKJV).

Webs: Calling: "Here Pig" (Mar.), Purpose Series (May), Words (Oct.), Presumption (Oct.).

Gleanings: "And kneeling before him, they mocked him, saying 'Hail, King of the Jews!' And they spit on him and took the reed and struck him on the head" (Matt. 27:29–30).

DAY 17

Farmers

Mr. Zuckerman . . . drove into the field.[41]

A farmer is a person who deals with uncertainty. He knows that ultimately he has no authority to plough his destiny. As author Lisa Prater explains, "Despite research and scientific breakthroughs, and despite innovations in technology, farming remains largely an act of faith. You plant a seed and you harvest a crop. You care for your livestock and they provide you with offspring. So much of what happens in between is out of your control."[42]

Nothing is really in Mr. Zuckerman's control either; a spider pulls his strings. And nothing is really in our control. Instead, as believers we know that God is in control and works in all circumstances and situations "for the good of those who love him, who have been called according to his purpose" (Rom. 8:28 NIV).

God must have a very tender place in His heart for those who tend the land. Human life began in a garden: "The LORD God planted a garden in Eden, . . . and there he put the man whom he had formed" (Gen. 2:8). One day, the garden will be restored, and we'll live in a place where the Tree of Life grows with leaves that will heal the nations.

If you're a Christian, you're a farmer, a sower of gospel seeds in God's field. We are commissioned and empowered to teach and disciple. We can plow and we can water, but always it is God who produces the crop of souls. He is the one glorified. "I planted, Apollos watered, but God gave the growth. So neither he who plants nor he who waters is anything, but only God who gives the growth . . . You are God's field, God's building" (1 Cor. 3:6–7, 9).

> *"The farmer knows just what to do, for God has given him understanding"* (Isa. 28:26 NLT).

Prayer: Dear God, help me prepare my fields. Prosper the good seeds I plant. Where do You want me to sow crops of Your Word?

Radiant Action: Journal Entry: Brains storm strategies for problems. I will not allow uncertainty to keep me from "farming." For a gospel harvest, like the farmer, I will trust the Lord for wisdom, power, and effectiveness.

Webs: Clean and White: Moral Freedom (July), Land (Aug.), Uncertainty (Aug.)

DAY 18

Hero: The Protector

The sheep stayed near the barn, too, for protection.[43]

Charlotte protects Wilbur from becoming pork chops by weaving silvery words on high. Her eight legs resemble the eight spokes of an open umbrella. An umbrella, like a canopy, is a means of protection. Charlotte's web is a canopy, protecting Wilbur from the expected future for a spring pig on a farm.

Canopy is the way Scripture describes the sky, which is translated in the KJV as "defense." God is like a canopy, sheltering us sovereignly from Satan's schemes. God protects and covers us, weaving us into the story of salvation as we become part of a new family and a new destiny. His love bears all things. The word *bears* also means "roof" or "protective covering" as used in Mark 2:4: "They removed the *roof* above him." His love protects from the enemy.

Charlotte weaves four sets of words for Wilbur in a web that eventually deteriorated. God speaks words of life over us that will never change: Redeemed, Child, Chosen, Holy, Washed, Conformed.

> "For the LORD God is a sun and shield; the LORD bestows favor and honor;
> no good thing does he withhold from those whose walk is blameless"
> (Ps. 84:11 NIV).

Prayer: Jesus, You are the perfect hero and canopy, who sings a new song over me, who speaks new words over me, who protects me from the Evil One, and who bears my weakness with a sheltering love to protect me from life's storms.

Radiant Action: An umbrella will remind me to stay near the Lord for protection. I will honor those in authority over me as earthly "umbrellas."

Webs: Relationships: Charlotte's Web (Jan.), Food and Feasting (Nov.), Provision (Nov.).

Gleanings: "Keep me, O keep me, King of kings, beneath thine own almighty wings."[44]

> "The eyes of the LORD are in every place, keeping watch on the evil and the good" (Prov. 15:3).

DAY 19

Transportation: The Farm Truck

The big truck . . . backed slowly down toward the barnyard.[45]

The big farm truck is a minor but essential "character." It carries everyone to the fair; it steals the spotlight as it begins to roll downhill by itself; it's a respite from the heat as the family meets for lunch and a nap; and it gains one more spotlight as it carries the group to the grandstand— "let the truck pass."[46]

The last we hear of the truck, Wilbur is loaded onto it, with Avery aboard and drenched from Lurvy's misaimed pail of water, making a wet spot on the seat. Then off trundles the truck back to the pigpen. The farm truck is a humble piece of equipment meant to transfer an unpretentious pig from his big trial and return him to the Zuckerman farm.

The Bible refers to the Christian as being transferred from one realm to another: "He has delivered us from the domain of darkness and transferred us to the kingdom of his beloved Son, in whom we have redemption, the forgiveness of sins" (Col. 1:13–14). Jesus, the humble servant, has transferred us from one kingdom to another. He is our transportation, our way out of an evil kingdom into one of light and wholeness. When the old farm truck took Wilbur to the fair, he was still under a penalty of death for being a pig. When the truck took him home, he had a medal and a secure future.

Jesus takes us from our place as sinners under the penalty of death to the place where our future is secure. The new location means we can receive blessing, forgiveness, and treasure beyond our imaginings. Our freedom is won. But only because He has transferred us.

Can you picture an old farm truck with pumpkins loaded into every corner and piled high? Think of Jesus transporting us to the new kingdom where the harvest is marvelously abundant.

> "But, as it is written, 'What no eye has seen, nor ear heard, nor the heart of man imagined, what God has prepared for those who love him these things God has revealed to us through the Spirit" (1 Cor. 2:9–10).

Prayer: Help me appreciate the humble way You served me and died on the cross to transport me all the way from one kingdom to another.

Radiant Action: When I see a farm truck, I will think of how You have transferred me.

Webs: Utopia (Dec.), Coming Kingdom (Dec.), Prophecy (Dec.)

(Photo by Ann K. Ayers)

189

DAY 20

Grace

"I'd be only too glad to help in any way I can."
"Oh, I'll work it out alone," said Charlotte.[47]

Charlotte promises Wilbur that she will not let him die and that she is working on a plan. Wilbur trusts Charlotte will fulfill her pledge.

We are like Wilbur who is not able to save himself or come up with a plan. He depends solely on his friend, Charlotte—on her plans, abilities, and wisdom. Paul wrote about us: "But God, being rich in mercy, because of the great love with which he loved us, even when we were dead in our trespasses, made us alive together with Christ . . . For by grace you have been saved through faith. And this is not your own doing; it is the gift of God, not a result of works, so that no one may boast" (Eph. 2:4–5, 8–9).

Grace's unsurpassable beauty is that it is a free gift from the only One who could plan for the means of redemption and also execute the plan. He accomplished it alone.

Humility is the key to access grace for salvation for eternity and grace for living abundantly on earth. Wilbur won his special prize with the word "Humble." To win at life and to enter God's presence forever, we must humble ourselves before Him, admit our sin that separates us from Him and admit our utter dependence upon Him. We will find grace that leads to eternal life. He will not turn us away. He is our Friend who saves us.

Prayer: Help me to remember that You alone opened the gate of grace. Give me humility to ask for the grace of salvation and then to walk in grace to do whatever You ask.

Radiant Action: I will set reminders to thank God for His indescribable gift of grace (2 Cor. 9:15). I will thank God for small blessings that are really wells of strengthening grace (for example, exercise, hot water, good food, friendship, and music).

Webs: Humble (Feb.), Blood (Apr.), Purpose I (May), Power of One (May)

Gleanings: One definition of grace, besides the grace of salvation, is the power and desire to do God's will.

> *"And God is able to make all grace abound to you, so that having all sufficiency in all things at all times, you may abound in every good work"* (2 Cor 9:8).

SEPTEMBER
TRIALS AND VICTORY!

At last there are delectable apples on the apple tree. September is the month of victory in *Charlotte's Web*. Wilbur secures his prize and his future. He gains maturity in time to use logic to lure Templeton into his saving act for the egg sac. But there are tears, trials, and terror before the harvest is ready, before the magnum opus is complete, before the glory of the last day.

Before Triumph

Anxiety: Dizziness, *p. 192*
Trials before Triumph, *p. 193*
Tears, *p. 194*
Failure, *p. 195*
Death of a Vision, *p. 196*
Choices, *p. 197*

Triumph

Planning, *p. 198*
Apples, *p. 199*
Rewards, *p. 200*
Harvest, *p. 201*
A Legacy That Lasts, *p. 202*
Magnum Opus, *p. 203*
The Last Day, *p. 204*

Finishing Well

Weight of Glory, *p. 205*
Victory, *p. 206*
Fame, *p. 207*
Goodbyes, *p. 208*
Renewal of Vision, *p. 209*
Cheerleaders, *p. 210*
Quarterly Review: July–September, *p. 211*

DAY 1

Anxiety: Dizziness

Wilbur fainted away.[1]

As the crickets lament the passing of summer, melancholy settles over the farm. Mrs. Zuckerman, the crickets, Wilbur, and the maple tree all sense an angst of changing seasons moving from warm to cold, easy to structured.

Change can rouse up anxiety. It also nests in that sense of inadequacy, as when Wilbur hears that big Uncle won the blue ribbon. Webster's defines anxiety as "an apprehensive uneasiness or nervousness usually over an impending or anticipated ill" or "an abnormal and overwhelming sense of apprehension and fear often marked by physical signs, by doubt concerning the reality and nature of the threat, and by self-doubt about one's capacity to cope with it."

God's promise is that His grace is enough: "But he said to me, 'My grace is sufficient for you, for my power is made perfect in weakness'" (2 Cor. 12:9). And we know His presence is always with us, that He will never leave us nor forsake us (Heb. 13:5). Focusing on God's greatness and presence will bring peace.

The sky in its power of cloud and wind, the ocean in its agitation, the towering mountains in their hues of blue and green and brown—all these are but mere shadows of God's greatness. The lion's majesty, the whale's colossal size, man's unstoppable technology are less than a midget aphid compared to God's all-encompassing Being. As He is the passport to everything good and eternal, we can confidently put our hope and trust in Him.

God calls us to cast all our anxieties onto His immense shoulders (see Isa. 9:6), for they uphold not only our own lives, but the government of the entire world with its changing fortunes and power structures and the unreliability of human bonds. To Him we must cling as our anchor in life, our peace in death, our hope for eternity.

Prayer: Help me to fix my eyes on You. I acknowledge You to be my faithful partner in life. I ask that peace, not anxiety, will rule my heart (Phil. 4:6–7).

Radiant Action: Anxieties are like ticks. When one attempts to latch on, I will flick it off with a promise from God and think about excellent things (see Phil. 4:8). I won't allow a tick of anxiety to steal a single tick of a clock. When I see a tick, I will think to cast my anxieties on to the Lord.

Webs: Crisis (Mar.), Tears (Sept.), Plot and Providence (Nov.)

Gleanings: "When my spirit faints within me, you know my way!" (Ps. 142:3).

DAY 2

Trials before Triumph

"I guess you're licked, Wilbur."[2]

Catastrophe often precedes victory. But seldom are goals realized and victory secured without a royal battle. A mischievous Avery almost captures Charlotte and the rotund, rude Uncle wins first place.

Before the promised land there was slavery and the desert. Before the resurrection was the cross. "[Look] to Jesus, the founder and perfecter of our faith, who for the joy that was set before him endured the cross" (Heb. 12:2).

What can we do when disasters like land mines lay between us and triumph? We can cry or simply give up in defeat. But if we surrender without resistance, we may well discover that what *could* have been *won* is lost. We give up too soon!

Battle Strategies:
- *Assess* whether the battle is critical or if the conflict can be put aside.
- *Lament* in healthy ways: grieve, write out thoughts and feelings, talk to a close friend.
- *Take hope* that there is a way out as God promised (see 1 Cor. 10:13).
- *Reframe* the disaster. In this case, one can expand the definition of winner. *Charlotte's Web* is instructive here: Could there possibly be a win beyond Uncle's obvious blue ribbon?
- *Take a positive step* under the guidance of God and others. Mr. Zuckerman gave Wilbur a bath after Uncle won the blue ribbon, and then Wilbur won the special prize!
- *Don't believe the lie* that all is lost and God has abandoned you.
- *Believe* God can heal and give unimaginable abundance.
- *"Cease recalling disappointments,"* as author Kim McNeal urges us to do.[3]

The prophet Joel wrote: "I will restore to you the years that the swarming locust has eaten" (Joel 2:25). The psalmist assures us of God's abiding presence and encourages us to "tell the next generation ". . . that this is God, our God forever and ever. He will guide us forever" (Ps. 48:13–14).

Prayer: Father, whatever trial is the stepping stone for me, give me faith to obey, a way to go, and strength that does not turn belly-up from the devil's discouragements.

Radiant Actions: Stepping stones will remind me that my trials, which so often seem to go nowhere, are leading to the good God has for me and ultimately to a glorious future. If the "a" and "i" in trials are reversed, the word "trails" is the result. God will give us new trails because of our trials.

Webs: Perseverance (Aug.), Time and Seasons (Aug.), Tears (Sept.)

DAY 3

Tears

He began to cry.[4]

Tears intertwine the joys in the barnyard. At times, Wilbur feels threatened, lonely, confused, and grieved. He easily cries.

Tears come to us, too, when we face death and loss. Tears can also be evidence of intense internal struggle—a yanking at and testing of our emotional seams, threatening to rip the garment of our souls apart.

There is no grief that God doesn't understand. He longs to hold and comfort us. He will not allow the world to crush our faith and catapult us into darkness. What reassurance we find in the words of this beloved hymn:

> The soul that on Jesus hath leaned for repose,
> I will not, I will not desert to his foes.
> That soul, though all hell should endeavor to shake,
> I'll never, no, never, no, never forsake.
>
> When through the deep waters I call thee to go,
> the rivers of sorrow shall not overflow;
> For I will be with thee, thy troubles to bless,
> and sanctify to thee thy deepest distress.[5]

God sees our tears, even as He saw and pitied Hagar, sobbing in the desert, having been driven off with her son, Ishmael. His eye is even on the sparrow (see Matt. 10:29–31). He sent the Comforter to minister to us (see John 14:16). He also sends angels (see Heb. 1:7, 14). His very presence, never in a rush to attend to the universe, lingers over your soul and mine, and lifts us up.

> *"He will wipe away every tear from their eyes, and death shall be no more, neither shall there be mourning, nor crying, nor pain any more, for the former things have passed away"* (Rev. 21:4).

Prayer: Dear Father, I cast all my sorrow upon the cross and ask You to quiet my wounded heart. Let Your Holy Spirit into the brokenness and the silence, and even into the confusion. Embrace me, gentle Savior, and reassure me. Thank You for putting my tears in Your bottle.

Radiant Action: I will give Jesus my tears and the burdens too heavy to carry.

Webs: Tears (Sept.), The Spidery Myth (Oct.), Words (Oct.), Grief (Nov.), Journey (Nov.).

Gleanings: "You have kept count of my tossings; put my tears in your bottle" (Ps. 56:8).

DAY 4

Failure

Wilbur landed with a thud.[6]

Wilbur believes he can spin a web *if he tries*. Everyone knows, however, that pigs can't fly or spin a web. But in trying, Wilbur discovers he doesn't need to spin a web.

Failure provides a better understanding of our identity, stepping stones for future accomplishment and guidance. As Maya Angelou said, "You may encounter many defeats, but you must not be defeated. In fact, it may be necessary to encounter the defeats, so you can know who you are, what you can rise from, how you can still come out of it."[7]

Many have harnessed the power of failure to lead them to extraordinary success. Reggie Jackson had 2,600 strikeouts, but he is known for the home runs that landed him in the Baseball Hall of Fame. Thomas Edison's light bulb was possible only because "the team at Edison's 'invention factory' in Menlo Park, New Jersey, tested more than 6,000 possible materials before finding one that worked: carbonized bamboo."[8] Denzel Washington failed to get parts after many auditions, but was awarded a Tony in the same theater where he had failed an audition.[9] Michael Jordan was cut from his high school's varsity basketball team as a sophomore.

If you fail in one calling, role, or stage in your life—that does not negate your overall purpose. It might cause you to turn down one avenue. But keep adjusting the course as you continue. As some say, Churchill Winston quipped "Success is not final; failure is not fatal. It is the courage to continue that counts" and, "Success is stumbling from failure to failure with no loss of enthusiasm."[10]

"*For though the righteous fall seven times, they rise again*" (Prov. 24:16 NIV).

Prayer: Dear Father, please give me enough faith to keep trying and enough wisdom to know when to try something else. Give me courage, humility, inspiration, and a sense of humor. When You died on the cross, all the world thought You had failed. But You had won over all the wolves of hell, and the kingdom dawn was just beginning to twinkle and stretch into day.

Radiant Action: As God leads, I will *try* something.

Webs: Equipping (May), Initiative (Aug.), Mustard Seed's Journey (Nov.), Prophecy (Dec.).

Gleanings: God gives "a future and a hope" (Jer. 29:11).

DAY 5

Death of a Vision

"I'm going to capture it," said Avery . . . Then he picked up a stick.[11]

One of the most terrifying obstacles to Wilbur's deliverance was Avery's plot to capture, and perhaps, exterminate Charlotte. Later, Charlotte, severely weakened, questions whether she can even make it to the fair to help Wilbur. After the rescue of her egg sac and her death, her children eventually hatch and all but three fly away.

Closely related to obstacles and failure is the "death of a vision." Evidently, if there is to be a fruitful plan or project, it can be so pummeled by obstacles that the vision dies. If your project is to be very, very effective, then a double death may ensue.

The Jews thought their Messiah would overthrow Rome. Then this Jesus died on a Roman cross. He was laid in a tomb; the heavy stone rolled over the opening. And then there was the resurrection. The resurrection changed everything forever.

Sometimes when a plan believed to be the Lord's will dies because of obstacles, disappointments, and lack, we're dismayed. But God is always in control, and He may well have an inconceivably wider plan. Jesus didn't just come to restore the Jewish nation. He came to die for sin to buy back all sinners everywhere from eternal separation from God.

God wants His children to trust Him rather than push forward in fleshly strength. A death of a vision is the time to stop and to patiently wait for Him to accomplish His good intentions, even as a dream crumbles.

Mr. Zuckerman saw Uncle's blue ribbon not as a death of a vision, but as an impediment to be overcome. Quickly, he called for buttermilk and began grooming Wilbur. Rather than give up hope, he acted to do all that he could as fast as he could. Fern received her runt pig; Mr. Zuckerman received his prize. Wilbur received a reprieve.

Prayer: Father, sovereign refuge, give me wisdom to know when to overcome and when to halt. Give me discernment, for giving up prematurely is as disastrous as pressing on when we are supposed to wait.

Radiant Action: When I see a spider, I will ask God to sharpen my vision and give me patience when I go through a death of my vision.

Webs: Uncertainty (Aug.), Renewal of Vision (Sept.), Victory (Sept.).

DAY 6

Choices

"I will let you have your choice of everything."[12]

When Wilbur promises the rat that he can forevermore have first choice of all the slops, he's not only being unselfish, but he's also yielding his power of choice and preference. Choice represents control. In a gesture of friendship, Wilbur gives up control over his most important possession—food—and with it, security.

Among humans today, many cleave to what they think is their most precious possession: the right to choose what benefits themselves. Actually, we're all guilty sometimes of protecting our Templetonian selves, preferring autonomy and personal preference over friendship. Wilbur sacrificed his first choice to extend goodwill to a rat.

Jesus sacrificed His precious life because He chose us, deeming us of infinite value. "Greater love has no one than this: to lay down one's life for one's friends" (John 15:13 NIV). Seeing our potential despite our sin, He yielded control of His life to see the joy of believers entering into an eternal relationship with God.

God's ways are opposite ours. Heavenly wisdom teaches us to willingly inconvenience ourselves for the good of others. Moses is another compelling example of one who chose to be inconvenienced for a higher good: "He regarded disgrace for the sake of Christ as of greater value than the treasures of Egypt, because he was looking ahead to his reward" (Heb. 11:26 NIV). By contrast, natural wisdom not only has us preserve our own conveniences but even causes others to be inconvenienced for us.

Choosing to give up our own pet choices for the good of God and others is impossible without God's grace. Even Jesus had to pray to the point of sweating blood to align His will with the Father's. On what values do we base our choices? Do those choices align with the world and relieve us of any inconveniences, or do they align with God and His ways?

Prayer: Help me yield my will to Yours and to make right choices in life.

Radiant Actions: Journal Entries: 1. Am I willing to give up my right to choose (control) to follow God wherever He leads? 2. What are my favorite preferences and choices? Am I willing to give them up if necessary to encourage someone else? 3. Am I being faithful in my friendships and my marriage? 4. How can I rely more fully on God's strength, so I am more like Christ in my choices and less like Templeton?

Webs: Liberty (July), Work and Diligence (Aug.), Harvest of Gluttony (Nov.)

DAY 7

Planning

Wilbur had planned to go out.[13]

Wilbur is a planner. He time-blocks his activities. He assigns certain times to eating, napping, scratching itchy places, and thinking about the meaning of life. Charlotte is the planner par excellence. To build her web of words, she weaves together timing, forethought, and skills of artistry, reasoning, and verbal acuity.

God, the Alpha and Omega, is the ultimate and sovereign planner. He planned for Jesus, His beloved Son, to bear the judgment for all humanity. From the beginning, God knew the need and planned for it. Even the constellations aligned at His birth to tell the story. Nothing under the eye of God is coincidence.

God also promises that when we need wisdom for a plan, He will give it to us. As James reassures us, "If any of you lacks wisdom, let him ask God, who gives generously to all without reproach, and it will be given him" (James 1:5).

Rain rerouted Wilbur's plans. Sometimes the Lord interrupts our personal plans to redirect us for our good. Jonah was determined to get as far away as possible from God's summons to preach repentance to Nineveh. So God sent a storm and a great fish to get him back on task. Saul planned to go to Damascus to persecute believers, but God stopped him with a vision and turned his plans and his life and the world upside down.

> God's plans are those that will remain: "Many are the plans in the mind of a man, but it is the purpose of the LORD that will stand" (Prov. 19:21).

Prayer: As a pastor has said, "I put my 'yes' on the table and say 'yes' to Your plans and welcome Your interruption as You see best. Help me to think out and plan the things of my life under the Holy Spirit's guidance, trusting You enough to obey."

Radiant Action: I will take twenty minutes today to start a plan and will set a daily, monthly, quarterly, and yearly time to review and pray through all my goals and plans.

Webs: Vision (Mar.), the month of May, Wilbur Force (Dec.), Utopia (Dec.).

Gleanings: "The heart of man plans his way, but the LORD establishes his steps" (Prov. 16:9).

God's plan: God created; man rebelled. Jesus—God in human form—came, taught, died on the cross to pay for our sin. He rose again from the dead. Accepting and believing in Jesus leads to eternal life and abundant life on earth. His Holy Spirit indwells, empowers, comforts, guides, and restores His children. If you have questions or if you have come to God through this book, please let me know: amanda@alabastersinkwell.com.

DAY 8

Apples

The red little apples lay thick.[14]

Wilbur is born in the spring, the season of apple trees in bloom. But another season's coming, autumn, when the apples are ripe and dropping from the branches. And autumn is the season when Charlotte's plan bears fruit, assuring Wilbur's victory.

Many Scriptures refer to fruit as a symbol for either good or bad results. Good fruit include character traits as listed in the Bible: "**love, joy, peace, patience, kindness, goodness, faithfulness, gentleness, and self-control**" (Gal. 5:22–23). Good "apples" could mean sharing the life-transforming gospel with someone who has no hope or sharing your birthday cake with someone hungry for fellowship. Rotten apples are associated with fleshly desires like sexual immorality, idolatry, strife, and jealousy (Gal. 5:19–21).

In the following compilation of good (spiritual) fruit, it's as if we're turning over a bushel basket and letting the splendid apples roll out.

>Fruit symbolizes
>>spiritual understanding,
>>>repentance,
>>>>character,
>>>>>future mysteries,
>>>>>>offspring,
>>>>>>>general blessings,
>>>>>>>>rewards and more.

Good soil that produces fruit is like the soul "who hears the word and understands it. He indeed bears fruit" (Matt. 13:23). Jesus also said, "You will recognize them by their fruits" (Matt. 7:16). When we meditate on God's Word, we're "like a tree planted by streams of water, which yields its fruit in season and whose leaf does not wither—whatever they do prospers" (Ps. 1:3 NIV).

Prayer: Let the bushel basket of my life overflow with all kinds of good fruit.

Radiant Action: When I take a bite of fruit or, when at the grocery store, pass by the produce section with strawberries, grapes, bananas, apples, and cherries, I will pray for fruitful living.

Webs: Work and Diligence (Aug.), Harvest (Sept.), Weight of Glory (Sept.), Joy (Dec.)

Gleanings: "In the same way, the gospel is bearing fruit and growing throughout the whole world" (Col. 1:6 NIV).

DAY 9

Rewards

Mr. Zuckerman took the medal from Wilbur's neck and hung it on a nail.[15]

Wilbur, although usually a humble pig, glories in the medal around his neck as the outer manifestation of his security. Charlotte is really the one who deserves the reward, but in this scene she is no longer alive. Unthanked, she completes both of her missions with courage, resourcefulness, flexibility, and love. Her reward was Wilbur's safety. In the beginning of the story, Fern received a piglet as a reward for her reaction to injustice.

Just like Charlotte, who receives no recognition, you and I may experience times when we're involved in a work of critical importance, but our efforts go unnoticed. Perhaps we are even upbraided or rebuked for our efforts. We can take comfort in knowing that God sees everything and will compensate the unseen work done for Him in obedience. He will see to it that our rewards are fitting for us and that we will receive an eternal glory:

> *So we do not lose heart. Though our outer self is wasting away, our inner self is being renewed day by day. For this light momentary affliction is preparing for us an eternal weight of glory beyond all comparison, as we look not to the things that are seen but to the things that are unseen. For the things that are seen are transient, but the things that are unseen are eternal.* (2 Cor. 4:16–18)

God rewards laborers who, as Paul did, win and disciple new members for His family. These people are his reward. "What is our hope or joy or crown of boasting before our Lord Jesus at his coming? Is it not you? For you are our glory and joy" (1 Thess. 2:19–20). Truly, the greatest reward is the Lord Himself.

> *"After this, the word of the L*ord *came to Abram in a vision: 'Do not be afraid, Abram. I am your shield, your very great reward'"* (Gen. 15:1 NIV).

Prayer: Dear Father, make me cling to Your promises of Your sure reward so that naysayers, trials, and even my own mind won't keep me from receiving what You want to give.

Radiant Action: Journal Entries: 1. What are some of my rewards resulting from faith? 2. What rewards may I look forward to in heaven?

Webs: Insignificance (Feb.), Naysayers (Aug.), Apples (Sept.), Coming Kingdom (Dec.), Utopia (Dec.)

DAY 10

Harvest

Mr. Zuckerman took fine care of Wilbur.[16]

Charlotte's Web embraces a bounty of harvests: baby spiders, Wilbur's peace and golden age, Zuckerman's fame, Fern's friendship with Henry Fussy, and a beloved book that has sailed through the decades and continues to do so.

The fair is held at harvest time—the season of gathering squash and pumpkins and good things from the earth. For believers, harvest means bringing in the sheaves of new souls. As Jesus told His disciples, "The harvest is plentiful, but the laborers are few; therefore pray earnestly to the Lord of the harvest to send out laborers into his harvest" (Matt. 9:37–38). If we open our spiritual eyes when we're at the grocery store, the basketball game, the university, and the movie theater, we will see that the fields are indeed full of ripe souls hungry for truth and real sustenance.

A Scottish minister made it a practice to watch farmers at labor, for they inspired him to work hard for a spiritual harvest. "According to his biographer, [Duncan] Campbell rose each morning as the farmers harnessed their horses to the plows. He was convicted by their work ethic and determined to be as diligent with his spiritual harvest as they were with their crops."[17]

How will we reap a harvest for the Lord? How are we using our resources of time, money, and talent? Will we reap a personally fulfilling harvest in our own lives and finish strong? What harvest can we expect from our personal lives? In the day-to-day dailiness, do we ask ourselves, "What will be the harvest from this decision?"

> "This is what the Lord says to the people of Judah and to Jerusalem: 'Break up your unplowed ground'" (Jer. 4:3 NIV).

Prayer: Holy Spirit, I plead with You to show me the harvest of my life. Expand my usefulness for Your kingdom. Show me the fields white for harvest and empower me by the Holy Spirit to bring You abundant crops.

Radiant Action: I will ask someone who needs to know the love of Jesus to coffee or brunch—my treat.

Webs: Apples (Sept.), Rewards (Sept.), Choices (Sept.), The Last Day (Sept.), Legacy That Lasts (Sept.)

Gleanings: "Israel was holy to the Lord, the firstfruits of his harvest" (Jer. 2:3).

DAY 11

A Legacy That Lasts

Many more happy, tranquil days followed.[18]

Charlotte left a legacy of words. Blooming with creativity, tenacity, and clever adaptations from the scraps of Templeton's reluctant scrounging, her words transformed Wilbur's destiny. Charlotte's legacy was a changed future for a pig, a changed farm, a changed community, and changed readers who continue to delight in White's story, spun not with spinnerets but with ink. The various characters in his book found their common perceptions altered as to the purpose and personality of pigs.

Charlotte's legacy shows us that our words may change the future of someone who's been taken for granted—an outcast, a person rejected and without hope. Are words bubbling up from your soul decrying injustice? Do they cry out against it (but without hate for the perpetrator)? Or will your angst be remembered but not the taking of action because emotions ruled and constructive measures didn't follow the heat?

What is one positive step you can take today toward your enemies?

What is one forward step toward a goal for your physical, emotional, and mental well-being?

What small steps can you take for your faith life, family life, community life? In your business, your home, your finances? Or in using a gift?

Small, forward steps impact your legacy for generations, multiplying your efforts and bringing glory to your Creator and relief to yourself and others.

Prayer: Dear Father, You know the plans You have for me are for good (see Jer. 29:11); give me insight to count all things as loss except for knowing You, so I can leave behind a highway for others to follow for glory and eternity (see Phil. 3:8-10). All that is seen is transitory; what is unseen is eternal (see 2 Cor. 4:18). Help my heart to seek Your grace, to firmly march to the call of the unseen, abandoning the toys of worldly pursuits, addictions, and habits.

Radiant Action: I will make sure my earthly affairs are in order and pursue an eternal legacy.

Webs: Changed (Apr.), Easter (Apr.), Justice (July), Mustard Seed's Journey (Nov.), Signs and Wonders (Dec.), Generations (Dec.)

Gleanings: "Now to him who is able to do immeasurably more than all we ask or imagine, according to his power that is at work within us" (Eph. 3:20 NIV).

DAY 12

Magnum Opus

"This egg sac is my great work."[19]

Charlotte uses all her strength to produce her greatest creation. Not only has she guaranteed a life of peace for Wilbur, but she's also succeeded in bringing a new generation into being. The Bible awards her species a noble standing: "The spider taketh hold with her hands and is in kings' palaces" (Prov. 30:28 KJV). Charlotte takes hold with her "hands" and brings about a king-size deliverance and a changed community. The wise and kindly spider achieves the impossible.

During the many weeks of her word-weaving, Charlotte matures in interdependence. She begins by working alone, refusing Wilbur's help, but later works with others, drawing on the strengths of the barnyard community. She even demands that the despicable Templeton come to the fair with her and Wilbur to be of service. Charlotte calls her egg sac her "magnum opus." But it's in securing both Wilbur's and her children's future through the teamwork of friends in the old barn that we recognize her real magnum opus.

Though a bloodsucking predator, Charlotte becomes a tenderhearted friend. Though at first an independent worker, she learns to rely on others to help her. Though weak, she uses what she has: her wit, her words, her weaving. Though an imaginary character, she has wisdom for us.

Jesus gave the last remnant of His human strength to complete His magnum opus: the cross upon which He sacrificed His life to become the Savior of the world, crying out in triumph, "It is finished!" (John 19:30). Jesus's finished work and resurrection made the way for us to have enduring hope and a relationship with the God of the universe. He invites us to a new life, one endowed with lasting purpose and access to the grace allowing us to accomplish works planned by God that will outlive our time on earth.

Prayer: Father in heaven, with You, growth is possible. Help me to take hold with my hands the things You have planned for me.

Radiant Action: Journal Entries: 1. What is God asking me to take hold of that requires deeper interdependence with others? 2. Who else might be a part of this?

Webs: Teamwork (Feb.), Specific Goals (Aug.), Work and Diligence (Aug.), Trials before Triumph (Sept.)

Gleanings: "You who once were far off have been brought near by the blood of Christ" (Eph. 2:13).

DAY 13

The Last Day

"A special award will be made . . . Everyone is invited."[20]

It's the last day of the fair, and the judges are making their final decisions. Wilbur is about to receive a special medal, and the Zuckermans will receive more fame—and twenty-five dollars to boot. Wilbur is so excited he faints.

In the grand scheme of God's dealings with humanity, there will be a last day for life on earth, when the righteous Judge will give just rewards based on each person's belief concerning the atonement of Christ. Jesus is that Judge (see John 5:22–23). He promises, "Whoever hears my word and believes him who sent me has eternal life. He does not come into judgment, but has passed from death to life" (John 5:24).

Peter, caught off guard on the night of crisis, learned a hard lesson from his betrayal. His stern warning to readers of his day reaches through time to us today: Be prepared, for the day of the Lord that "will come like a thief. The heavens will disappear with a roar; the elements will be destroyed by fire, and the earth and everything done in it will be laid bare" (2 Peter 3:10 NIV). He exhorts the church to live with the perspective of that day approaching: "Since all these things are thus to be dissolved, what sort of people ought you to be in lives of holiness and godliness, waiting for and hastening the coming of the day of God" (2 Peter 3:11–12).

Luke likewise writes of the coming judgment: "In the past God overlooked such ignorance, but now he commands all people everywhere to repent. For he has set a day when he will judge the world with justice by the man he has appointed. He has given proof of this to everyone by raising him from the dead" (Acts 17:30–31 NIV).

On that day, "each one's work will become manifest, for the Day will disclose it, because it will be revealed by fire, and the fire will test what sort of work each one has done" (1 Cor. 3:13).

"It is appointed for man to die once, and after that comes judgment" (Heb. 9:27).

Prayer: God, help me to live with that day in mind.

Radiant Action: Journal Entry: How will my work be judged? Do I have assurance for that day?

Webs: Time and Seasons (Aug.), Legacy That Lasts (Sept.), Harvest (Sept.), Coming Kingdom (Dec.).

Gleanings: "I will raise him up on the last day" (John 6:40).

DAY 14

Weight of Glory

Templeton grew . . . fatter.[21]

There is a kind of weight that leads to death. A big pig, for example, equals delectable sides of bacon and pork roasts, pork chops, barbecue, and country ham. And then there's unhealthy human weight, that, as with Templeton, leads to preventable diseases.

But there's another kind of weight, a good weight, a weight of glory. The word "weight" refers to substance. C. S. Lewis describes it in this way: "To please God . . . to be a real ingredient in the divine happiness . . . to be loved by God, not merely pitied, but delighted in as an artist delights in his work or a father in a son—it seems impossible, a weight or burden of glory which our thoughts can hardly sustain. But so it is."[22]

This kind of abundance doesn't lead to weight gain or health problems. The weight of glory brings honor to Jesus and brings to us satisfaction beyond what temporal glory can give. But the weight of glory is also molded in us through times of suffering. A grace-filled response to suffering, empowered by the Holy Spirit, yields something far more valuable than any precious possession or accolade.

> "For our momentary, light distress [this passing trouble] is producing for us an eternal weight of glory [a fullness] beyond all measure [surpassing all comparisons, a transcendent splendor and an endless blessedness]!" (2 Cor. 4:17 AMP).

Prayer: Dear Father, for those of us who are weighed down with the world and its troubles, with the voice of the devil accusing us day and night, darkening our hearts with shame and guilt we can't seem to shake—turn our vision to the weight of glory—the delight and wonder of what You have for us that lasts forever, an abundance that far exceeds our imaginations.

Radiant Action: Pastor Spurgeon challenged: "Believer, you are anticipating the time when you will join the saints above in ascribing all glory to Jesus, but are you glorifying Him now?"[23]

Webs: Rewards (Sept.), Radiance and Light (Dec.), Presence (Dec.)

Gleanings: "I glorified you on earth, having accomplished the work that you gave me to do. And now, Father, glorify me in your own presence with the glory that I had with you before the world existed" (John 17:4–5).

DAY 15

Victory

Then he tied the medal around Wilbur's neck.[24]

Charlotte's Web is a treasured story for many reasons but especially for its joyful victory. Wilbur lives on. He is fed and not the food.

For us, Jesus won the ultimate victory and destroyed the works of the devil (see 1 John 3:8). How awesome it is that we have the ultimate victor on our side and His Spirit lives within us. As John wrote, "He who is *in* you is greater than he who is in the world" (1 John 4:4; emphasis mine).

One day all our enemies, including death, will be vanquished. God will make all that is bittersweet to be sweet even as He did for the Israelite prophets whose water was poisoned. Elijah cast a log into the bitter waters and made them drinkable. God has made a way to change our heartaches into heavens through the log of the cross. Hold your head high and cast your sighs behind you, for your Prince draws you with everlasting love and crowns your head with glory (see Ps. 103:4; 2 Tim. 4:8).

> O sing to the Lord a new song,
> for he has done marvelous things!
> His right hand and his holy arm
> have gotten him victory.
> The Lord has made known his victory.
> (Ps. 98:1–2 RSV)

As I read this psalm, a stunned, comatose sparrow revived and made a triumphant flight from her box on the porch to the holly tree in my yard. She flies around the porch still to remind me of victory!

Prayer: Thank You for the victory in Christ.

Radiant Action: I will use my imagination (shaped by Scripture) to move toward victory over addiction, bitterness, sadness, and failure, believing that God will use hard things for His glory.

Webs: Imagination (July), Transportation: The Farm Truck (Aug.), Rest (Oct.)

Gleanings: "We shall find peace. We shall hear angels. We shall see the sky sparkling with diamonds." —Anton Chekhov

> "The Lord is on my side as my helper; I shall look in triumph on those who hate me" (Ps. 118:7).

> "And we know that for those who love God all things work together for good, for those who are called according to his purpose" (Rom. 8:28).

DAY 16

Fame

It is deeply satisfying to win a prize in front of a lot of people.[25]

Mr. Zuckerman's best day is the day Wilbur wins the grand prize—in front of a lot of people. White pours the tonic most of us want to drink. A little glory, please—a few minutes in the place of honor. Bow, grin, and scrape a little. Again. Spotlight, please.

If Mr. Zuckerman had concentrated on farming, not fame, he would have had blackberry jam and a healthy crop of corn. Instead, he had a well-fed pig and a farm that was the center of attention, or rather, distraction.

Today, the distraction of social media is a popular way to garner glory. It's all about appearances, the outward show, the photoshopped image. In that medium, the inner self rarely is displayed. But see a negative comment on what you posted with hopes of gaining a little honor and feel the searing pain of shame and embarrassment that follows. Besides putting a cloud on your day, the distraction upsets the cart of productive work and service.

Only honest prayer, seeking God's presence, and meditating on His Word will convict and redirect our paths away from seeking ephemeral fame. One way we can know we are working for the Lord with a servant's heart is to check how we react if someone else gets the credit for our planning and execution of a job. Do we feel anger or self-pity if our contributions are ignored? Or can we, like Charlotte, do an excellent job, despite lack of praise or pay? Ultimately, are we doing it for the Lord?

If we do get praise, do we acknowledge it with a humble spirit?

> "It is dangerous to be concerned with what others think of you, but if you trust the LORD, you are safe" (Prov. 29:25 GNT).

Prayer: God, give me a humble heart and help me commit my work to You.

Radiant Action: The next time my opinion is ignored, or I'm denied praise for a job well done, I will give up my right for recognition and glory for the greater good of pleasing God. I will prefer His reward (see John 8:50).

Webs: Insignificance (Feb.), Trapping (July), The Dump (July), Weight of Glory (Sept.).

Gleanings: "Yes, LORD . . . your name and renown are the desire of our hearts" (Isa. 26:8 NIV).

DAY 17

Goodbyes

"Good-bye!" she whispered. [26]

The song of the crickets is a song of goodbye to summer. Goodbye means "God be with you." Charlotte's goodbye to Wilbur is sad, but her weakness gives him opportunity to display maturity and strength. He becomes Wilbur Force, the pig of determination and self-sacrifice. He becomes the hero who delivers the egg sac to the haven of the old barn. Goodbye is a gate to a new beginning. Wilbur's second spring arrives, and soon after the last threads of Charlotte's web are gone, the baby spiders begin to hatch. The old is making way for the new.

When Jesus left the earth, He sent the promised Holy Spirit to live inside us, His followers, so we would not be orphans. The Holy Spirit, called the Comforter and Helper, is with us even though Jesus said "goodbye" physically for now. This power and new life of the Spirit became available only after Jesus departed.

When the believers at Ephesus said farewell to Paul, they grieved that they would never see him again. Like Charlotte, he departed without regrets. He had frankly given advance notice of what he was facing and committed the disciples to God, praying fervently with them. Paul's prayer for them provided protection and empowerment when he had to leave them. There will be no more goodbyes in heaven.

> *"When Paul had finished speaking, he knelt down with all of them and prayed. They all wept as they embraced him and kissed him. What grieved them most was his statement that they would never see his face again. Then they accompanied him to the ship"* (Acts 20:36–38 NIV).

Prayer: "May [Christ] dwell in your hearts through faith—that you, being rooted and grounded in love, may have strength to comprehend with all the saints what is the breadth and length and height and depth, and to know the love of Christ that surpasses knowledge, that you may be filled with all the fullness of God" (Eph. 3:17–19). (Paul wrote these powerful words of encouragement to the Ephesians after his departure.)

Radiant Action: I will thank the Lord for blessings of the past, but I will not cling to them. I will embrace the new.

Webs: Time and Seasons (Aug.), Evenings (Nov.), Aging (Nov.)

DAY 18

Renewal of Vision

A web gets torn every day . . . and a spider must rebuild it.[27]

The stress of all those bugs kicking around in a spider web, even if it's strong, puts holes in it. As Christians, even if we're strong in our belief, we can be certain that those bugs (or what bugs us) will tear holes every day in our emotional and spiritual webbing.

But we can take heart because God has given us ways to reboot and reknit. Such things as reading and meditating on Scripture, singing, having fellowship with other believers, praying and listening to God, journaling, and reviewing our progress and failures all contribute to our spiritual and mental well-being. We can take other positive actions as well, such as being faithful and obedient to do what the Lord says to do, and loving and serving our family, neighbors, and enemies. Sometimes a good meal, exercise, nap, and a hot bath is the best medicine.

Though as humans we're a trinity of spirit, soul, and body, these aspects of our being comprise one unit, and each affects the other. Taking care of one's being in its different dimensions is godly. Consider Jesus who washed the disciples' feet, a loving act rendered in the physical dimension but with spiritual implications.

Peter was torn and tormented after denying three times that he knew Jesus. After His resurrection, Jesus, ever seeking to restore and reconcile, asks Peter three times, "Do you love me?" (see John 21). With each affirmation, Peter's confidence rises again. Restored, he becomes the preacher for Pentecost. No longer afraid, he gives out the gospel in the power of the Spirit, and three thousand people respond to his message.

Prayer: Lord, renew my mind, my vision, my strength, my peace. Cleanse me and lead me to walk where You want me to walk. Fill me again with Your Spirit and affirm me. Help me to positively affirm myself too.

Radiant Action: I will take time today to refresh by doing something I enjoy. After losing a job and finding freedom again, E. B. White correlated grapes with rededication. I'll let eating grapes remind me to rededicate myself to the Lord.

Webs: The Last Day (Sept.), Victory (Sept.), Death of a Vision (Sept.), Prophecy (Dec.).

Gleanings: "Be transformed by the renewal of your mind" (Rom. 12:2).

DAY 19

Cheerleaders

"Congratu-congratu-congratulations!" they cried. "Nice work!"[28]

The geese, although too chatty, are encouragers. But sometimes they're a little edgy in their encouragement. The goose tells Wilbur to push on the loose board in his pen, declaring that he doesn't have to stay in his "dirty-little yard"[29] but can escape to freedom. The freedom ends in panic and with Wilbur's perfect resolve to return to the pen. But the geese indeed are cheerleaders for Wilbur. One goose even comes up with the second word for the web, "Terrific," a word characteristic of their own good humor.

Overall, those somewhat annoying geese are good models for us as believers. As we work through our callings and life goals, the pressing thing is to "encourage one another and build one another up" (1 Thess. 5:11). The Lord Himself refreshes us every day. The Holy Spirit is our advocate and champion.

One day, the Lord will say, "Well done, good and faithful servant. You have been faithful over a little; I will set you over much. Enter into the joy of your master" (Matt. 25:21). In other words, "Nice work!"

"Therefore encourage one another with these words" (1 Thess. 4:18).

Prayer: As You have encouraged me, enable me to encourage others.

Radiant Action: I will reach out to someone today to encourage them.

Webs: Liberty (July), Servanthood (July), Words (Oct.), Self-Control (Nov.).

Gleanings: "Whatever you do, work at it with all your heart, as working for the Lord, not for human masters, since you know that you will receive an inheritance from the Lord as a reward. It is the Lord Christ you are serving" (Col. 3:23–24 NIV).

DAY 20
Quarterly Review

July–September

1. July: Fern and Avery took off for the merry-go-round at the fair, exulting in their freedom. How do you define freedom? Does freedom mean doing what you want or does freedom mean having the ability to make right choices?
2. July: Have you found greater freedom in making moral choices? How does self-control impact freedom? What does victory look like to you?
3. July: Fern was enraged over the idea of a baby pig being executed because it was small. What injustices rile you to action?
4. July: How do you determine truth? Do you swing? Are you asking enough questions?
5. July: Avery kept the crowd at the Fair laughing. How are you honing your humor? Investing in play? Keeping healthy?
6. August: The barn in *Charlotte's Web* is a character itself. Do you have any experience with barns or other humble places that have brought forth great stories?
7. August: Charlotte and Templeton were able to say no, but with different motivations. How are your boundaries? Healthy? Rigid to keep people out? Or are they good ones that help you be who you are without being swallowed up or entangled with emotionally unhealthy people?
8. August: Do you feel secure that God is eternal, and He holds time in His hands? How do you understand that salvation is by faith, yet works are a part of our faith?
9. August: Charlotte had to decide to either go to the fair or stay home when her egg sac was due. What decisions do you need to make? What are your specific goals? How can you start? What rhythms and routines can help keep you keep balanced? What will be your "magnum opus"? What will be your legacy on the real "last day"?
10. September: Wilbur often fainted and cried hysterically. When are you most anxious? How do you manage your anxiety now?

Challenge: Keep a record of Scriptures that are special to you, answers to prayer, and songs that encourage. Make notes on God's timing, wisdom (understanding), grace, and provisions. Even note where you find God breaking through in the ordinary, sometimes with humor!

OCTOBER
WRITING AND NATURE

In the Northern hemisphere, the earth pivots from one season to another, and here we've come to October, what Keats in his beautiful poem "To Autumn" called the "season of mellow fruitfulness." The apple tree begins its fluttery shedding, flinging off its last golden leaves. The branches are laden with good, ripe fruit. Apples are thump, thump, thumping to the ground. Such fruitfulness is an apt metaphor for writing fruitful words. In this section, we explore the human ability to wield the powerful, persuasive gift of writing and communication. Writing is power for change.

Writing

Calling: The Writer, *p. 213*
Opus, *p. 214*
Scriptures on Writing, *p. 215*
Charlotte's Web: Tips for Writing, *p. 216*
The Spidery Myth of *Charlotte's Web*: A Vehicle for Gospel Truth, *p. 217*
Parables, *p. 218*
The Glory of Story, *p. 219*
Poetry, *p. 220*
Words, *p. 221*
Reading, Education, and Vocabulary, *p. 222*

Nature in a Fallen World

Autumn, *p. 223*
Longing, *p. 224*
Animals, *p. 225*
Foxes, *p. 226*

Nature and Human Nature

Rooting Around, *p. 227*
Presumption, *p. 228*
Shame, *p. 229*
Fishing, *p. 230*
Rest, *p. 231*
The Glory of the Ordinary, *p. 232*

DAY 1

Calling: The Writer

"I'm not a writer any more myself."[1]

E. B. White had given in to a sense of failure in 1937 as he penned those dispirited words to James Thurber. Thurber wrote back, "You may be a writer in farmer's clothing, but you are still a writer . . . This is not a time for writers to escape to their sailboats and their farms. What we need is writers who deal with the individual plight . . . You are not the writer who should think that he is not a writer." White replied by calling himself "the second most inactive writer living, and the third most discouraged."[2]

Despite his frustration, White affirms his own calling as a writer at the closing of *Charlotte's Web*. He writes of Charlotte, "She was in a class by herself. It is not often that someone comes along who is a true friend and a good writer. Charlotte was both."[3] These lines were taken and adapted from a letter his wife wrote defending his work.[4]

The calling is costly. As Madeleine L'Engle explains,

> We do have to pay, with hours of work that ends up in the wastepaper basket, with intense loneliness with a vulnerability that often causes us to be hurt . . . If we're given a gift—and the size of the gift, small or great, does not matter—then we are required to serve it, like or not, ready or not. Most of us, that is, because I have seen people of great talent who have done nothing with the talent, who mutter about "when there's time" . . . , or who bury their talent because it's too risky to use.[5]

Prayer: Creator, help me hear Your creative calling. Nothing is made without You (see John 1:3).

Radiant Action: I will schedule time now to write (or paint, create in any medium, or play). I will believe the investment will be fruitful.

Webs: Childlike (July), Imagination (July), Words (Oct.)

DAY 2

Opus

"Remember that writing is translation and the opus to be translated is yourself."[6]

White's understanding is that as you write, you write yourself into the story. Possible "translations" of E. B. White into *Charlotte's Web* include the following:

- Wilbur's emotional reactions (White had times of psychological strain.)
- Templeton's loner tendencies (E. B. didn't receive a reward in person or go to his wife's funeral.)
- Charlotte's ability to spin a web (White wrote a poem to his wife about being a spider.)
- The demise of the pig and the meaning it had in White's own life (see introduction, page 4)
- Dr. Dorian and the minister's belief in wonders (White reveled in the wonders of the world.)
- Fern's youthful anger at injustice (White wrestled with the injustice of a pig dying while he himself was recovering from an illness.)
- Mr. Arable's final turning to believe in Fern's ability to listen to animals (White loved them and seemed to listen to them too.)

Some even interpret *Charlotte's Web* as White's metaphor for writing. The opening sentence "Where's Papa going with that ax?" could be said to represent the brutal process of revision, of hacking off words and thoughts of lesser importance to the work as a whole.

God is the ultimate Story Writer who translated Himself by the Incarnation into our human story. "The Word became flesh and dwelt among us, and we have seen his glory, glory as of the only Son from the Father, full of grace and truth" (John 1:14).

> *"Long ago, at many times and in many ways, God spoke to our fathers by the prophets, but in these last days he has spoken to us by his Son"* (Heb. 1:1–2).

Prayer: Lord, please help me to understand all that You have translated by Your Son, who came to live in our story. Help me in my own life to see what darkness You have translated into Your light.

Radiant Action: I will ask close friends to affirm my calling, and I will dedicate my creative work to further translate His story.

Webs: Cheerleaders (Sept.), Words (Oct.), Calling: The Writer (Oct.)

Gleanings: "He is the image of the invisible God, the firstborn of all creation" (Col. 1:15).

DAY 3

Scriptures on Writing

"Thus says the Lord, the God of Israel: Write in a book all the words that I have spoken to you" (Jer. 30:2).

"It seemed fitting to me as well, having investigated everything carefully from the beginning, to write it out for you in an orderly sequence, most excellent Theophilus" (Luke 1:3 NASB).

"Moses finished writing the words of this Law in a book until they were complete" (Deut. 31:24 NASB).

"So in the morning David wrote a letter to Joab and sent it by the hand of Uriah" (2 Sam. 11:14 NASB).

"Beloved, this is now the second letter I am writing to you in which I am stirring up your sincere mind by way of a reminder" (2 Peter 3:1 NASB).

"Then Moses turned and went down from the mountain with the two tablets of the testimony in his hand, tablets which were written on both sides; they were written on one side and the other. The tablets were God's work, and the writing was God's writing engraved on the tablets" (Ex. 32:15–16 NASB).

"Your eyes saw my unformed substance; in your book were written, every one of them, the days that were formed for me, when as yet there was none of them" (Ps. 139:16).

"They were saying this to test Him, so that they might have grounds for accusing Him. But Jesus stooped down and with His finger wrote on the ground" (John 8:6 NASB).

"You are our letter, written in our hearts, known and read by all people" (2 Cor. 3:2 NASB).

"Let this be written for a future generation, that a people not yet created may praise the Lord" (Ps. 102:18 NIV).

DAY 4

Charlotte's Web: Tips for Writing

"Somebody's got to go along who knows how to write."[7]

Charlotte goes to the Fair with Wilbur because she can write. Just as Charlotte spins a web to draw people into her plan, human writers also spin wordwebs to draw readers into their stories. The following are some of the techniques that White uses in his book:

Action keeps a reader's pulse accelerating with the drama. Here are a few examples from scenes at the fair: the danger of the hideaways being discovered, Wilbur feigning a fight while getting in the crate, the truck rolling away, Avery's acting up, Wilbur's fainting, the nailing of the crate.

Beginning words, the hook, draw the reader in with a gasp, making them anxious to know what's going to happen: What's up with the ax?

Crisis crashes into the pastoral setting with the revelation of impending murder.

Empathy for the pig caused White to write *Charlotte's Web*, and many of his characters are sensitive and caring beings. The geese are cheerleaders; the Zuckermans give Wilbur buttermilk baths to help his standings; Mrs. Arable provides a bottle for baby Wilbur to nurse.

Suspense, a vital element of fiction, rises as Charlotte is dying, the farmers are heading home, and the egg sac is high in the loft. The villain is Templeton, the only character who can climb, and we see him lying in gluttonous repose from gratuitous feasting.

Surprise: Ironically, Templeton finally saves the day. The victory rests with the unlikely.

God, the author of language itself, sent a **Word**: "In the beginning was the Word, and the Word was with God, and the Word was God" (John 1:1). God chose the perfect Word at the perfect time to speak to us about Himself. And now we, His messengers, "are an epistle of Christ . . . written not with ink but by the Spirit of the living God . . ." (2 Cor. 3:3 NKJV).

Prayer: Lord, You created words as well as complexities of personalities and relationships. Give me the right words to communicate love and justice, and have the patience to listen to the words of others. Give me "apples of gold in settings of silver" (Prov. 25:11 NASB). Make me and Your followers everywhere "winds" of fire with Your messages (Ps. 104:4).

Radiant Action: I commit to investing a certain amount of time at my craft per week.

Gleanings: "Cast your bread upon the waters, for you will find it after many days" (Eccl. 11:1).

Webs: Work and Diligence (Aug.), Perseverance (Aug.), Opus (Oct.)

DAY 5

The Spidery Myth of *Charlotte's Web*: A Vehicle for Gospel Truth

"Wilbur's destiny and your destiny are closely linked."[8]

Survival is one of ten classic themes of literature. Others are judgment, peace, love, heroism, good and evil, the circle of life, suffering, deception, coming of age, and war. White includes all of these themes in the story or "myth" of *Charlotte's Web*. This myth of the spider that saves a pig has within it intimations of truth.

Further, C. S. Lewis made the connection between myth and Christianity, calling Christianity the "True Myth," the archetype of other myths; in pagan myths, "there is a real but unfocused gleam of God's truth falling on human imagination."[9] Early in C. S. Lewis's life he noticed the parallels between pagan myths and classic Christianity.

In Lewis's education it was assumed that the pagan myths were false and Christianity true. He resolved the problem and wrote about myth in a number of places. A key to his resolution was the increased understanding that if God created the world in a certain way and the human mind with a definite structure, it is not surprising that patterns reoccur. The only question is, are any of these myths truer than others or, more precisely, are any of these myths also fact? He came to believe that Jesus was the "myth become fact."[10]

"For with you is the fountain of life; in your light do we see light" (Ps. 36:9).

Prayer: Lord, You are the fountain of life; all human longing is really a longing for Your truth. Open my eyes to see wonders in the stories I read and gleams of divine truth on their pages. Help me to see Your image in the humans that populate our world.

Radiant Action: I will analyze a creative work outside my usual taste and compare it with Scripture.

Webs: Imagination (July), Poetry (Oct.), The Glory of Story (Oct.), Parables (Oct.)

Gleanings: "They serve a copy and shadow of the heavenly things" (Heb. 8:5).

DAY 6

Parables

"Home is the part of our life that's arable, / home is a pledge, a plan, and a parable."[11]

Knowing that White had thought his pig's death held implications for himself, we can suppose he had an inkling that he was writing a kind of parable. A parable, according to one definition, is "a story that uses everyday imagery and activities to communicate a spiritual truth."[12] Another definition is this: "The word 'parable' (Gk. parabole) by derivation means 'saying things in a different way.' The object of teaching parables and allegories is the same. It is to enlighten the listener by presenting him with interesting illustrations, from which he can draw out for himself moral and religious truth."[13]

God wrapped His truth in vivid comparisons so the hearers seeking Him could understand: "I spoke to the prophets; it was I who multiplied visions, and through the prophets gave parables" (Hos. 12:10). The believer finds meaning in the parables' shadows.

As Jesus began to use this teaching methodology, His disciples asked Him, "Why do you speak to them in parables?" (Matt. 13:10). Howard Z. Cleveland, general editor of the *Zondervan Pictorial Bible Dictionary*, explains: "It was an effective method of revealing truth to the spiritual and ready mind and at the same time of concealing it from others."[14] God reveals truth to those who want to seek Him, but by divine design, His detractors remain in the dark. Paul prays for God's people to have the "Spirit of wisdom and of revelation in the knowledge of him" (Eph. 1:17).

> "I will open my mouth in a parable; I will utter dark sayings from of old"
> (Ps. 78:2 RSV).

Prayer: Dear God, please open my heart to receive Your revelation. Where I am blinded by the world and deceived, heal my spiritual eyes so I can see.

Radiant Action: I will commit a date for prayer and fasting, and in reading Your Word to seek Your truth.

Webs: Truth (July), Thinking (July), The Glory of Story (Oct.)

Gleanings: "That same day Jesus went out of the house and sat beside the sea. And great crowds gathered about him, so that he got into a boat and sat down. And the whole crowd stood on the beach. And he told them many things in parables" (Matt. 13:1–3).

DAY 7

The Glory of Story

"What finally happened?" asked her mother.[15]

Story can include a wide spectrum of expressions, such as myth, parable, allegory, fable, proverb, tragedy, comedy, mystery, history, and poetry. Fern relates Charlotte's story about the fish caught in Charlotte's cousin's spider web with great animation, but Mrs. Arable rebukes her, calling it a wild tale. (But her mother's curiosity soon overcomes skepticism. She wants to hear more!) Those stories Charlotte tells Wilbur and Fern are fascinating and they're also instructive. As for the fish story, the lesson is the reward of persevering through the struggle. Charlotte's Queensborough Bridge account compares building a web overnight to the eight years it took men to build the bridge in New York City. It's a telling example of inherent design.

Storytelling is so effective for teaching, writes *Harvard Business Review* author Vanessa Boris, because

> storytelling forges connections among people, and between people and ideas. Stories convey the culture, history, and values that unite people. When it comes to our countries, our communities, and our families, we understand intuitively that the stories we hold in common are an important part of the ties that bind . . . They build familiarity and trust and allow the listener to enter the story where they are.[16]

Good stories do more than create a sense of connection. They allow the listener to enter the story where they are, making them more open to learning. Good stories can contain multiple meanings so they're surprisingly economical in conveying complex ideas in graspable ways. And stories are more engaging than a dry recitation of data points or a discussion of abstract ideas. How could a well-placed story enliven a company meeting and give clarity to major points?

Story has the power to shape opinion, rework thinking, and influence emotions and motivations. It can help very different people find common ground.

Prayer: Lord, thank You for coming to our world to be in the story of salvation that You wrote and for being in *my* story. Please help me to finish my earthly story well.

Radiant Action: Journal Entries: 1. I will begin to write down my story. When did I meet God or when did I first began to realize there must be something more to life than what I see? Some call this a testimony and I will try to write a sixty-second version. 2. I will set aside time to write a story just for fun.

Webs: Longing (Oct.), Autumn (Oct.), Poetry (Oct.), The Spidery Myth (Oct.)

DAY 8

Poetry

Charlotte writes one—and two-word poems.[17]

"Poetry is that impassioned arrangement of words, whether in verse or prose, which embodies the exaltation, the beauty, the rhythm and the truth of life," wrote English author and poet Richard Le Gallienne.[18]

Charlotte's minimalist poems are not the regular variety. But they make an impact. Blogger Robin Bates writes that Charlotte's last poem "is Wilbur to the core," and goes on to say that "the poem also manages to reshape the narrative around Wilbur so that he can no longer be regarded as future bacon and ham. Zuckerman looks at him and says, '"Humble." Now isn't that just the word for Wilbur!'"[19]

Poetry can touch and even change us by providing channels into the deepest reaches of our being through the truth, beauty, and emotional allure of its words. Scripture is full of poetry that expresses the full range of human existence. About a third of the Old Testament is poetry (Job, Psalms, Proverbs, Song of Solomon, Ecclesiastes), and we find pockets of poetry in benedictions (Genesis 49) and the epic poetry of Israel's history.

John Piper defines poetry as "a kind of verbal resistance to the impenetrability of human experience. The poet will at least try."[20] Charlotte did indeed try, weaving the essence of a pig in words that spoke volumes. Through her poems she changed destiny.

Jesus's life is the perfect poem of love: cadenced by truth, balanced with the rhythm of Creation's song, and rhymed and synced with the vibrations of the past, present, and future.

Prayer: Written during a dry season, I share it with the thought that you, too, have felt the grit and might pray these words of supplication: *Restless deserts shimmy on my horizon; grit grinds into my eyes. You—the Lord of time and trial—break open Your vast, unlimited grace from vials of power You made to inhabit me.*

Radiant Action: I will write a poem today, even if it is one word. Or, I will read one or even sign up for an email with a poem-a-day (https://poets.org/poem-a-day) or at least leave a poetry book handy for me to pick up and read once a day.

Webs: Truth (July), Weaving (July), Words (Oct.)

Gleanings: "Naphtali is a deer let loose; He uses beautiful words" (Gen. 49:21 NKJV).

DAY 9

Words

"I haven't got your gift for words."[21]

Each word Charlotte weaves in her web is a step toward securing life for a doomed pig, but her words also shape Wilbur's view of himself, his abilities, and his future expectations. You could say he builds his house on the "rock" of those words. But it isn't just Wilbur who benefits from those carefully crafted words: *Some Pig* turns the entire farming community upside down.

Terrific, suggested by the goose, is the next word Charlotte spins, and it's Wilbur's heightened status as terrific that changes Mr. Zuckerman's perception of him, prompting Zuckerman to prohibit Lurvy from throwing any more manure into the pigpen. It's also what makes him decide to take Wilbur to the fair.

Radiant, Templeton's first contribution retrieved from a soap box in the dump, has Wilbur living up to the word with running, backflips, and jumping.

Humble is Templeton's final contribution, reluctantly fetched from an old newspaper wrapped around a discarded lunch, a word true to Wilbur's real nature. Wilbur finally gets to be himself. *Humble* is the winning word that gains him the special prize and the guarantee of his freedom.

Proverbs 18:21 proclaims that words have the power of death and life. Words can cause others to swoon or flourish. For example, when his friend Bildad insisted Job must have done something wrong to justify his suffering, Job answered, saying, "How long will you ... break me in pieces with words?" (Job 19:2).

The word *word* has such living power that John, inspired by the Holy Spirit, used it to describe the Son of God Himself: "In the beginning was the Word and the Word was with God, and the Word was God" (John 1:1). God spoke the world into being with words: "Let there be . . ." (Gen. 1:3, 6, 14). Scripture affirms that "he upholds the universe by the word of his power" (Heb. 1:3).

Prayer: Dear Word of Life, help me to be wise in how I use this powerful gift of language. Help me to find great joy in Your Word (Ps. 119:162).

Radiant Action: I will be aware of my words and their effect on myself and others.

> *"Death and life are in the power of the tongue, and those who love it will eat its fruits"* (Prov. 18:21).

Webs: Asking Questions (July), Choices (Sept.), Charlotte's Tips for Writing (Oct.)

Gleanings: "Lord, to whom shall we go? You have the words of eternal life" (John 6:68).

DAY 10

Reading, Education, and Vocabulary

"What does 'versatile' mean—full of eggs?"[22]

Templeton reads a word (*crunchy*) he found in the dump to Charlotte, but she rejects it based on its nuance as too reminiscent of bacon![23] Throughout the story there's a continuous discussion of words and definitions, such as *untenable, versatile, humble,* and *salutations.* When Wilbur is desperately lonely and pleads for even Templeton to play with him, he takes a rational moment and defines *play* for the rat.

Our ability to use words well is a tremendous asset in communicating with others and with the culture at large. Greater ability to communicate helps one succeed in gaining greater influence and position. One of the greatest means of developing this skill is to have companions who value reading, education, and words, for they can increase our desire to learn. Charlotte loves knowledge and is a patient and willing teacher of many subjects. Wilbur is hungry for her explanations. His eagerness to learn over time transforms him into a passionate pig who makes a fine speech when the spiderlings, Aranea, Joy, and Nellie, fasten their webs to the barn.

Reading good books, new and old, enables us to gain knowledge and wisdom, and can be life changing. In *Guernsey Literary and Potato Peel Pie Society,* Isola Pribby makes this wise observation: "Reading good books ruins you for reading bad books."[24] Good writers read good books. E. B. White believed that "a good literary education leads to other discoveries, wider in scope, among them the discovery that the works of great writers nourish the imagination and augment the wisdom of experience."[25]

But the best book to read of all is the Bible, because of its sublime language, range of genres from history to poetry to prophecy and more, and its practical applications, providing an education for eternity that has, to use terms from business, the most long-lasting returns on your investment.

Prayer: Stir my mind and heart with eagerness to learn. Give me friends who love to learn too. Make me hungry to read Your Word that teaches the things that last.

Radiant Action: I will develop a reading list and make time to read.

Webs: Truth (July), The Glory of Story (Oct.), Glory of the Ordinary (Oct.), Finances (Nov.).

Gleanings: "For whatever things were written before were written for our learning, that we through the patience and comfort of the Scriptures might have hope" (Rom. 15:4 NKJV).

DAY 11

Autumn

The crickets sang . . . the song of summer's ending.[26]

The dawning of autumn and the year's maturing elicit in us deep emotions and elusive longings that rise like mists. In autumn, "deep calls to deep" (Ps. 42:7). There's a pensive air in autumn that woos us, stirs us into knowing there's something beyond our brittle days. In Wilbur's life, the cricket's song signals the time of decision. Autumn is a season for considering mortality. As White wrote, "Everybody heard the song of the crickets."[27]

Matt Cardin, author of the blog *The Teeming Brain*, examines the feeling autumn elicits:

> This autumnal mood is inextricably bound up with a certain, strange longing . . . it is always characterized by a kind of nostalgia for something I have never really known, as if I possess some vestigial memory of a lost knowledge or emotion that flits maddeningly and elusively on the edge of my ability to recall directly . . . It's an experience that makes me feel as if I've come into brief contact with some sort of transcendent spiritual truth. It tends to generate the impression of an absolute, unmediated experience of supernal beauty hovering just beyond the edge of my inner grasp. All the flickering hints of this beauty that I sometimes encounter in literature . . . seem to reach their apotheosis in this ungraspable ultimacy, as if they are merely finite carriers that filter and refract partial glimpses of an infinite reality."[28]

Beatrice Potter's *Squirrel Nutkin*, a winsome autumnal tale, wooed C. S. Lewis into this same sense. Its conveyance of the essence of autumn gave Lewis a deeper longing for something beyond himself. Lewis describes it as "that unnameable something, desire for which pierces us like a rapier at the smell of a bonfire, the sound of wild ducks flying overhead, . . . the morning cobwebs in late summer, or the noise of falling waves."[29]

Prayer: Father, please fill my autumn wistfulness within the deep caverns in my spirit, with You.

Radiant Action: Journal Entry: Daily write about a blessing in the present season.

Webs: Time and Seasons (Aug.), Longing (Oct.), Poetry (Oct.).

Gleanings: "Rejoice in the Lord your God, for he has given you the autumn rains because he is faithful. He sends you abundant showers" (Joel 2:23 NIV).

DAY 12

Longing

If you have the poetic temperament, you go on groping toward something which will express all this . . . and our own inarticulateness only hastens the final heart attack.[30]

White's "groping toward something," of deep calling to deep, C. S. Lewis called *sehnsucht*, a German word meaning longing or desire. In the autobiography *Surprised by Joy*, Lewis describes the flood of feelings that overtook him as a student when he read a book of Norse mythology. He writes, "And with that plunge back into my past there arose at once, almost like heartbreak, the memory of Joy itself, the knowledge that I had once had what I now lacked for years, that I was returning at last from exile and desert lands to my own country."[31]

At the core was his understanding that there was something more than earthly existence. As Lewis expressed it, "If I find in myself a desire which no experience in this world can satisfy, the most probable explanation is that I was made for another world."[32] "*Sehnsucht* is a feeling of nostalgia that faces towards the future," observes blogger Daniel Motley.[33]

Motley explains that Lewis's feeling was "a permanent sense of longing that characterized his deepest held beliefs about Christianity."[34] Desires "for love, safety, security, belonging—are never truly satisfied here in this life . . . Like the 'forward-facing nostalgia' of *sehnsucht*, this feeling points us toward the heavenly home for which we were created."[35]

God "has put eternity into man's heart" (Eccl. 3:11). We yearn with a wordless song in our deepest souls for something bigger, more lasting, than the thing we want most in this life. That yearning is met in the love of God through Jesus Christ. Through Him we find restoration, purpose, and hope for eternity. Knowing Him satisfies all our yearnings.

> "He satisfies the longing soul, and the hungry soul he fills with good things" (Ps. 107:9).

Prayer: Lord, You see the longing in my heart. Fill me.

Radiant Action: Journal Entry: What am I feeling and for what am I longing?

Webs: Life Goals (May), Imagination (July), Autumn (Oct.), Utopia (Dec.)

DAY 13

Animals

The rat had no morals.[36]

Templeton is committed solely to his own good. He's the quintessential rat and, in those terms, perhaps he is immoral only as rats are naturally immoral. But White paints him as the darkest character, one who "would kill a gosling if he could get away with it."[37]

Charlotte, on the other hand, we regard as selfless and caring. But White says he didn't intend to show her decision as a morally principled choice. He explains in a letter that the story of *Charlotte's Web* "is essentially amoral, because animals are essentially amoral . . . [Charlotte] does what she does. Perhaps she is magnifying herself by her devotion to another, but essentially she is just a trapper."[38]

But clearly his barnyard animals act on far more than instinct; White created them to resemble characters we have all likely met in real life. They engage in goals, planning, communication, and equipping. In fact, the animals are the ones who are really running the Zuckerman farm. Although Lurvy brings the food and Zuckerman calls the orders, it's Charlotte, together with the creatures acting under her direction, who ultimately directs the plot.

From its very beginning, the Bible shows the importance of animals and God's pleasure in them. He fills the empty skies and lands with creatures; they are Adam's first companions. They are servants: a talking donkey rebukes Balaam; a donkey carries the mother of God to Bethlehem; another donkey carries the Son of God into Jerusalem for His Passion Week. They are witnesses to the miraculous: animals surrounded the infant Jesus in a stable. God fondly cares for animals and provides for them. He feeds the birds of the air and knows when a sparrow falls and even when it rises to fly again.

Prayer: Dear God, thank You for our animal friends. Thank You for how they can reveal Your character and how they'll be a part of our eternal good future. Show us how to be kind shepherds of their lives. Thank You for how they have served You and how they serve us.

Radiant Action: I will consider the needs of my pets or animals (see Prov. 12:10).

Webs: Play (July), Imagination (July), Journeys (July), Plot and Providence (Nov.)

Gleanings: "But ask the beasts, and they will teach you" (Job 12:7).

DAY 14

Foxes

Foxes came in the night.[39]

We can imagine White's foxes hunting at night and inspecting fallen wild apples.

There's much to admire in a fox. Known for its ability to outwit predators, it can lead a pack of dogs onto thin ice and a group of horses and huntsmen on a fruitless chase or tag-team to wear out hunting dogs.[40] Known for its ability to make quick and effective choices, a fox exemplifies decisiveness in crisis and is a loyal mate for life.

But a fox can represent negative qualities. A fox can damage a harvest. As Solomon warns, "Catch the foxes for us, the little foxes that spoil the vineyards, for our vineyards are in blossom" (Song 2:15). Every day, Satan, the world, and our own desires are like foxes that thwart our spiritual progress and outreach to others who need the ministry of Christ's love through us.

Prayer: Lord, as I go through my day, make me aware of what I can do to further your kingdom and help others, even if they are very small things. I ask You to disable the enemy so he can't outfox me from fulfilling Your will in my everyday life. May I not be a simpleton wandering imprudently into situations.

Radiant Action: When I see a fox, I will ask for wisdom to keep any "foxes" from spoiling my vines. The vines represent my relationship with God and others, and also any plans I have conceived of to carry the gospel to others or to use my gifts for Your kingdom. I will aim to think like a fox to avoid capture by the enemy.

Webs: Small Things (Feb.), Distractions (July), Decisiveness (Aug.), Established (Dec.).

DAY 15

Rooting Around

Wilbur was poking the straw with his snout.[41]

Wilbur is doing what pigs do—using his snout to find food. He is rooting around. The word "root" has several meanings. One, according to Dictionary.com is to become "established deeply and firmly." Wilbur is putting down roots on Zuckerman's farm. He's becoming established, so no one will eat him as smoked bacon or a ham at Christmastime.

God takes the believer into His gracious care and plants him firmly in the ground of eternal security where the Evil One cannot devour him. Although while on earth the enemy is constantly pursuing those who love God, Jesus promises that no one can separate them from Him.

> "I give them eternal life, and they will never perish, and no one will snatch them out of my hand. My Father, who has given them to me, is greater than all, and no one is able to snatch them out of the Father's hand" (John 10:28-29).

Prayer: Pray these words from Ephesians 3:16-19, and let them take root in your heart:

> Father God, according to the riches of Your glory, may You grant me to be strengthened with power through Your Spirit in my inner being, so that Christ may dwell in my heart through faith—that, being rooted and grounded in love, I may have strength to comprehend with all the saints what is the breadth and length and height and depth, and to know the love of Christ that surpasses knowledge, that I may be filled with all the fullness of God" (Eph. 3:16-19).

Radiant Action: I will plant a tree or bulbs and watch them grow. Plants will remind me to plant myself in the Bible and grow roots in my faith.

Webs: Farmer (Aug.), Land (Aug.), Mustard Seed's Journey (Nov.), Established (Dec.)

Gleanings: "You brought them in and planted them on the mountain of your own possession" (Ex. 15:17 NRSVUE).

DAY 16

Presumption

"Got a little piece of string I could borrow?" asked Wilbur. "I need it to spin a web."[42]

Do pigs fly? Or spin webs? Do we as humans define our own meaning and purpose? Can we save ourselves? Presumption arises from ignorance or pride. Whether from lack of wisdom or lack of humility, a fall is coming.[43]

There was a creature, Lucifer, of highest heaven who presumed to outrank God, and from that great height, he fell. The day is coming when that enemy of God will be cast away forever.

The builders of Babel presumed they could find God their way by building a tower to heaven. God's power handily thwarted their plan, their tower, and their ability to collaborate.

Likewise, the plan to make our own meaning and find God on our own terms is futile. Cain, Israel's religious leaders, and countless others have sought to sew "fig leaves" like Adam. Adam foolishly tried to cover his sin with the fig leaves, a fruitless effort not only to hide his nakedness but also as a counterfeit "salvation" to redeem his relationship with God. He tried to make himself acceptable to God by covering up. And so, we have been in the same habit since Eden. Presumption is to have no need for a personal relationship with God. Such a person knows how to handle life without Him and is certain of his own goodness. He has no need of the Savior or His costly salvation He provided as our only way back to God.

> *"So the LORD dispersed them from there over the face of all the earth, and they left off building the city"* (Gen. 11:8).

Prayer: God, heal my blinded eyes and keep me from pride, ignorance, and presumption. Thank You that the adversary is defeated by the blood of Christ and has no power over me.

Radiant Action: I will pray for wisdom, humility, and for truth to guide my way.

Webs: Asking Questions (July), Fences (Aug.), Foxes (Oct.)

Presumption

The lump of clay blinked,
perceiving five extremities on the ends
of his ... "arms"?
Oh the glory of his legs that lifted him
above the other creatures!
How marvelous he was!
And how he shook his fantastic fist
at the Sovereign sky
when the rain reduced him to mud again.

—*Ann K. Ayers (2021)*

DAY 17

Shame

"Pigs mean less than nothing to me."[44]

Both the lamb and Templeton shame Wilbur when he is innocently and hopefully seeking a playmate. Shame is the "intensely painful feeling or experience of being fundamentally flawed, defective, unworthy, and deficient in some vital way as a human being."[45] Shame says you are worthless. Shame or a sense of worthlessness can be at the root of addiction.[46]

Abdu Murray explains that whole cultures are based on shame. An honor and shame culture (usually found more in Muslim countries) is different from an innocence and guilt culture (the West).[47] In the former, *the person is* the sin and is defined by sin. This condition cannot change. In the innocence/guilt culture, the sin *can* be fixed and the guilt removed. Sin does not and cannot define a person. However, the West is fast changing into a shame-based culture.

There is a fruitful shame or Holy Spirit led conviction that leads to positive and eternally consequential results. If we become convicted that our actions and inner bent are in rebellion to the Creator, and we repent, we can find forgiveness and new life. Repentance means turning back to God and heaving ourselves entirely on His mercy, relying on the unspeakably costly payment of the cross for that shame. We receive relief for both the inner man corrupted by sin and the guilt of all the outer manifestations of that nature. We become a new creation.

The Holy Spirit, not legalistic tradition, convicts us of the inner shame that needs to change so we can become who we are meant to be. Legalism, or adding to what God expects of us, can frighten, and turn people away from true faith. Legalism focuses on what we do rather than on what Jesus has already done through the cross. The devil's shame is often cloudy and unspecific.

Prayer: Free me of shame because of the cross (see Rom. 8:1).

Radiant Action: I will not let the devil accuse me of my old sin. I belong to God. Reminders of my past sin bring me closer to God instead of estranging me.

Webs: Sin (April), Clean and White: Moral Freedom (July), Weight of Glory (Sept.), Rest (Oct.)

DAY 18

Fishing

Avery often brought a trout home.[48]

Fishing is fun but also practical. It's a welcome summer activity that can supply supper. We can imagine Avery casting out his line and a fish taking the bait then giving up the struggle after a short battle and landing in Avery's pocket. Being summer, there is still time to play, and Avery has fun swinging and playing with his frog. Eventually he goes home, where we read that he offers the fish, warm and stiff, to his mother.

Jesus tells us as His followers that we will be fishers of men. But it's not a game—there's eternity on the "line." The fish we catch will be fellow human beings, and the stakes are forever.

If you are a fisher of men, what kind of irresistible bait do you use? Is it the joy and peace you possess, even when you're enduring pain? Is it perseverance in times of struggle? If you think of your fishing pole as the means of influence by which you direct your bait into the population you wish to catch, what is your pole; namely, your avenues of influence?

Other questions to ask yourself are the following:

1. Is your line of reasoning and your understanding of Jesus, the Scriptures, and salvation solid?
2. Can you effectively articulate these truths?
3. Do these truths reach down far into your soul?
4. What about the hook at the beginning to catch the attention of your reader?
5. Do you know how to close a discussion of faith with clarity?
6. Do you speak the language of the person you want to reach?
7. Do you need other believers to help reel in the fish who might be foundering?

Go fishing this season and bring home a new friend in Christ to your Father.

Prayer: Lord, show me the person I need to love and spend time with so that they can begin to understand Your goodness and saving grace.

Radiant Action: I will "go fishing," considering the best ways to "catch" people around me and learning to "speak their language" as the disciples did on the day of Pentecost (see Acts 2:4).

Webs: Trapping (July), Weight of Glory (Sept.), Harvest (Sept.).

Gleanings: "And he said to them, 'Follow me, and I will make you fishers of men'" (Matt. 4:19).

DAY 19

Rest

"Get some sleep!"[49]

Wilbur sleeps. Charlotte sleeps. Animals and plants sleep. When winter comes to the Zuckerman farm, the cows stay in the barn, and quiet descends upon the fields. Rest allows us to disconnect from life's demands and brings out greater creativity. "Ideas, be they scientific or artistic, come when the cognitive mind is at rest, and suddenly it will awake to an idea that has been given it by the interior, creative, often unrecognized area of the brain."[50]

But we live in a restless society where barriers to rest are legion. Besides obvious irritants like the urgent vibrations and pings of smartphones, there can be emotional and spiritual anxiety or physical and mental pain. Sometimes people can't rest because they're trying to prove their worth through endless activity, or maybe because they feel guilt, real or imagined. In all these conditions, creativity is stymied.

One of God's most precious promises is for rest. God created everything, and when He finished, He rested. He commands His people to honor the Sabbath. He invites us to spiritual rest as well. "Come to me, all who labor and are heavy laden, and I will give you rest. Take my yoke upon you, and learn from me, for I am gentle and lowly in heart, and you will find rest for your souls. For my yoke is easy, and my burden is light" (Matt. 11:28–30).

Prayer: Lord, help me to receive Your peace and find rest in the midst of life. Give me a big enough vision of who You are and any wisdom from Your Word for strategies that would allow me to rest more.

Radiant Action: I will prepare for and practice Sabbath and believe You will provide what I need even if I make the time to rest, reflect, and worship a priority.

Webs: Routines and Rhythms (Aug.), Initiative (Aug.), Work and Diligence (Aug.), Peace (Nov.)

Gleanings: "O may my soul on thee repose / and with sweet sleep mine eyelids close."[51]

> "Return, O my soul, to your rest; for the LORD has dealt bountifully with you" (Ps. 116:7).

DAY 20

The Glory of the Ordinary

"I don't see why you say a web is a miracle—it's just a web."[52]

Dr. Dorian proposes that the ordinary web Mrs. Arable takes for granted is a wondrous creation beyond understanding. How well this scene illustrates that in the things we take for granted in our world lay seeds of the extraordinary. Reading *Charlotte's Web*, a story about an ordinary spider, carries us much farther into the divine than the author might ever have imagined.

Cynthia Maus writes, "If we focus on the ordinary and small things of life we find the glow of eternal things."[53] To explain the unseen, Jesus used everyday things like bread, fish and fishnets, a pearl, a lost son, money, a fig tree, a mustard tree, sparrows, salt, a vineyard, and regular people. When the Samaritan woman was performing the everyday duty of filling her water jugs, she met Jesus, and everything changed.

> "For since the creation of the world God's invisible qualities—his eternal power and divine nature—have been clearly seen, being understood from what has been made" (Rom. 1:20 NIV).

Prayer: God, assist me in understanding and practicing Your presence every day as I observe creation. Use me in my ordinariness.

Radiant Action: I will look for inspiration both in the natural world around me and in everyday life.

Webs: Childlike (July), Imagination (July), Contentment (Nov.), Signs and Wonders (Dec.)

Gleanings: "True ministry is about common, ordinary people involved in little, very human missions."[54]

Theologian N. T. Wright wrote about the ordinary:

> All truth can be twisted to serve the ends of human pride and arrogance, and that happens far too frequently. But it can be straightened out again; and the way to do that is to "take it captive," to make it change armbands, to bring it on to the right side. There is no insight, no vision of truth, so noble and lofty that it cannot be perverted and made an instrument of human pride. Likewise, there is no small glimmer of light, no faint echo of reality, so small or corrupt that it cannot be taken into the service of the world's creator and rightful Lord.[55]

NOVEMBER
GRATITUDE, REST, AND REFLECTION

Our apple tree begins its rest. November is the season for quiet reflection—a time to sift through the graces that gave strength in testing, to examine one's heart for generosity, to foster gratitude for food, community, and unlikely treasures.

Gratitude I, *p. 234*
Gratitude II: Collected Prayers of Thanksgiving, *p. 235*
Finances, *p. 236*
Generosity, *p. 237*
Food and Feasting I, *p. 238*
Food and Feasting II, *p. 239*
Milk and Meat, *p. 240*
Harvest of Gluttony or Piggly Wiggly Jiggly, *p. 241*
Greed and Bribes, *p. 242*
Scraps and Slops, *p. 243*
Self-Control Scriptures, *p. 244*
Contentment: The Deep Freeze, *p. 245*
Peace, *p. 246*
Plot and Providence, *p. 247*
Provision, *p. 248*
Aging, *p. 249*
Evenings, *p. 251*
Grief, *p. 252*
The Mustard Seed's Journey I, *p. 253*
The Mustard Seed's Journey II, *p. 254*

DAY 1

Gratitude I

"Many, many, many thanks!" they always said.[1]

Mr. and Mrs. Geese are grateful for food and the hatching of seven of eight eggs. Even though one is a dud, they rejoice in what they do have. Their positivity is an example to us, for it is a key to living an abundant life. To focus on disappointment allows sadness to sap the energy of forward spiritual and practical progress.

Gratefulness has been defined as "making known to God and others the ways they have benefited my life."[2] We are in debt to others. "What do you have that you did not receive? If then you received it, why do you boast as if you did not receive it?" (1 Cor. 4:7).

Our debt of gratitude extends even to those who harm us and cause us to suffer, because through suffering we grow in grace. "Count it all joy, my brothers, when you meet trials of various kinds. For you know that the testing of your faith produces steadfastness. And let steadfastness have its full effect, that you may be perfect and complete, lacking in nothing" (James 1:2–4).

Gratitude is often in short supply. We see it in our culture: at the store or restaurant when the cashier fails to thank us for our business or when children take without thanking. A powerful example of ingratitude is found in the biblical account of the ten lepers whom Jesus healed, but with only one expressing thankfulness.

"Then one of them, when he saw that he was healed, turned back, praising God with a loud voice; and he fell on his face at Jesus' feet, giving him thanks" (Luke 17:15–16). Why was this man the only one to give God glory?

Prayer: I will enter Your gates with thanksgiving and enter your courts with praise: I will be thankful to You and bless Your name (see Ps. 100). I will determine to give thanks, for benefits or trials: "Give thanks in all circumstances; for this is the will of God in Christ Jesus for you" (1 Thess. 5:18).

Radiant Action: I will think of good things others have done and thank them. I will be a good steward, count blessings and not losses, and affirm that God is at work in my life. I will work through lament, anguish, and the grief as the psalmists did, and quiet my heart and focus on loving others.

Webs: Patience (Aug.), Words (Oct.), Peace (Nov.)

DAY 2

Gratitude II: Collected Prayers of Thanksgiving[3]

Give thanks to the Lord, *for he is good; his love endures forever* (Ps. 107:1 NIV).

"Thanksgiving is a time of gratitude to God, our Creator and Provider, whose guidance and care go before us, and whose love is with us forever. Thanksgiving is a time to reflect on change, to remember that we, too, grow and change from one season of life to another. Thanksgiving is a time of changing seasons, when leaves turn golden in autumn's wake and apples are crisp in the first chill breezes of fall. Let us remember the true meaning of Thanksgiving. As we see the beauty of autumn, let us acknowledge the many blessings which are ours, let us think of our families and friends, and let us give thanks in our hearts." —Author Unknown

"Let us therefore proclaim our gratitude to Providence for manifold blessings—let us be humbly thankful for inherited ideals—and let us resolve to share those blessings and those ideals with our fellow human beings throughout the world. On that day let us gather in sanctuaries dedicated to worship and in homes blessed by family affection to express our gratitude for the glorious gifts of God; and let us earnestly and humbly pray that He will continue to guide and sustain us in the great unfinished tasks of achieving peace, justice, and understanding among all men and nations and of ending misery and suffering wherever they exist." —John F. Kennedy

"O, heavenly Father: We thank thee for food and remember the hungry. We thank thee for health and remember the sick. We thank thee for friends and remember the friendless. We thank thee for freedom and remember the enslaved. May these remembrances stir us to service, that thy gifts to us may be used for others. Amen." —Abigail van Buren, a.k.a. "Dear Abby"

DAY 3

Finances

When he heard that the price was only six dollars, he said he would buy the pig.[4]

Mr. Zuckerman thinks he can make money on the six dollars he invests in the runt but can't imagine how his investment will eventually pay out. Dividends can be collected from intangibles too. How we earn our bread and how we use it reveal much about character and the values of the heart.

Financial Principles:

1. Be alert and resourceful. Charlotte catches her own dinner while Wilbur waits to be served.
2. "Keep your life free from love of money, and be content with what you have" (Heb. 13:5).
3. Don't borrow: "The rich rules over the poor, and the borrower is the slave of the lender" (Prov. 22:7). "Owe no one anything" (Rom. 13:8).
4. "Lay up for yourselves treasures in heaven" (Matt. 6:20).
5. Believe that "God shall supply all your need according to his riches" (Phil. 4:19 KJV).
6. The Lord gives the power to gain wealth (see Deut. 8:18).
7. Practice "godliness with contentment" (1 Tim. 6:6), for Jesus "will never leave you nor forsake you" (Heb. 13:5).
8. Work (2 Thess. 3:10), but don't overwork (Prov. 23:4).

Prayer: Thank You, God, for giving me exactly what I need for each day. Make me wise and rich in every way so I can share generously with others.

Radiant Action: I will decide on a specific charitable cause and fill up my piggy bank so I can give to that cause. I will leave out a piggy bank to remind me to save and give.

Webs: Generosity (Nov.), Contentment (Nov.), Scraps and Slops (Nov.), Provision (Nov.)

DAY 4

Generosity

Wilbur let the rat eat first.[5]

Out of love, Wilbur gave up first dibs on his beloved slops in response to Charlotte's generous outpouring of love. Wilbur gave the best he had for his friend, and so we should give to God all we have: time, money, talent, relationships. Everything we have is from Him anyway. David wrote, "But who am I, and who are my people, that we should be able to give as generously as this? Everything comes from you, and we have given you only what comes from your hand" (1 Chron. 29:14 NIV).

We respond to the love of Christ because of His amazing outpouring of love for us. "For while we were still weak, at the right time Christ died for the ungodly" (Rom. 5:6). Because of His love, we lay all we have at His feet.

Prayer: Gracious God, help me to hold nothing back from You since You gave all for me. I am Yours and all I have is Yours. Show me how to give to others wisely so Your kingdom will come.

Radiant Action: Journal Entry: I will assess my time, talents, and assets, and will pray for and about opportunities to invest them in the service of God and record the results.

Webs: Scraps and Slops (Nov.), Contentment (Nov.), Joy (Dec.)

Gleanings: "I cannot do much, but as the widow put in her two mites, which were all her living, so, Lord, I cast my time and eternity into Your treasury."[6]

> *"Do not neglect to do good and to share what you have, for such sacrifices are pleasing to God"* (Heb. 13:16).

DAY 5

Food and Feasting I

There are plenty of things for a child to eat and drink and suck and chew.[7]

Charlotte's Web celebrates food, joining merriment and play with eating good things. Even Wilbur's slops are a wonderful mix of such things as middlings, apple parings, meat gravy, and upside-down cake. It was the smell of those slops that brought young Wilbur back into his pen after his wild escape. Food and joy are close friends.

Scripture recounts the joy of food as a sign of God's care. From the beginning, the Lord provided for His people (see Gen. 2:9). He fed the Israelites manna in the wilderness and sent Elijah bread and meat by ravens.

Jesus was compassionate about hungry people: "Lifting up his eyes, then, and seeing that a large crowd was coming toward him, Jesus said to Philip, 'Where are we to buy bread, so that these people may eat?'" (John 6:5). On the road to Emmaus with two unnamed followers, He ate broiled fish (see Luke 24:42). He hosted a cookout after his Resurrection (John 21:9-13).

God's gracious provision of food and necessities for humans and creatures is ongoing, for He "fills the hungry with good things" (Ps. 107:9 NIV). "The eyes of all look to you, and you give them their food at the proper time. You open your hand and satisfy the desires of every living thing" (Ps. 145:15–16 NIV).

But His spiritual food and drink have far richer and greater implications. He prepares a table of blessings and peace before unbelievers (see Ps. 23:5). He is the bread of life who satisfies. Jesus proclaimed, "Whoever comes to me shall not hunger, and whoever believes in me shall never thirst" (John 6:35). At the Communion table, the great thanksgiving to our God, we draw close to Him in celebration of the gifts of His body and blood that satisfy our spiritual hunger.

Prayer: Thank You for inviting us to Your table to feast on Your goodness!

Radiant Action: I will enjoy preparing food as a symbol of what You do for us and as a "fellowship offering," also called a peace offering in the Old Testament book of Leviticus. With this in mind, I plan to make a special meal and invite unbelievers, that I might show God's love for them, and if a door is opened, I will share the gospel. (I call this *apolospaghetics*—apologetics and spaghetti).

Webs: Longing (Oct.), Provision (Nov.), Generosity (Nov.), Joy (Dec.)

DAY 6

Food and Feasting II

"You will find a veritable treasure of popcorn fragments [and] frozen custard dribblings."[8]

The old sheep depicts for Templeton the unimaginable pleasures that await him at the fair. The rat is headed for rodent heaven! Good food signifies abundance, security, and contentment.

God will feed His people in heaven beyond what we can imagine too.

Besides physical satisfaction, food is a metaphor for finding fulfillment by doing the will of God. Jesus told His friends, "My food is to do the will of him who sent me and to accomplish his work" (John 4:34).

Even more vital than our physical food is God's Word, as Jesus demonstrated when tempted by the devil: "It is written, 'Man shall not live by bread alone, but by every word that comes from the mouth of God'" (Matt. 4:4).

Food and its enjoyment is a means of celebrating community. Nehemiah exhorted his people, saying, "Go your way. Eat the fat and drink sweet wine and send portions to anyone who has nothing ready, for this day is holy to our Lord. And do not be grieved, for the joy of the LORD is your strength" (Neh. 8:10).

All these images of provision and feasting and joy are reminders that God's plan for us is to experience and rejoice in life: "God . . . *richly* provides us with everything *to enjoy*" (1 Tim. 6:17, emphasis mine). The rising tide in the early morning fills the marsh and sets the boats on high paths of the water's fullness. Full tables, full waterways, fullness is what God invites us to enjoy.

"Open your mouth wide, and I will fill it" (Ps. 81:10).

Prayer: "Give us this day our daily bread" (Matt. 6:11).

Radiant Action: Because it's good to enjoy food and fellowship with others, I will try to eat with someone once a day or several times a week. I'll also plan to fix a meal and include others. I will plan, shop, and cook as ministry to the Lord.

Webs: Play (July), Longing (Oct.), Generosity (Nov.)

Gleanings: "But he would feed you with the finest of the wheat, and with honey from the rock I would satisfy you" (Ps. 81:16).

DAY 7

Milk and Meat

Carrying a bottle of milk, Fern sat down under the apple tree . . .
Wilbur ran to her and she held the bottle for him.[9]

Like infant Wilbur who craved milk, Christians are to crave milk too, but of a certain type: "Like newborn babies, crave pure spiritual milk, so that by it you may grow up in your salvation" (1 Peter 2:2 NIV). Instead of piling down the doughnuts or getting "fed" emotionally and mentally through various forms of media (especially social media), we're exhorted to develop an appetite for spiritual nourishment by ingesting God's Word.

In another Scripture, we're told to advance from milk to meat. Meat is a picture of spiritual maturity. We're to go on to deeper matters of the faith.

> "Everyone who lives on milk is unskilled in the word of righteousness, since he is a child. But solid food is for the mature, for those who have their powers of discernment trained by constant practice to distinguish good from evil. Therefore, let us leave the elementary doctrine of Christ and go on to maturity, not laying again a foundation of repentance from dead works and of faith toward God" (Heb. 5:13–6:1).

Prayer: Father, help me to crave spiritual milk and be able to digest spiritual meat. Give me discernment to know the difference between good and evil. Help me move on from repentance to doing works of faith.

Radiant Action: When I see milk and meat, I will ask God to help me crave the milk of His Word and to be able to tell good from evil. Milk reminds me to grow, and meat reminds me to grow up.

Webs: Truth (July), Apples (Sept.), Food and Feasting (Nov.)

Gleanings: "Let us grow as babes do, nourished by unadulterated milk—steadily, slowly—but surely and certainly. Little each day, but much in years. Oh that we may grow as a child does in strength, till the little tottering limbs of our faith shall be firm muscular legs with which the young man may run without weariness."[10]

DAY 8

The Harvest of Gluttony, or Piggly Wiggly Jiggly

Templeton . . . was gigantic.[11]

When rebuked for his gluttony, Templeton retorts: "Who wants to live forever? . . . I am naturally a heavy eater and I get untold satisfaction from the pleasures of the feast."[12] He's going to continue fully worshiping the feast, and he will reap the benefits.

Selfishness and stubbornness are Templeton's hallmarks. His gigantic stomach and self-centered attitude are impediments to service. He has a hard time climbing with that protruding gut! Another of his traits accompanying his gluttony is self-pity. Templeton feels sorry for himself when he thinks he's unappreciated, and this contributes to riotous, gluttonous indulgence.

Paul says of gluttons, "Many live as enemies of the cross of Christ. Their destiny is destruction, their god is their stomach, and their glory is in their shame" (Phil. 3:18–19, NIV). Consumed with desire for immediate gratification, their indifference to the Lord of all betrays a pernicious lack of trust.

The practice of gluttony exchanges fruitful purpose for sensual indulgence, and can be an emotional denial, indicating loss of hope and loss of connection with the Creator. We have choices to make: we can gorge ourselves on pleasures that seem to make us full *or* deny our tendencies to overindulge and thereby discover deeper joys of service and lasting legacy. We will be more dependable. We won't miss out on blessings because of gluttonous dopiness.

Templeton failed to realize that the true feast is not food, but fellowship and love, like that shared by Charlotte and Wilbur. Wilbur chose friendship over his beloved slops, yielding his right to them to entice Templeton to save Charlotte's egg sac. At one point, Wilbur unpiggishly saves a whole noodle for Templeton. Wilbur experienced freedom from the enslaving greed of hogging his food and discovered blessings that came not from food but from friendship (see 1 Cor. 10:23–33).

Prayer: Grant me self-control when I'm tempted to be gluttonous so I can remain sober and alert to pray and set a good example. "So, whether you eat or drink, or whatever you do, do all to the glory of God" (1 Cor. 10:31).

Radiant Action: I will "put a knife to [my] throat" (Prov. 23:2) by practicing self-control and remembering the consequences of overindulgence in food or drink, before I get into tempting situations. I will do an inventory of my soul to determine my triggers and give forgiveness to myself and others.

Webs: Thinking (July), Weight of Glory (Sept.), Food and Feasting (Nov.), Greed (Nov.)

DAY 9

Greed and Bribes

He remembered Templeton's fondness for food.[13]

Templeton can be easily bribed. The old sheep tantalizes Templeton with the description of fair food as "a rat's paradise."[14] Gluttony and greed not only make the glutton susceptible to bad health and boredom, but also to manipulation. Merriam-Webster defines the word *greedy* as being "acquisitive, grasping, avaricious, having or showing a strong desire for especially material possessions." It is marked by "a selfish and excessive desire for more of something (such as money) than is needed." It's the opposite of contentment.

Paul warns against the greed of desiring advantages and possessions owned by others, writing, "Put to death therefore what is earthly in you: . . . covetousness, which is idolatry" (Col. 3:5). A blogger who identifies simply as Geoff explains the concept well: "Covetousness is the notion that created things are the primary point of human desire. It arises from the attempt, whether implicit or not, to fill the infinite void in the human soul with the limited field of creation."[15]

Things break, rust, can be stolen, cause heartburn, or grow useless. A focus on money is not only futile, but destructive. Solomon wrote, "He who loves money will not be satisfied with money" (Eccl. 5:10). Scripture warns, "For the love of money is a root of all kinds of evils. It is through this craving that some have wandered away from the faith and pierced themselves with many pangs" (1 Tim. 6:10).

The opposite of covetousness is hard work motivated by giving. "Let the thief no longer steal, but rather let him labor, doing honest work with his own hands, so that he may have something to share with anyone in need" (Eph. 4:28).

Prayer: Dear God, kill in me desires for someone else's belongings or physical appearance (see Acts 20:33–35). Give me my daily bread and not more than what I need to serve You (see James 4:2–3).

Radiant Action: I will thank God for my blessings and be content with what I have, forgoing major purchases for thirty days.

Webs: Fame (Sept.), Contentment (Nov.), Generosity (Nov.), Harvest of Gluttony (Nov.).

Gleanings: "Keep your lives free from the love of money and be content with what you have, because God has said, 'Never will I leave you; never will I forsake you'" (Heb. 13:5 NIV).

DAY 10

Scraps and Slops

Apple parings, meat gravy, carrot scrapings.[16]

A scrap is something left over. It could be defective and rejected like the unhatched goose egg. It could be something as unlikely as a scrap of a soap box that turned out to be a treasured source for the right words. Mrs. Zuckerman's scraps grew Wilbur into Some Pig. Scraps delight greedy old Templeton at the fair.

Some people throw away scraps. Others find in them value and even beauty as Fern discovered in the almost-thrown-away Wilbur. God can use all the scraps of our experiences, including our sufferings. He takes the small things, the shunned things, the clumsy, awkward things, the little bits of our lives, and even the rotten things, and weaves them into a remarkable tapestry for His glory. He blessed a little boy's lunch to feed thousands with twelve baskets of scraps left over.[17] We marvel at the widow's gift and a friend who can make a stunning necklace from old safety pins. I love to see what comes up in my yard when I plant seeds left over from dinner. One year I reaped a prize pumpkin I gave away as a birthday present.

Movers and shakers in history have worked "scraps" of jobs. Inventor and businessman R. G. LeTourneau worked a wide range of manual tradesman's jobs, and all these experiences combined led to designing earth-moving equipment that led to winning World War II.[18]

A scrap could be the key to a new life for you, a new ministry, a new relationship, a new vocation. With God, anything is possible! He redeems us, recycles us, and rejoices over us.

"*Gather up the leftover fragments, that nothing may be lost*" (John 6:12).

Prayer: Dear Lord, I offer You all the scraps of my life, from material blessings to my experiences good and bad. As You changed water into wine, I'm thankful You will take my rags of failure and disappointment and transform them into something new and lovely. Whatever scrap I give You will become a thing of purpose.

Radiant Action: I will think positively about the potential of the scraps of my life. (These devotions are made of scraps, ideas from here and there). Scraps will remind me to be resourceful in using leftover things.

Webs: Small Things (Feb.), Death of a Vision (Sept.), Glory of the Ordinary (Oct.), Finances (Nov.)

DAY 11

Self-Control Scriptures

All through *Charlotte's Web*, we see Wilbur learning self-control in his emotions and thinking. At the critical moment of need to rescue the egg sac, his emotions are the catalyst for persuading the gluttonous and indifferent rodent to become an agent of deliverance.

> "Fools show their annoyance at once, but the prudent overlook an insult" (Prov. 12:16 NIV).

> "Therefore an overseer must be above reproach, the husband of one wife, sober-minded, self-controlled, respectable, hospitable, able to teach, not a drunkard, not violent but gentle, not quarrelsome, not a lover of money. He must manage his own household well, with all dignity keeping his children submissive" (1 Tim. 3:2–4).

> "Whoever is slow to anger is better than the mighty, and he who rules his spirit than he who takes a city" (Prov. 16:32).

> "A fool gives full vent to his spirit, but a wise man quietly holds it back" (Prov. 29:11).

> "Let us behave decently, as in the daytime, not in carousing and drunkenness, not in sexual immorality and debauchery, not in dissension and jealousy. Rather, clothe yourselves with the Lord Jesus Christ, and do not think about how to gratify the desires of the flesh" (Rom. 13:13–14 NIV).

> "Now the works of the flesh are evident: sexual immorality, impurity, sensuality, idolatry, sorcery, enmity, strife, jealousy, fits of anger, rivalries, dissensions, divisions, envy, drunkenness, orgies, and things like these. I warn you, as I warned you before, that those who do such things will not inherit the kingdom of God. But the fruit of the Spirit is love, joy, peace, patience, kindness, goodness, faithfulness, gentleness, self-control; against such things there is no law" (Gal. 5:19–23).

> "God gave us a spirit not of fear but of power and love and self-control" (2 Tim. 1:7).

> "As for you, always be sober-minded, endure suffering, do the work of an evangelist, fulfill your ministry" (2 Tim 4:5).

> "But since we belong to the day, let us be sober, having put on the breastplate of faith and love, and for a helmet the hope of salvation" (1 Thess. 5:8).

> "Therefore, preparing your minds for action, and being sober-minded, set your hope fully on the grace that will be brought to you at the revelation of Jesus Christ" (1 Peter 1:13).

DAY 12

Contentment: The Deep Freeze

Mrs. Zuckerman lay dreaming about a deep freeze unit.[19]

Mrs. Zuckerman couldn't wait to go to the fair to find a freezer. Everyone wants something or other. Getting our "want" satisfied will bring contentment. NOT. This thinking is deceived foolishness. The "deep freeze" brings with it a new want. And so it keeps on and on.

But Wilbur does find true contentment in the barnyard, despite his profound losses. Charlotte dies, Fern turns to growing-up things like being with Henry Fussy, all but three of Charlotte's offspring balloon away, and Wilbur gives up first choice on his slops. Instead of dwelling on what he's lost, he focuses on what he has, so in the end he is content.

What have we lost that God cannot redeem? Is it money or loved ones, health or opportunity? We will never want for His presence (see Heb. 13:5). We will never want for hope: "I will restore to you the years that the swarming locust has eaten" (Joel 2:25). We will not want for salvation: "He restores my soul" (Ps. 23:3).

Contentment isn't found in a deep freeze or a new boat or a new anything, although such things can be helpful or pleasurable enhancements to our lives. Contentment is found in knowing that God is present and will never leave. Contentment is usually wrapped in the robe of patience with the belt of gratitude.

"The LORD is my shepherd; I shall not want" (Ps. 23:1).

Prayer: El Shaddai (Almighty God), let me rest content in Your presence and Your love, knowing that You know what I need. Give me eyes to see the green in my pasture. Lead me to sip from the still waters You provide. Help me believe You are in control. As Spurgeon prayed, "Lord, help me to glorify You. I am poor; help me to glorify You by being content."[20]

Radiant Action: Journal Entries: 1. Thanksgivings for the Lord's provisions of simple blessings today, things like water and toilet paper. 2. What have I lost that I need to give over to God? 3. What do I need to focus on to be content? 4. What fears are snatching my contentment?

Webs: Emotional Self-Control (Mar.), Provision (Nov.), Generosity (Nov.), Scraps and Slops (Nov.)

Gleanings: "I am not saying this because I am in need, for I have learned to be content whatever the circumstances" (Phil. 4:11 NIV).

DAY 13

Peace

Every night was peaceful.[21]

Charlotte dies in peace knowing Wilbur will be safe. Wilbur looks to the future in peace. Even the farm animals knew the power of peace. How much more can we!

Steps to Peace

"*You will keep him in perfect peace whose mind is stayed on you*" (Isa. 26:3).

Focus on prayer for the government: "I urge, then, first of all, that petitions, prayers, intercession and thanksgiving be made for all people—for kings and all those in authority, that we may live peaceful and quiet lives in all godliness and holiness" (1 Tim. 2:1–2 NIV).

Focus on God's sovereignty and His omnipotence (Eph. 1:11).

Focus on Christ's guidance: Jesus is "the light of the world" (John 8:12) and "the way, the truth, and the life" (John 14:6 NKJV).

Focus on His love: His love is poured into our hearts. "He loved us and sent his Son as an atoning sacrifice for our sins" (1 John 4:10 NIV).

Focus on loving your neighbor: "Love your neighbor as yourself" (Mark 12:31 NIV).

Remember, we can't overcome troubles and failures by ourselves, but **we overcome through Christ in us** (see Col. 1:27; John 15:5).

Prayer: "I realize that the evil I encounter is more than my humanity can bear. So cleanse me of any sadness, negativity, or despair. Come Holy Spirit, renew me, fill me anew with Your power, life, and joy. Strengthen me where I have felt weak and clothe me with Your light. Fill me with life, and Lord Jesus, please send your holy angels to minister to me and my family and to guard and protect us from all sickness, harm, and accidents. I praise you now and forever, Father, Son, and Holy Spirit." —Francis McNutt

Radiant Action: I will say aloud: "In peace I will both lie down and sleep; for you alone, O Lord, make me dwell in safety" (Ps. 4:8). At the end of the day, at the end of a turbulent episode, or in the midst of one, in peace I will both lie down and sleep. I can admit, Lord, I can't handle this situation, nor control my bent to sin, nor forgive my enemy, but You can. (The apostle Paul says the same in Romans 7.)

Webs: Anxiety: Dizziness (Sept.), Rest (Oct.), Gratitude (Nov.), Plot and Providence (Nov.).

Gleanings: "Let the peace of Christ rule in your hearts, to which indeed you were called in one body. And be thankful" (Col. 3:15).

DAY 14

Plot and Providence

There was a dull explosion as the egg bork, and then a horrible smell.[22]

Fern is in the kitchen at just the right time to see her papa going out to the barn with an ax. The geese hatch one rotten egg during Wilbur's first spring, which Templeton pockets away in precisely the right place for Avery to break it at just the right time to save Charlotte. Templeton retrieves Charlotte's egg sac at the very last second after Wilbur ferociously commands him to do it and bribes the rat with his food. What if Fern hadn't left the house to chase her father? What if the goose egg *had* hatched? What if Templeton hadn't kept the rotten mass in a treasure trove right below the place where Avery fell?

As surely as E. B. White masterfully crafted his book, God is even more carefully crafting His own "forever story." "Providence concerns God's directing everything to its divinely appointed goal. By His providence, God works out His decree for all actual things."[23]

God's providence brought the right number and species of animals to the ark. Joseph was guided through slavery and imprisonment to become the ruler of Egypt and save the lives of many during the famine. Esther became queen just in time to deliver the Jews from destruction. David slew Goliath before the Philistines could overwhelm his people. Jesus came in the fullness of time to open the gates of salvation.

We experience "coincidences" that actually are answers to prayer. Prayer was at work when a bread vendor and a milk seller happened to break down in front of an orphanage when the orphans had nothing on their plates. As Spurgeon famously said, "Prayer moves the arm that moves the world."

> "The Most High is sovereign over the kingdoms on earth . . . He does as he pleases with the powers of heaven and the peoples of the earth. No one can hold back his hand or say to him: 'What have you done?'" (Dan. 4:17, 35 NIV).

Prayer: Creator of heaven and earth, help us to trust in Your providence.

Radiant Actions: Journal Entries: 1. How is God's providence is at work despite problems, chaos, anarchy, suffering? 2. How does belief in His providence help me to step out in faith to fulfill the calling He has for me?

Webs: Time and Seasons (Aug.), The Spidery Myth (Oct.), The Glory of Story (Oct.)

DAY 15

Provision

... Mr. Zuckerman would keep him as long as he lived.[24]

Wilbur is a well-cared-for pig. He basks in Fern's protective babying and thrives under Charlotte's wise counsel, teaching, and loving friendship. He always has plenty to eat and is rescued from being eaten himself. For the rest of his days, Mr. Zuckerman "took fine care of Wilbur," who had frequent visits from friends, and was very happy.[25]

So it is that God provides for His children. His love is boundless. He is a faithful friend and a friend of sinners. He provides spiritual and physical food to nourish our souls and bodies. He is our teacher, our sustainer through tribulation, the perfecter of our faith, and the guarantor of a forever future with Him of perfect peace and joy.

> *"Consider the lilies, how they grow: they neither toil nor spin; and yet I say to you, even Solomon in all his glory was not arrayed like one of these"* (Luke 12:27 NKJV).

Prayer: You are Jehovah Jireh, my Provider (see Gen. 22:14). Help me to not set my hopes on the uncertainty of riches, but on You, who richly provides me with everything to enjoy (see 1 Tim. 6:17). Thank You for the daily bread You give me that represents not only bread but carrots and potatoes, roast beef and chicken, apples, and ice cream (see Matt. 6:11).

Radiant Action: Bread of all kinds will remind me of God's provision and my dependence on Him. I will ask God for what I need.

Webs: Food and Feasting (Nov.), Faithfulness (July), Hero (Aug.), Plot and Providence (Nov.)

Gleanings: "And my God will supply every need of yours according to his riches in glory in Christ Jesus" (Phil. 4:19).

> *"Every good and perfect gift is from above, coming down from the Father of the heavenly lights"* (James 1:17 NIV).

We will have all we need if we seek first His kingdom and His righteousness (see Matt. 6:33), for the earth is the Lord's and the fullness thereof (see Ps. 24:1), and every beast of the forest is His and the cattle on a thousand hills (see Ps. 50:10).

> *"God . . . giveth us richly all things to enjoy"* (Tim. 6:17 KJV).

DAY 16

Aging

"Springtime," said the old sheep.[26]

White's image of the newborn lamb following its aging mother is archetypal, for the theme of youth and age is an enduring one in literature as in life. Now what used to *seem* old, like my doctor or teacher, is actually very young, and what used to *be* old is for many just another stage of productivity.

Friends and relatives in their nineties are still sending birthday cards and praying diligently. They don't have time to wash in the what-ifs and the if-onlys—regrets from possibly poor choices of years past. They don't lament over what they can't do; they rejoice in every blessing and make their gratitude known. They keep on being thankful despite obstacles. Their legacies are treasures of gold, heaping with diamonds.

Gray or white hair can remind one of the whiteness of the crest of a powerful ocean wave or of a plump, sweet marshmallow. White hair testifies to God's faithfulness.

> "Even to your old age I am he, and to gray hairs I will carry you. I have made, and I will bear; I will carry and will save" (Isa. 46:4).

Prayer: Help me to age gracefully and with dignity, relying on the power You give.

Radiant Action: Journal Entries:1. How do I feel about aging? Sometimes the subject causes panic, poor choices, and soaking in regrets. 2. How can I be thankful and productive as time progresses? 3. What are my goals to glorify God until the day I see Him face-to-face?

Webs: Childlike (July), Perseverance (Aug.), Gratitude (Nov.), Peace (Nov.)

Gleanings: God Himself is the Ancient of Days whose "number of . . . years is unsearchable" (Job 36:26).

"There is beauty both in the sunrise and the sunset. Believe that the night is as useful as the day. The dew of grace falls heavily in the night of sorrow. The stars of promise shine forth gloriously amid the darkness of grief. Continue your service under all changes . . . My soul, your evening of old age and death is drawing near. Do not dread it, for it is part of the day; and the Lord has said, 'I will cover him all the day long.'"[27]

Finale

To her, will death come as a grand surprise
As much of life has done—most of all
The serendipity of uncommon love
That only deepened during loss and pain?

Confounding to her were the aftershocks
When logic buckled, caving in to luck.
When old age came, it quite astonished her
At seventy years plus nine, she yet was young
Then eighty somehow meddled with her mind.
Most denial faltered: she was forced

To view the mirror's truth, cross-hatched and foxed;
To accommodate her gait, her slack controls—
Upending dignity, deflating pride.

Still she is grateful for these winter days,
For all her days of summers, springs, and falls
Spent reveling in a world enthralled by time—
Where, come tomorrow, scarcely will she care
Who might be climbing down her family's tree,
Each with a story overtopping hers.

How will, perchance, her own story end
O she with pending hope would be there when
This finite act unveils infinity.

Ruth Calhoun (1925–2020)
In *Linear Perspective: Collected Poems*

DAY 17

Evenings

Sometimes at night he would have a bad dream.[28]

Worries and unresolved conflicts we experience during the day often are magnified threefold and more when we try to fall asleep. Sometimes we wake in the middle of the night grasped by terror or grave concern. Distractions of routine and responsibility keep some anxieties at bay during the daylight hours. With the quieting of life's necessary functions, the brain is more open to pressing distresses.

One evening in Israel, He, the Light, dispelled the darkness of troubled minds and situations caused by the master of darkness, and Jesus literally scattered all the demons. "That evening after sunset the people brought to Jesus all the sick and demon-possessed" (Mark 1:32 NIV).

Prayer: "O Lord, support us all the day long until the shadows lengthen, and the evening comes, and the busy world is hushed, and the fever of life is over, and our work is done. Then in thy mercy, grant us safe lodging, and a holy rest and peace at the last. Amen."[29] Please soothe the stresses of the day and help me to give thanks.

Radiant Action: I will try to resolve any conflict before going to bed, keeping in mind this wise admonition: "'In your anger do not sin': Do not let the sun go down while you are still angry, and do not give the devil a foothold" (Eph. 4:26–27 NIV). I will expect You to work even in the evening.

Webs: Goodbyes (Sept.), Aging (Nov.), Peace (Nov.)

Gleanings: "If I say, 'Surely the darkness shall cover me, and the light about me be night,' even the darkness is not dark to you; the night is bright as the day, for darkness is as light with you" (Ps. 139:11–12).

DAY 18

Grief

Wilbur threw himself down in an agony of pain and sorrow.[30]

Wilbur openly displayed dismay about Charlotte's impending death. When grief overpowers him though, he gathers his wits and determines to do what he can—save the egg sac. He makes the ultimate sacrifice for a pig: he gives up food. And while you, too, might find that an act of love on behalf of someone else lessens your grief, at least for a little while, remember that it's okay to grieve. Your journey of loss is unique, and God understands.

It is good to acknowledge pain, and counterproductive to deny or conceal it. God expects us to lament; He knows and understands the heavy weather of grief and arrows of fiery pain. He longs to comfort us, for "the LORD is near the brokenhearted and saves the crushed in spirit" (Ps. 34:18).

The Lord treasures us and gently recovers our broken pieces. "The sacrifices of God are a broken spirit; a broken and contrite heart, O God, you will not despise" (Ps. 51:17). He is the One who wipes away our tears: "He will swallow up death forever; and the Lord GOD will wipe away tears from all faces" (Isa. 25:8).

He teaches us to focus on blessing and to realize that each day is a new gift—we aren't promised any certainty of days for ourselves or our loved ones. A widower and pastor speaking about his grief on a podcast commended the practice of the Discipline of Celebration from Philippians 4:4. "'Rejoice always.' Celebrate milestones; find the good in the day. Keep eternity in perspective. Paul expressed his life as 'sorrowful, yet always rejoicing.'"[31]

Jesus, despised and rejected, empathizes with our grief (see Isa. 53:3–5).

Prayer: Dear Father, take and hold my heart when it breaks, and give me faith to live, to do whatever You desire, and to trust You. "Out of the depths I cry to you, O LORD!" (Ps. 130:1).

Radiant Action: Journal Entry: I will write out my feelings and consider joining a grief support group.

Webs: Emotions Series (Jan.), Tears (Sept.), Scraps (Nov.), Generations (Dec.)

DAY 19

The Mustard Seed's Journey I

"I will bring the runt when I come in. I'll let you start it on a bottle, like a baby."[32]

Wilbur begins his journey as a tiny pig. He eats and grows and adjusts. His life is fraught with danger, but his deliverer conquers those who plot against him. Wilbur prevails, not because of his own strength, but because of the love of his friend.

We are invited on such a journey as well. It all begins with faith, even if it is only a "runt" faith the size of a mustard seed. The apostle Peter describes what is required for the journey of faith: "For this very reason, make every effort to supplement your faith with *virtue,* and virtue with *knowledge,* and knowledge with *self-control,* and self-control with *steadfastness,* and steadfastness with *godliness,* and godliness with *brotherly affection,* and brotherly affection with *love*" (2 Peter 1:5–7; emphasis mine).

He continues with an assurance and an admonition:

> For if these qualities are yours and are increasing, they keep you from being ineffective or unfruitful in the knowledge of our Lord Jesus Christ. For whoever lacks these qualities is so nearsighted that he is blind, having forgotten that he was cleansed from his former sins. Therefore, brothers, be all the more diligent to confirm your calling and election, for if you practice these qualities you will never fall. (2 Peter 1:8–10)

Faith is the beginning. Grace is the path.

> *"I have been crucified with Christ. It is no longer I who live, but Christ who lives in me. And the life I now live in the flesh I live by faith in the Son of God, who loved me and gave himself for me"* (Gal. 2:20).

Prayer: Father, my little mustard seed of faith thrives and grows only because Your grace is always available.

Radiant Action: I will water my mustard seed of faith today with fellowship, Scripture, and by listening to Bible-based teachers.

Webs: Seed Life (July), Faithfulness (July), Transportation: The Farm Truck (Aug.), Fern: Apples and Growth (Dec.)

DAY 20

The Mustard Seed's Journey II

God puts a seed of faith in our hearts. The foundation of our faith rests in the reality of Easter. Jesus was dead but rose again to redeem us and intercede for us. We are made clean in His blood and live by the power of the Holy Spirit.

God changes lives and gives
purpose,
    passion, and
        peace.
He
    equips and
        designs,
            granting us vision and life goals,
                dreams, calling, and mission, and

                gets us unstuck and energized with hope so we can lift,
                    launch, and
                        fly.

Prayer: By Your grace, help me fly.

Radiant Action: The mustard seed comes to life through the work of the Holy Spirit, and through Him grows and bears fruit in character and good works.

Webs: Life (July), Life and Health (July), Specific Goals (Aug.)

DECEMBER
PROMISE AND PROPHECY

In December, an apple tree's finery has fallen in rags to the orchard soil, but a first snow may now clothe its nakedness. It is a month for waiting, for promise and prophecy, as the Christmas season descends with its rich, royal goodness and anticipation of a time to come when all will be made well and right. The aging year dwindles and passes by to say farewell. The Grand Weaver, the One who enables all spiders to spin their webs, weaves all time and fact, thought and hurt, and every event into His redemptive plan.

> *Of the Father's love begotten, ere the worlds began to be,*
> *Alpha and Omega, the source, the ending He,*
> *Of the things that are, that have been*
> *And that future years shall see,*
> *Evermore and evermore!*
> —A. C. Prudentius (fifth century)

Signs and Wonders I, *p. 257*
Signs and Wonders II, *p. 258*
Radiance and Light, *p. 259*
Presence, *p. 260*
Fern: Apples and Growth, *p. 261*
Wilbur Force, *p. 262*
Temple Ton: Physical Growth, *p. 263*
Generations and Descendants, *p. 264*
Christmas, *p. 265*
Coming Kingdom, *p. 267*
Utopia, *p. 268*
Prophecy, *p. 269*
Memories, *p. 270*
Ethnic Barriers Broken, *p. 271*
Joy I, *p. 272*
Joy II, *p. 273*
Established, *p. 274*
The Trough, *p. 275*
Quarterly Review: October–December, *p. 276*
Yearly Review, *p. 277*

> "That which was from the beginning, which we have heard, which we have seen with our eyes, which we have looked at and our hands have touched— this we proclaim concerning the Word of life The life appeared; we have seen it and testify to it, and we proclaim to you the eternal life, which was with the Father and has appeared to us" (1 John 1:1–2 NIV).

His Promise

His promise,
Before the beginning,
Rolled through the expanse of time,
Propelled by the force of surging Love.

His promise,
When it had reached its full salvific potency,
Crashed onto a foreign and hostile shore,
Split open the night,
Swept up kings and generals, lowly shepherds, a teenage girl,
Leaving nothing and no one unaltered.

His promise,
After the Living Water had flooded the earth
And angels' songs had ebbed away,
God's Promise born, lay in a manger,
The Word made flesh.

Ann Kinsland Ayers
2021

DAY 1

Signs and Wonders I

Watch for the coming of wonders.[1]

Wonders abound as Charlotte's plan unfolds. The minister can't explain the wonders of the worded webs, but he exhorts people to watch for wonders anyway. And, as the miracle of a spider's web, there are signs of wonders and grace in all of creation.

Our problem is that we faint from a want of wondering, not a want of wonders. When the Israelites lost their wonder of God, and the Northern Kingdom's identity was mingling with Assyrian culture, God sent a promise to the Southern Kingdom of Judah about a wonder that would be their future: "Therefore the Lord himself will give you a sign. Behold, the virgin shall conceive and bear a son, and shall call his name Immanuel" (Isa. 7:14). And so, the prophecy was fulfilled, and the wonder came to be centuries later.

God performs wonders today. Missionaries, pastors, doctors, children, prisoners—people across all spectrums and in all cultures—can give accounts of His supernatural dealings in our time. But is it not also miraculous when He confirms His truth and presence, refreshes our sense of wonder, grants us faith and courage, and perhaps the greatest miracle of all, gives new hearts and new birth in Jesus Christ? God is even revealing Himself through dreams to peoples traditionally resistant to His grace.[2]

"I will show wonders in the heavens above" (Acts 2:19).

Prayer: Lord, help me recover a childlike sense of wonder and stand in awe of Your creation. Even more, may I be awed by Your work of salvation that makes someone like me a new creation. "Open my eyes, that I may behold wondrous things out of your law" (Ps. 119:18).

Radiant Action: On dull days, I will watch. Miracles are blooming, but I might not see them unless I look in unlikely places. I will let spider webs cause me to pause and contemplate the wonder of their engineering. I will marvel at everyday things like windshield wipers, garbage disposals, Velcro, and cell phones. I even wonder at our ability to think, see, create, walk, relate, and breathe. I will look with a child's eyes at the stars.

Webs: Glory of the Ordinary (Oct.), Prophecy (Dec.), Coming Kingdom (Dec.)

Gleanings: "If we lose our sense of wonder, our capacity to worship will atrophy."[3]

DAY 2

Signs and Wonders II

Lurvy felt weak . . . "I'm seeing things."[4]

Lurvy is the first to see the miracle. He experiences shock as he observes a wonder his mind does not, cannot comprehend. Like Mary Magdalene, Lurvy is the first eyewitness of a grand miracle, although one of course is fiction and the other, the historical resurrection. Both witnesses were humble servants.

You and I are everyday Lurvys, created with a capacity for wonder. May God open our eyes to see the awesomeness of His creation and the marvels of the spiritual realm. The Lord brings about miracles of new birth, changed lives, healings, and deliverances. There is nothing too hard for Him.

After Jesus came, signs and wonders accompanied the preaching of the Word. Where Jesus went, "the blind receive their sight, and the lame walk, lepers are cleansed, and the deaf hear, and the dead are raised up, and the poor have good news preached to them" (Matt. 11:5).

The first "manifestation of His glory" or miracle, sign, or wonder, was at a wedding, where, as H. W. Watkins writes in his commentary on John 2:11, "That at his will water became wine, is as natural as . . . the rain passing though earth and vine and grape should become wine. From his [Jesus'] point of view both are equally explicable; from any other, both are in ultimate analysis equally inexplicable."[5] The disciples also had God's power working through them to perform miracles.

> "And they went out and preached everywhere, while the Lord worked with them and confirmed the message by accompanying signs" (Mark 16:20).

Prayer: Lord, may I be where You want me to be so I can witness the signs and wonders that confirm Your truth. Stir my faith to believe and expect.

Radiant Action: Journal Entry: What wonders do I feel as I observe the marvels of both natural and spiritual worlds? An answer to prayer is a wonder and not a coincidence.

Webs: Childlike (July), Glory of the Ordinary (Oct.), Prophecy (Dec.)

Note: Jesus does not want our faith to rely only on signs and wonder but on a living relationship with Him. See John 4:48.

DAY 3

Radiance and Light

"With New Radiant Action."[6]

After racing around, jumping into the air, touching the ground with his ears, and doing a backflip with a half twist, Wilbur lives up to the "radiant" label. The scene is humorous, but the truth is, Wilbur is radiant already in his creatureliness and has no need to prove himself with silly antics.

So it is that God pronounces His people radiant: "And those who are wise shall shine like the brightness of the sky above; and those who turn many to righteousness, like the stars forever and ever" (Dan. 12:3). As we abide in Him, our countenance reflects His light. We shine only because of His presence and radiance in us, for the Son "is the radiance of God's glory and the exact representation of his being, sustaining all things by his powerful word" (Heb. 1:3 NIV). Like a light bulb, we need an outside power source, and that Source is described in Acts 1:8.

Prayer: Father of lights, the giver of every good gift in whom there is no shadow or changing, shine in my darkness. Help me to walk in fellowship with my brothers and sisters in Christ and keep me from stumbling in the dark. Let my light radiate so others may know You. Make my path brighter each day. I praise You that one day I will have no need of sun or light bulbs, for You will be the light and the glory. "And night will be no more. They will need no light of lamp or sun, for the Lord God will be their light" (Rev. 22:5).

Radiant Action: When I change a light bulb, I will think of my need for the Holy Spirit to shine through me. Same for when I light a candle or turn on a light.

Webs: Weight of Glory (Sept.), Calling: The Writer (Oct.), Presence (Dec.)

Gleanings: "Light, however, life-giving light, life that is light itself, overcomes that fear. Rather than draw away from the Lord and his will when times are hard, we press into him instead. Rembrandt famously painted in such a way; the bright source of light in his paintings came from Jesus. The other sources of light pale into insignificance by comparison." —Michael Ramsden

"He is the radiance of the glory of God" (Heb. 1:3).

DAY 4

Presence

"I knew you wouldn't forsake me just when I need you most."[7]

For a time, Wilbur doesn't know if Charlotte will go with him to the fair. Her presence has always brought life to Wilbur, and the fair is his most desperate time. Her promise to go is Wilbur's comfort. Later, her death closes the era of her presence with him.

In contrast, our God is eternal; His presence is promised and everlasting. Jesus's very name is Immanuel, God with us. He promises, "I will not leave you as orphans; I will come to you" (John 14:18 NIV). "For I am sure that neither death nor life, nor angels nor rulers, nor things present nor things to come, nor powers, nor height nor depth, nor anything else in all creation, will be able to separate us from the love of God in Christ Jesus our Lord" (Rom. 8:38–39).

God's presence brings **deliverance**: "He brought you out of Egypt by his Presence and his great strength, to drive out before you nations greater and stronger than you" (Deut. 4:37–38 NIV).

His presence brings **security**: "And [Moses] said to him, 'If your presence will not go with me, do not bring us up from here'" (Ex. 33:15).

His presence gives us **renewal and joy** when people make fun of us for our belief in God's Word: "You prepare a table before me in the presence of my enemies" (Ps. 23:5).

His presence gives **hope and purpose** in suffering. Joseph spoke peace to his brothers who had caused his terrible, deep suffering: "And God sent me before you to preserve for you a remnant . . . So it was not you who sent me here, but God" (Gen. 45:7–8).

His presence brings **power**.

> *"But you will receive power when the Holy Spirit has come upon you, and you will be my witnesses"* (Acts 1:8).

Prayer: Help me to practice Your presence and receive all the blessings that come with knowing You are near; You are in my spirit, and You go before me and behind me. Assist me in using my imagination to practice remembering that You are always present with me.

Radiant Action: I will be conscious of Your Presence with me wherever I go. I will imagine you with me as I wash dishes or run errands, even at Costco.

Webs: Friendship (Feb.), Longing (Oct.), Joy (Dec.), Signs and Wonders (Dec.)

Gleanings: "My presence will go with you, and I will give you rest" (Ex. 33:14 NIV).

DAY 5

Fern's Apples and Growth

"Fern was up at daylight . . . As a result, she now has a pig."[8]

Fern's reward for her courage and willingness to make a stand is not only a helpless, hungry, baby pig, but the expansion of her world. Because she acts to save a life, she becomes part of the barn community and a part of the miracle.

After a year of maturing, Fern begins to be interested in Henry Fussy. Indeed, our priorities change as we discover more of who we are and are meant to be. To find ongoing purpose and fulfillment, we need to turn our thoughts from the matters of childhood to mature horizons. Certain relationships, resolutions, or commitments may only be for a season, and letting go of them to move forward is the only way to make good progress. However, for covenant relationships, letting go is not an option.

Fern is like her name—a graceful plant that the wind blows in one direction and then another. Sometimes this blowing is a sign of double-mindedness. Sometimes it's a sign of maturing and leaving behind the old for the fresh leading of God.

> "When I was a child, I talked like a child. I thought like a child, I reasoned like a child. When I became a man, I put the ways of childhood behind me" (1 Cor. 13:11 NIV).

Prayer: Dear Father, thank You for designing me uniquely. Help me to know who I am and that I belong to You because I believe in You. Give me grace to embrace each season of life. Help me also to grow in ways that bring life to me and others, and joy to You. Lead me in the letting go of whatever You want me to release so I can do Your will. Let neither home, friend, nor comfort keep me tucked in when You want me to move out like Moses leaving Egypt. After all, I am just "renting" here.

Radiant Action: Journal Entries: 1. How do I need to grow? 2. Where am I stuck? 3. How can I examine my emotions, thoughts and beliefs, identity, relationships, boundaries, and obstacles? When I see a fern, I will ask God to make me single-minded and not wavering back and forth in my beliefs and commitments, nor blow around with the wind of emotions. I will also ask Him for His new directions for my life.

Webs: Specific Goals (Aug.), Apples (Sept.), Choices (Sept.)

Gleanings: "Therefore, if anyone is in Christ, the new creation has come: The old has gone, the new is here!" (2 Cor. 5:17 NIV).

DAY 6

Wilbur Force

". . . does the pig have a name?"[9]

The name Wilbur means "resolute." In this sense, the pig is like his cousin the wild boar who's considered tough, strong, and difficult to hunt. But it takes growing pains for Wilbur to live up to his name. He grows from operating primarily out of feelings to relying on reason. As Charlotte is dying, his screaming dramatics give way to rational thinking.

Wilbur shows maturity as he sacrifices his most beloved slops for Charlotte's well-being. He is finally beyond the "all about me" stage. Once passive, with everything served to him, he takes initiative to do for someone else. These words, drawn from his innermost being, are the story's central truth: "I would gladly give my life for you."[10]

We observe other signs of Wilbur's transformation. He accepts the loss of his best friend. He sobs, when some of Charlotte's spiderlings balloon away, but focuses on the three who stay. He learns hope, contentment, self-sacrifice, and the power of rational thinking over tremendous despair. Growth occurs in Wilbur after many tears. He has backbone. He is a Wilbur Force.

As with our lovable pig, our own trials nurture growth. The Israelites survived the desert before reaching the promised land. Joseph had his brothers; David had his adversary, Saul; Nehemiah had the naysayers; Jesus contended with the devil and the religious aristocracy. Our tormentors and obstacles mold us into soldiers if we allow God's grace to reign in us and not bitterness.

Prayer: As I think of Wilbur's shaky beginnings, I thank You, that like Wilbur, no matter where I've come from, no matter what demons I battle in my mind, body, or emotions, Your redemption, Holy Spirit, grace, love, and people can help me make forward progress. You free me from what pens me up; You give me the mind of Christ and make me a Wilbur Force.

Radiant Action: When I see a pig or a picture of a pig, I will remember to pray to be strong and resolute.

Webs: Trials (Sept.), Rest (Oct.), Self-Control Scriptures (Nov.)

Gleanings: "Abide in me, and I in you. As the branch cannot bear fruit by itself, unless it abides in the vine, neither can you, unless you abide in me. I am the vine; you are the branches. Whoever abides in me and I in him, he it is that bears much fruit, for apart from me you can do nothing" (John 15:4–5).

DAY 7

Temple Ton: Physical Growth

"I must have eaten the remains of thirty lunches."[11]

Templeton grows in several ways. The most obvious is that he swells to the size of a woodchuck. In the end, his bodily temple weighs a ton. This stomach, gorged with goodies at the fair, makes the climb up to the egg sac grueling.

We also note that Templeton never again laments his perceived lack of appreciation from others. His pity parties seem to end. At the end of the story, he's even included as being a part of "the glory of everything."[12] "In all things [even rats] God works for the good" (Rom. 8:28 NIV).

If rats can improve, there's hope for everyone!

Prayer: Father, reveal to me if I'm growing too much girth. Show me how to grow my sense of humor (and perspective at challenges). Help me to be physically, mentally, and spiritually strong for whatever challenges await.

Radiant Action: Journal Entries: 1. What meager, selfish gains mold my goals and prevent real growth and blessing in my life? 2. Where do I need to be inconvenienced for the sake of others? Remind me that in refreshing others, I will be refreshed.

Webs: Asking Questions (July), Clean and White: Moral Freedom (July), Harvest of Gluttony (Nov.)

Gleanings: "God chose what is low and despised in the world . . ." (1 Cor. 1:28).

DAY 8

Generations and Descendants

But Charlotte's children and grandchildren and great grandchildren, year after year, lived in the doorway.[13]

For generations, Charlotte's descendants hatch and populate the old barn, but not only Charlotte's children. Even the old sheep have offspring. The geese have an even greater clutch in Wilbur's second spring. God promised Abraham descendants as populous as the stars in the sky and the sands by the sea. By faith Abraham and Sarah believed, and through Isaac, the Jews came. Through the Jews, Jesus came.

Scriptures to pray for your children and grandchildren:

"His offspring will be mighty in the land; the generation of the upright will be blessed" (Ps. 112:2).

"Each will be like a hiding place from the wind, a shelter from the storm, like streams of water in a dry place, like the shade of a great rock in a weary land" (Isa. 32:2).

"But the steadfast love of the Lord is from everlasting to everlasting on those who fear him, and his righteousness to children's children" (Ps. 103:17–18).

"One generation shall commend your works to another and shall declare your mighty acts. On the glorious splendor of your majesty, and on your wondrous works, I will meditate. They shall speak of the might of your awesome deeds, and I will declare your greatness" (Ps. 145:4–6).

Prayer: God, grant me grace to walk righteously so my offspring will see You in me and will want to draw near to You.

Radiant Action: I will pray for my children and descendants every day and keep a notebook for each with answers to prayer.

Webs: Magnum Opus (Sept.), Death of a Vision (Sept.), Victory (Sept.)

Gleanings: "And his mercy is for those who fear him from generation to generation" (Luke 1:50).

DAY 9

Christmas

One evening, just before Christmas . . .[14]

Not much is said about Christmas in *Charlotte's Web*. White notes the snow that falls before Christmas and after, but the day just passes by without festivity. And while the event is understated, the celebratory fact is that Wilbur does not become the Christmas ham. His salvation is secure. He survives. He lives another spring and the year after that and beyond. Instead of death, Wilbur embraces life.

For those who trust in the Lord for salvation, there is no fear from a lack of safety or security. A believer's sins have been cleansed by the blood of Christ, and he has no fear of judgment. We will receive the fullness of our Christmas blessing of life forever in the presence of the Lord with perfect peace, love, and joy.

Advent and Christmas are reminders of the time Jesus will come again. For those who reject salvation offered through Him, their sins keep them from the blessing of abundant life forever.

> Where charity stands watching
> And faith holds wide the door,
> The dark night wakes, the glory breaks
> And Christmas comes once more.[15]

Which Christmas will you experience?

"'I am the Alpha and the Omega,' says the Lord God, 'who is and who was and who is to come, the Almighty'" (Rev. 1:8).

Prayer: Dear Lord, help me to be ready when You come again. I want to be prepared for Your second advent so that it will be a time of rejoicing, not wailing.

Radiant Action: I will rejoice in the cross at Christmastime and that all my sins have been taken away. Listening to Handel's *Messiah*, making an Advent wreath, and selecting Christ-centered Christmas cards to send are just a few things I could do to honor the birthday of Jesus.

Webs: Blood (Apr.), Last Day (Sept.) Utopia (Dec.), Coming Kingdom (Dec.), Prophecy (Dec.), Signs and Wonders (Dec.)

Gleanings: "Behold, I am coming soon, bringing my recompense with me, to repay each one for what he has done" (Rev. 22:12).

Advent

Through the needle's eye
the rich man came
squeezing through stars of razor light
that pared his body down to thread.
Gravity crushed his heart's chime
and his breath that breathed out worlds
now flattened as fire between walls.
The impossible slit stripped him,
admitting him
to stitch the human breach.

Suzanne U. Rhodes
(in *What a Light Thing, This Stone*)

DAY 10

Coming Kingdom

Life in the barn was very good.[16]

Charlotte's Web ends with a commentary on the glory of life on Zuckerman's Farm: "This warm delicious cellar, with the garrulous geese, the changing seasons, the heat of the sun, the passage of swallows, the nearness of rats, the sameness of sheep, the love of spiders, the smell of manure, and the glory of everything."[17] The narrator's eloquent paean of praise celebrates an idyllic place, but like a spider's web that floats away, the glory of Wilbur's barnyard exists only in the memories of those who read this story.

Those who seek their own kingdom and ultimate satisfaction in this world are writing their own gossamer story. The mirage of perfect earthly satisfaction floats ever onward, even while pursued. Victory here, like Wilbur's, is elusive. If established, it will vanish. The Israelites hoped that the Messiah would restore their nation's earthly kingdom. But God had in mind a kingdom infinitely better, one that would last forever. While we suffer on earth, we know His will is for us to be with Him forever where death and tears will be no more.

Not only is God's kingdom in the future, but it is also among us now (see Luke 17:21). On earth, one day the kingdom of this world will become the kingdom of our Lord (see Rev. 11:15). We live to do His will while we are on this earth: "Your will be done, on earth as it is in heaven" (Matt. 6:10). Although we await the day when God will establish His kingdom, we abide in His grace and live fruitfully now as He leads. We can't just do nothing and wait; that would not be His will.

Prayer: Father, may Your kingdom come. Help us, Your followers, to prepare for Christ's return and the glorious new kingdom He'll bring with Him. Give us wisdom to be like Noah who lived in a violent and unbelieving generation and help us to be faithful like him. Take the veil from the spiritual eyes of those who cannot see so they can belong to a kingdom so wonderful that eyes and ears and hearts cannot imagine what You have prepared for them.

Radiant Action: I will practice sharing the good news of Your coming again today.

Webs: Longing (Oct.), Radiance and Light (Dec.), Utopia (Dec.), Prophecy (Dec.)

Gleanings: "Behold, the dwelling place of God is with man. He will dwell with them, and they will be his people" (Rev. 21:3).

DAY 11

Utopia

It was the best place to be.[18]

In the end, everything in Wilbur's barnyard is sunlight and joy, portrayed as a communal utopia where rats and geese live together in harmony. And such an ending is perfect for this beloved children's story. But Charlotte dies a lonesome death, and her departure is a reminder that every earthly creature will pass away. The most wonderful situations in life are marred in varying degrees by conflict, loss, sickness, and other ills.

The only perfect utopia will be when Jesus reigns as King. The millennium, or thousand-year reign of Christ on earth, is the first part of the coming kingdom. After the millennium, the division between earth and heaven will be removed. The river of life will flow through the new Jerusalem, and the tree of life will provide healing for the nations; there will be no more night, and the light will be the light of God (see Rev. 22:1–5). Unshakable, unending. Rivers of life and light, flourishing and love. It will truly be the best place to be. We cannot begin to explore its delights.

Prayer: Dear Father, help me to remember this unshakable, unimaginable kingdom where peace and harmony will reign forever, especially during the times I am suffering or experiencing criticism, persecution, heartaches, and rejection. Help me bring a taste of your goodness and coming perfect kingdom by relieving those who suffer, by showing compassion, by giving practical help and prayerful support, and by sharing the good news, all by your power and wisdom.

Radiant Action: Journal Entry: A prayer asking God to show His goodness to me in just the time and place I most need it. I will seek to look less and less to this life for the fulfillment of my hopes, and more and more to the heavenly kingdom that awaits me. And yet, I will also seek balance by following the words of the psalmist: "I believe that I shall look upon the goodness of the LORD in the land of the living!" (Ps. 27:13).

Webs: Glory (June), Childlike (July), The Last Day (Sept.), Coming Kingdom (Dec.).

Gleanings: "'Behold, the days are coming,' declares the LORD, 'when the plowman shall overtake the reaper and the treader of grapes him who sows the seed; the mountains shall drip sweet wine, and all the hills shall flow with it. I will restore the fortunes of my people Israel" (Amos 9:13–14).

DAY 12

Prophecy

The crickets . . . sang the song of summer's ending.[19]

Charlotte's Web is full of prophecy: the crickets foretell summer's passing; the old sheep tells Wilbur the usual fate of the spring pig. In the opening scene, the kitchen smells of bacon, a hint of what could happen! Charlotte's words spun in her web became prophecies of Wilbur's identity. He becomes what she spoke over him.

The Bible, too, is full of prophecy. One of the ways God distinguishes Himself is through His capacity to reveal the future. As noted in *The Encyclopedia of Biblical Prophecy*, "By one count, about 27 percent of the Bible is predictive. This means that, when written, over one fourth of the Bible—more than one in four verses— was prophetic. Professor and theologian J. Barton Payne lists 1,817 prophecies in the Bible . . . The consistent relation of prophecy in the Bible is staggering; on top of that is the amazing accuracy of those detailed prophecies."[20]

God sent many prophets to warn His people of the consequences or blessings of their ways that would occur in years to come. What greater blessing than the news John's father prophesied, that Jesus was God's salvation (see Luke 1:67–75)!

> *"And beginning with Moses and all the Prophets, he explained to them what was said in all the Scriptures concerning himself"* (Luke 24:27 NIV).

Prayer: Oh Lord, open my ears to hear what Your prophets are saying.

Radiant action: Journal Entry: Begin to research the prophecies of the Messiah.

Webs: Expectations of Others (Feb.), Weight of Glory (Sept.), Victory (Sept.), Words (Oct.), Plot and Providence (Nov.)

Gleanings: "He said to them, 'This is what I told you while I was still with you: Everything must be fulfilled that is written about me in the Law of Moses, the Prophets and the Psalms'" (Luke 24:44 NIV).

DAY 13

Memories

Wilbur never forgot Charlotte.[21]

The last rags of Charlotte's web disappear, but the presence of her children keeps Wilbur aware of her faithful friendship. We can keep Ebenezers, or stones of remembrance, to recall what God did through and for us and our loved ones.[22] What do you have that helps you remember the good in the life of your loved one? Carl Sandburg, Lincoln biographer and famed poet, wrote, "There are certain old poems, old stories, old books, clocks, and jackknives, old rose and lavender keepsakes with musk and dusk in them, with a sunset smoke loitering in the faded shine of their walnut and mahogany stain and embellishment."[23]

It is also life-giving to make Ebenezers to remember when God provided answers to specific prayers. When we see a remembrance of prayer answered, it can prompt us to act in giving thanks, encourage someone else, or grant courage to move ahead in faith. We can recollect that God is the God of grace, who cares, and who answers prayer. Spurgeon reminds us that in each person in the hour of need, "there lingers in his memory shadows of what he was and remembrances of where his strength must still be found. Therefore, no matter where you find a man, you will meet one who will ask for supernatural help in his distress."[24]

Prayer: For today, Lord, help me remember my loved ones who have gone on, and keep a thankful heart for their influence and gifts in my life. For those who were more difficult, please inspire me to remember how You used them in my life to build character traits like patience, compassion, and humility. Thank You for the many reminders I have of Your protection, provision, direction, and mercy.

Radiant Action: Journal Entry: What have God and others done for me? I will let thanksgiving dominate my life. These lists will help me take courage for the future. I'll continue to keep a "blessings box" reminding me of these gifts and will make a list every November of the many great things God has provided for me.

Webs: Gratitude (Nov.), Generosity (Nov.), Utopia (Dec.)

DAY 14

Ethnic Barriers Broken

"How can I learn to like her?"[25]

Wilbur and Charlotte are best friends and deliverers for each other. Charlotte delivers Wilbur through words in webs, and Wilbur delivers Charlotte's egg sac via his mouth. Although they are of different species, they love one another.

Jew and gentile historically have lived in separate spheres, almost like different species. Through the cross of Jesus, that segregation ended (see Eph. 2:11–18). God called Peter, a Jew, to tell Cornelius, a gentile, the good news of Jesus. Peter announced to Cornelius, "You yourselves know how unlawful it is for a Jew to associate with or to visit anyone of another nation, but God has shown me that I should not call any person common or unclean" (Acts 10:28). The ethnic divide had come to an end.

Samaritans, a people of mixed race, were anathema to Jews, who would travel great distances out of their way to avoid that nation. Jesus broke tradition by traveling through Samaria where He engaged in conversation with a woman and asked her for a drink at Jacob's well. She answered, "'You are a Jew, and I am a Samaritan woman. How can you ask me for a drink?' (For Jews do not associate with Samaritans)" (John 4:9 NIV). Jesus's loving interactions with the woman in this remarkable scene of racial reconciliation and conversion make her a surprising deliverer as she then sought to rescue her people from spiritual ignorance.

Prayer: Holy Spirit, please give me a heart of thankfulness for people who are very different from me and show me how to love them. You work with the most unlikely people in the most unlikely ways to bring reconciliation. You love the impossible, for nothing is too hard for You.

Help me to hear their stories so I will grow in understanding and compassion. I will be enriched as I listen.

Radiant Action: The threesome in the crate going to the fair are a rat, a spider, and a pig. Journal Entries: 1. Am I avoiding an individual, a team, or a project involving others because deep down I think of them in some way as being a rat, a spider, or a pig? 2. What might not get done because of this prejudice? 3. What steps can I take to show the love of Jesus to someone I've felt alienated from?

Webs: Listening (Feb.), Barnyard Disciples (Mar.), Failure (Sept.), Evenings (Nov.), Generations (Dec.)

Gleanings: "For he himself is our peace, who has made the two groups one and has destroyed the barrier" (Eph. 2:14 NIV).

DAY 15

Joy I

"I'm trembling with joy."[26]

Wilbur treasures his friendship with Charlotte—the hatching of her 514 offspring is for him pure ecstasy, although his joy is to be short-circuited in a few days when the baby spiders launch out into the world on a warm updraft. But his joy returns when three spiderlings settle down in Charlotte's old corner. He even names one Joy.

Real joy, however, does not depend on circumstances. As Madison Perry, an Anglican priest who heads up a Christian study center at a university, explains:

> Even in our fearful days where tomorrow is always up for grabs, we can know the deepest of joys. This isn't a drunk over-the-top ecstasy. It is a rooted and peaceful appreciation of God's goodness, known in the ordinary meals, prayers, and passing of time with loved ones. This is the joy of a humble heart, a heart broken and restored by Jesus's life-changing death and resurrection.[27]

The psalmist declares, "You have put more joy in my heart than they have when their grain and wine abound (Ps. 4:7). James even admonishes believers to "consider it pure joy, my brothers and sisters, whenever you face trials of many kinds, because you know that the testing of your faith produces perseverance" (James 1:2–3 NIV).

Jesus's mission was to bring joy: "I have told you this so that my joy may be in you and that your joy may be complete" (John 15:11 NIV). God even exults over us with singing (see Zeph. 3:17).

> *"May the God of hope fill you with all joy and peace in believing, so that by the power of the Holy Spirit you may abound in hope"* (Rom. 15:13).

Prayer: Lord, lead me in the path of joy.

Radiant Action: Journal Entry: How will I practically love others so their joy will increase? (starting with those who are most challenging).

Webs: Victory (Sept.), Reading, Education, and Vocabulary (Oct.), Presence (Dec.).

DAY 16
Joy II

"My name is Joy."[28]

Joy is the first of the three spiderlings who stay after Charlotte's death to talk to Wilbur. He trembles with joy to hear the voice of a new little friend as his sorrow turns to delight. And so it is for believers: heavenly joy transforms us, even during life's uncertainties and losses.

Joy comes from the Lord. "I delight greatly in the Lord; my soul rejoices in my God" (Isa. 61:10 NIV).

Joy in the Lord gives us strength. As Nehemiah labored despite many obstacles and enemies, he admonished the people, "Do not be grieved, for the joy of the Lord is your strength" (Neh. 8:10).

Joy brings healing. "A joyful heart is good medicine, but a crushed spirit dries up the bones" (Prov. 17:22).

Joy comes after trials and is often doubled after our vision is renewed. Wilbur has much joy after enduring sorrow, death, and departures. Job lost his children, health, and possessions, but he remained a worshiper of God, and God returned all things to him. He didn't double the number of children because his original children, eternal souls, still existed in heaven.

Joy comes to inspire us to endure, "looking to Jesus, the founder and perfecter of our faith, who for the joy that was set before him endured the cross, despising the shame, and is seated at the right hand of the throne of God" (Heb. 12:2).

Joy comes after a finished fight, a job completed God's way. "His master said to him, 'Well done, good and faithful servant. You have been faithful over a little; I will set you over much. Enter into the joy of your master' (Matt. 25:23).

Fern delighted in Wilbur, and it led her on quite a path of imagination. Think about what joys you had in childhood. Remembering those experiences that caused joy to bloom in your heart may give you new insights into what lifts your spirit now. These insights may then guide you to an open door for a new ministry, creative work, business, or relationship.

Prayer: Father, may I experience the joy that comes from above. Grant me joy that isn't melted by circumstances nor stolen by trials. Let my sorrow be swallowed up in Your presence and comforted by Your promises. Send me a fresh anointing of joy.

Radiant Action: Journal Entry: What brought me joy in childhood? Even if I'm troubled today, I will practice the presence of God and rejoice in Him.

Webs: Presence (Dec.), Radiance and Light (Dec.), Prophecy (Dec.)

DAY 17

Established

"Your future is assured."[29]

Out of love and concern, Charlotte destroys all the farm folks' harmful intentions to eat Wilbur. She is the book's hero.

Our hero, Jesus, crushed the works of the devil (see 1 John 3:8). Any plot Satan means for evil God will weave into your good and His glory (see Gen. 50:20; Rom. 8:28). If you've found new life and protection through belief in Jesus, rest in joy. His Spirit lives in you to give you peace, power, assurance, and deliverance from sin and the Evil One. Your future is guaranteed.

If you haven't yet come into God's kingdom, please don't delay. God, the angels, and all who love His name are waiting for you to accept this one-of-a-kind salvation. Unlike the world's religions that require you to work your way to God, salvation through Jesus Christ is a free gift. There is nothing you can do to earn it. Like Wilbur, you can receive and rejoice.

> *"And after you have suffered a little while, the God of all grace, who has called you to his eternal glory in Christ, will himself restore, confirm, strengthen, and establish you . . . This is the true grace of God. Stand firm in it"* (1 Peter 5:10, 12).

Prayer: I rejoice in my salvation or enter Your kingdom simply by asking You to take away my sins. Let me live for You, and in coming to You, may laying down my life bring a great harvest, fruitfulness, and a future so wonderful I cannot fathom it.

Radiant Action: Journal Entries: 1. Review good progress for body, emotions, soul, thinking, identity, relationships, boundaries. 2. How have I handled disappointments, wobblestacles, bad news, crises, truth, friendships, victories? 3. What have I learned about puddle jumping? 4. How do I grow more hope? 5. Is my heart more "arable"?

Webs: Hero (Aug.), Victory (Sept.), Legacy That Lasts (Sept.)

Gleanings: May this be true of you: "My roots spread out to the waters, with the dew all night on my branches, my glory fresh with me, and my bow ever new in my hand" (Job 29:19–20).

> *"But now the LORD my God has given me rest on every side; there is neither adversary nor evil occurrence"* (1 Kings 5:4 NKJV).

DAY 18

The Trough

He . . . poured the slops into the trough.[30]

Wilbur's exuberance over his trough is a celebration of satisfaction. He finds his appetite pangs appeased. He's abundantly cared for more than any little pig could conceive or imagine.

God promises His followers that we, too, will enjoy what is beyond our imagining (see 1 Cor. 2:9). Our loving God has promised us satisfaction, joy, and delight from the inside out. Jesus, the trough that contains all a human needs for fulfillment, will satisfy and complete your heart's deepest longings (see Matt. 6:33)

> *"I am the bread of life; whoever comes to me shall not hunger, and whoever believes in me shall never thirst"* (John 6:35).

Prayer: Lord, satisfy me with Your dear presence. Feed me with Your Word. Thank You for being the trough of peace.

Radiant Action: Journal Entry: I will celebrate specific things God has provided according to the need and review these testaments of grace on a regular basis.

Webs: Planning (Sept.), Food and Feasting (Nov.), Contentment (Nov.), Established (Dec.), Coming Kingdom (Dec.)

Gleanings: "For God so loved the world, that he gave his only Son, that whoever believes in him should not perish but have eternal life" (John 3:16).

If you have come to the Trough or are coming back to the Trough, and you would like encouragement in your faith, please contact me at amanda@alabastersinkwell.com.

DAY 19
Quarterly Review

October–December

1. October: Journaling? How are you taking small steps to grow your vocabulary?
2. October: How does myth apply to spiritual life?
3. October: Can you write a poem about your life? Or write a short story to help others? How about three sentences? How has God rescued you, provided, and given abundant life?
4. October: What are your longings? Where do you find rest?
5. November: Do you keep a list of things to be thankful for and people to thank?
6. November: How is the health of your finances and giving?
7. November: Wilbur grieved for Charlotte and for her offspring who flew away. In what ways are you grieving?
8. November: What new recipe are you going to make for yourself and others to enjoy? Wilbur graciously offers Templeton a noodle and gives him first rights on his slops, all for a good cause. Maybe your hospitality will lead to unforeseen joys.
9. December: How has God established you?

Challenge: Keep up your journal routine: record Scriptures that are special to you, answers to prayers, and songs that encourage. Make notes on God's timing, wisdom (understanding), grace, and provisions. Even note where you find God breaking through in the ordinary, sometimes with humor! You will build a strong story to help others.

> "Then I saw a new heaven and a new earth, for the first heaven and the first earth had passed away, and the sea was no more. And I saw the holy city, new Jerusalem, coming down out of heaven from God, prepared as a bride adorned for her husband. And I heard a loud voice from the throne saying, "Behold, the dwelling place of God is with man. He will dwell with them, and they will be his people, and God himself will be with them as their God. He will wipe away every tear from their eyes, and death shall be no more, neither shall there be mourning, nor crying, nor pain anymore, for the former things have passed away" (Rev. 21:1–4).

DAY 20
Yearly Review

Look back through your journal.
1. What were your struggles, trials before triumph, wobblestacles?
2. How would you describe your emotions? Are you growing in self-control? Are you becoming more of a Wilbur Force rather than a squeamish fainting squealer?
3. Has your thinking changed?
4. How has your understanding of your identity been made new, been restored, grown?
5. Have your human relationships improved?
6. How has your relationship been strengthened with the timeless Center of the Universe, the Trinity of God the Father, Son, and Holy Spirit?
7. Do you know that you were sealed with the promised Holy Spirit for the Last Day because of Jesus, that you can have abundant life with Him now, and that you will one day live in heaven?
8. Can you share your findings with a friend? Look over the Scriptures that are special to you, answers to prayers, songs, notes on God's timing, wisdom (understanding), grace, provision, and funny ways that God broke through in the ordinary.
9. Do you understand that you were made to be more than "bacon" in a material world? Do you know you were made to be a friend to God and to others?
10. What does victory look like to you? Write your own prayer for your journey and your victory.

> "When all I see is the battle, You see my victory . . . And if You are for me, who can be against me? . . . When all I see is a cross, God, You see the empty tomb. O God, the battle belongs to You." —Phil Wickham, "Battle Belongs"

Pray, plan, practice patience, and persevere! I'm always collecting stories and thoughts at amanda@alabastersinkwell.com. You can share your struggles, victories, friends who have helped you, wobblestacles, and moments of peace.

ACKNOWLEDGMENTS

This book has been a five-year project. You might say I was thoroughly tangled in this web! To make good progress has required the encouragement and expertise of many incredible friends, family members, and expert readers/advisors. Thanks to the Piggy Prayer Partners who agreed to pray for their birthday month in *Some God!* They didn't know how many years they would be praying!

Thank you to my husband David, son David McCotter, and Luke for hearing about this project for a long time. For years, they discussed parades of ideas. And more ideas. And more. I played a game for a while where whenever I saw a pig, I would try to think of a devotional that could go along with it. (Inspiration from the ordinary! The refracted light in a pool inspired the whole project.) My husband, David, and Luke were especially long-suffering during Covid when there was no way to escape listening to ideas. Without them, though, this book would not have found momentum. My family also bore with my growing pig collection, notably the sizable plush pink pig dangling from the family car keys. Thanks to David McCotter Chambers for the wire web that says "Some Mom!" and was the source of the inspiration for the book's title.

Thanks to Steve West who encouraged me to stick with the original vision when I thought I would cast it into the sea because of some intense "wobblestacles," and to Frances Schoeling who was the first to say repeatedly that she wanted to read the book, even when I had a difficult time explaining it. That goes for Dot and John Bedor and Dot Andrews also.

Thanks to Ann K. Ayers for her constant cheerleading and for her excellent poetry contributions; and thanks to Mari Fitz-Wynn's mentoring in writing and the book business. They believed in me and the project when it was full of wobblestacles.

I am grateful for my late mother, Jo Jones, who loved people and loved writing. Right before Thanksgiving 2022, I received and listened to a cassette tape she made thirty-five years ago encouraging her listeners to write. What a mysterious blessing to hear her voice and advice on writing the night after the book's title was finalized.

Suzanne Underwood Rhodes, the editor, is the only one in the world who could edit this book. Her spiritual understanding, editing expertise, ear for poetry, intolerance of shoddy or muddy writing, perseverance, and kindness and encouragement gave life to this book. Her work on this project while engaged in her own teaching, writing, and work as poet laureate of Arkansas is a priceless gift. She acted as Charlotte, helping with word choice, undoing tangled threads, and reweaving sentences to help the reader understand the message. As a poet and the winner of many awards, she kindly supplied some of her poems for this study.

I am especially grateful for publisher Tim Beals, editor Elizabeth Banks, and the team at Credo House Publishers for bringing this book into the world.

My hope is that any heart that needs peace or spiritual or emotional growth may find a path to wholeness. These devotionals point to God, for He is the One who sustains and inspires. Though I take the blame for anything out of line, He is the source of anything good. He has changed me through working on this project. And I keep learning that He has such a sense of humor! One day when I wanted to give up, the next devotion was on endurance. A few minutes later, I wanted to quit again, but the entry was Work and Diligence. So, I kept going. Thank You, Lord, for Your hope and inspiration. May You alone be glorified in this work and may it kindle hope in Wilburish hearts.

RADIANT ACTIONS

Month/Day	Title	Reminder	Meaning
January			
Day 3	Identity: Fern	A fern	Examine who I am: Giftings, Purposes, Identity
Day 8	Identity: Wilbur	Mirror	My value lays in God's love, not what I do
Day 18	Identity: Charlotte	Spider	Trinity
February			
Day 7	Small Things	Pebbles	Small things/Victory
Day 19	Waiting for Dawn	Sunrise	Redemption
March			
Day 1	Vision: Timing	Timer	Time is short
Day 4	Darkness-Light	Flashlight	Go step by step
Day 14	Dreams	Freezer	Right desires
Day 18	Calling	Rose	Open Doors
April			
Day 3	Captured: Sin	Windshield Wipers	Sin wiped away
Day 4	Boards	Pile of boards	Tighten defenses
Day 6	Murder and Betrayal	Pig	Forgiveness
Day 11	Baptism	Buttermilk or Milk	Living the new life
Day 12	Death	Bulbs	New life
Day 14	Easter	New Clothes	Easter/new life
Day 17	Listening	Pouring water, Pitchers	Pour out heart to God
Day 19	Unstuck	Breeze	Holy Spirit in me
May			
Day 1	Passion	Tennis Shoes	Prayer for Passion
Day 2	Anointing	Dew	Prayer for Anointing
Day 14	Eggs	Egg	New opportunities
Day 15	Seed Life	Seeds	What's planted in me?
Day 18	Lament to Creativity	Darkness	Prayer for Creativity
Day 20	Flight	Airplane/Anything that flies	God's uplift in me
June			
Day 1	Wisdom	Sweets	Prayer for God's wisdom
Day 6	Ferris wheel	Ferris wheel/ceiling fan	God at center of time

Month/Day	Title	Reminder	Meaning
Day 7	Rain	Rain	Anointing/purpose
Day 8	Place	Table	My seat at God's table
Day 12	Frogs	Frogs	Strategies/beginnings
Day 18	Look up!	Sky	Look up to God
July			
Day 6	Play	Dog (or otter)	Play
Day 12	Weaving	Knitted blanket	God knits me together
August			
Day 4	Time and Seasons	Turtle	Slowdown or pivot
Day 14	Perseverance	Spider web	Persevere
Day 18	Hero	Umbrella	God's and authority's protection
September			
Day 1	Anxiety	Ticks	Send anxieties into God's hands
Day 2	Trials before Triumph	Stepping stones	Trails towards Future
Day 5	Death of a Vision	Spider	Patience in death of a vision
Day 8	Apples	Fruit	Prayer for fruitful life
Day 18	Renewal of Vision	Grapes	Renewal of vision/rededication
October			
Day 14	Foxes	Fox	Think like a fox
Day 15	Rooting Around	Trees/Bulbs	Grow roots of faith
November			
Day 3	Finances	Piggy Bank	Save and give
Day 7	Milk and Meat	Milk/Meat	Prayer for growth
Day 10	Scraps and Slops	Scraps	Resourcefulness
Day 12	Contentment: The Deep Freeze	Freezer	Contentment
Day 16	Aging	White hair	God's faithfulness
December			
Day 1	Signs and Wonders	Stars, Everyday things	Continue to be amazed
Day 3	Radiance	Lightbulb/candle	Holy Spirit shine
Day 5	Fern's Apples	A fern	Single-mindedness
Day 6	Wilbur Force	Pig	Resolve
Day 13	Memories	Blessing Box	Reminders of God

BIBLIOGRAPHY

A

Acha, Kenneth. "Calling vs. Vision: What Is the Difference Between Calling and Vision?" *Wise Christians Ministries* (blog). May 2, 2016. https://www.wisechristians.com/calling-vs-vision-what-is-the-difference-between-calling-and-vision.

Alcorn, Randy. *Heaven*. Carol Stream, IL: Tyndale House, 2004.

Arthur, Sarah, and Erin Wasinger. *The Year of Small Things: Radical Faith for the Rest of Us*. Ada, MI: Brazos Press, 2017.

B

Barackman, Floyd. *Practical Christian Theology*. Grand Rapids: Kregel, 2001.

Basham, Megan. "Denzel Washington Advises Crowd at Christian Event to 'Stay on Your Knees,' Says 'Strength and Leadership' Are Part of God's Role for Men." Dailywire.com. September 24, 2021.

Bates, Robin. "Charlotte's 'Web Poetry' Saves Lives." *Better Living through Beowulf*. December 20, 2013. https://betterlivingthroughbeowulf.com/charlottes-web-poetry-saves-lives.

Blackham, Paul. "Touch and Skin." YouTube video. 59:59, June 18, 2021. Creative Christianity Summit 2021. Day 4. https://www.youtube.com/watch?v=LHpE08PoFLY.

Boa, Ken. Reflections Ministries. https://kenboa.org.

Book of Common Prayer, Rite 2. Nashville: Abingdon, 1979.

Bray, Susan. "Chesterton—All Men Matter." In *The Grand Miracle: Daily Reflections for the Season of Advent*. Worcester, PA: Christian History Institute, 2019.

Brooks, David. *The Road to Character*. New York: Random House, 2015.

Brooks, David, Lydia Dugdale, and Andy Crouch. "Coronavirus and Quarantine: What Big Questions Can We Be Asking?" Veritas Forum. YouTube video. 1:25:22, March 26, 2020. https://www.youtube.com/watch?v=3RP4BKCKGwI.

Brooks, Philip. "O Little Town of Bethlehem." *The Hymnal of the Protestant Episcopal Church in America*. New York: Church Pension Fund, 1940.

Brown, Brené. *The Gifts of Imperfection*. Center City, MN: Hazelden Publishing, 2010. Quoted in Goodreads. Accessed July 17, 2023. https://www.goodreads.com/quotes/8765518-shame-resilience-101-here-are-the-first-three-things-that.

Buechner, Frederick. *Eyes of the Heart: A Memoir of Lost and Found*. San Francisco: HarperCollins, 1999.

Bundt, Dianne. *Blessings from Your New Year 50-pack: A Prayer Journey to Bethlehem*. Carol Stream, IL: NavPress Cards, 2006.

C

Cardin, Matt. "Autumn Longing: C. S. Lewis." *The Teeming Brain* (blog). October 16, 2006. https://www.teemingbrain.com/2006/10/16/autumn-longing-cs-lewis.

Carlson, Darren. "When Muslims Dream of Jesus." The Gospel Coalition. May 31, 2018. https://www.thegospelcoalition.org/article/muslims-dream-jesus.

———. "The Gardener." In *Weather of the House*. Abingdon, VA: Sow's Ear Press, 1994.

Cloud, Henry, and John Townsend. *Boundaries*. Grand Rapids: Zondervan, 1992.

Craig, Nick, and Scott Snook. "From Purpose to Impact." *Harvard Business Review* (Spring 2020): 95.

Crouch, Andy. "Lament Is the Seed of Creativity." Veritas Forum. YouTube video. 2:05, April 28, 2020. https://www.youtube.com/watch?v=URZBI7ycJa0.

D

Da Siena, Bianco. "Come Down, O Love Divine." Translated by Richard Frederick Littledale. *Hymnary.org*. Accessed December 4, 2023. https://hymnary.org/text/come_down_o_love_divine.

Davey, Stephen. "The Truth about Trouble." Sermon. Colonial Baptist Church, Raleigh, North Carolina. March 22, 2020.

Davis, Linda. *Onward and Upward: A Biography of Katherine S. White*. New York: Harper, 1987.

Dickens, Charles. *A Christmas Carol*. New York: Simon and Schuster Paperbacks, 2007.

Donovan, Blair. "Collected Prayers." CountryLiving.com. October 1, 2020.

Drucker, Peter. *The Effective Executive*. New York: HarperCollins Business, 2006.

E

Early, Justin Whitmel. *The Common Rule: Habits of Purpose for an Age of Distraction*. Downers Grove, IL: InterVarsity Press, 2019.

Edwards, Jonathan. "Such a Means of Promoting His Work amongst Us": *Evangelicalism and Autobiography in Early American Conversion Narratives*. Accessed June 28, 2023. http://xroads.virginia.edu/~MA05/peltier/conversion/edwards.html.

Eliot, T. S. *Four Quartets*. New York: Harcourt, 1943.

Elledge, Scott. *E. B. White: A Biography*. New York: W. W. Norton, 1984.

F

Fensham, F. C. *The New Bible Dictionary*. Grand Rapids: Eerdmans, 1962.

Fitz-Wynn, Mari. Holy Trinity Healing Prayer Training. Raleigh, North Carolina, April 27, 2021.

Fragos, Emily. *Poems of Gratitude*. New York: Penguin Random House-Everyman's Library Pocket Poets Series, 2017.

G

Geoff, "Why Is Covetousness Idolatry?" *Geoff's Miscellany* (blog). September 24, 2017. https://geoffsmiscellany.com/why-is-covetousness-idolatry.

Gordon, Arthur. "Prayer of a Writer." In *A Touch of Wonder*. Old Tappan, NJ: Spire, 1974.

Greear, J. D. "Distinguishing Good and Bad Distractions." Sermon. Summit Church, Raleigh-Durham, North Carolina. July 29, 2018.

Greenblatt, Drew. "5 Leadership Principles from UVA Basketball Coach Tony Bennett." January 14, 2015. https://www.inc.com/drew-greenblatt/five-core-principles-coach-tony-bennett-taught-for-basketball-will-help-your-lea.html.

Guth, Dorothy Lobrano, ed. *The Letters of E. B. White*. Rev. and updated by Martha White. New York: Harper, 2006.

H

Hartigan, Rachel. "Searcher of the Deep." *National Geographic*. May 20, 2021.

Havner, Vance. "Home Before Dark." Sermon. YouTube video. N.d. *Christian Library*. Accessed November 18, 2023. https://www.youtube.com/watch?v=2tk4Hp0okGs.

Herbert, George. "Easter Wings." In *The Works of George Herbert*. Hertfordshire, UK: Wordsworth Editions Ltd., 1994.

"Here, Where You Stand." *Magnolia Journal*. Spring 2020.

Herriot, James. *Treasury for Children*. New York: St. Martin's Griffin, 1992.

I

Institute in Basic Youth Conflicts. *Character Sketches*. Vol. 1. Big Sandy, TX: IBLP, 1976.

J

Jeremiah, David. *Ever Faithful*. Nashville: Thomas Nelson, 2018.

Johnson, Bill. *Strengthening Yourself in the Lord*. Shippenburg, PA: Destiny Image, 2007.

Johnson, James Weldon. "Prayer at Sunrise." In *Fifty Years & Other Poems*. Boston: The Cornhill Company, 1917. Accessed December 4, 2023, https://poets.org/poem/prayer-sunrise.

Jones, Jo. *Friends in the Kitchen*. Chesapeake, VA: Jo Jo Publications, 2003.

K

Keller, Timothy. *The Prodigal God*. New York: Random House-Penguin Books, 2008.

Ken, Thomas. "All Praise to Thee, My God, This Night." *The Hymnal of the Protestant Episcopal Church in America*. New York: The Church Pension Fund, 1940.

Koch, Kathy. Interview. *Focus on the Family Broadcast.* February 4, 2020. https://www.focusonthefamily.com/episodes/broadcast/are-your-five-core-needs-being-met-part-1-of-2/.

Kwik, Jim. "3 Simple Hacks to Remember Everything You Read." YouTube video. 0:14–0:18, September 14, 2019. https://youtube.com/watch?v=BTip4HCO2Lk.

L

Langberg, Diane. "The Ministry of Small Things." Lecture. Biblical Theological Seminary, Hatfield, PA. March 2009. Accessed September 22, 2021. http://wrfnet.org/resources/ 2009/05/ministry-small-things-wrf-member-dr-diane-langberg.

Latson, Jennifer. "How Edison Invented the Light Bulb—and Lots of Myths about Himself." *Time Magazine*, October 21, 2014. https://time.com/3517011/thomas-edison.

L'Engle, Madeleine. *The Rock That Is Higher Than I: Story as Truth.* Colorado Springs, CO: Convergent Books, 2018.

LeTourneau, L. G. *Mover of Men and Mountains.* Chicago: Moody Publishers, 1967.

Lewis, C. S. *Collected Letters (1905–1931).* Vol. 1. Edited by Walter Hooper. New York: HarperCollins, 2000.

———. *The Last Battle.* New York: Harper Collins, 1956.

———. *Mere Christianity.* San Francisco: Harper, 1952.

———. *Miracles.* New York: Touchstone, 1996.

———. *Pilgrim's Regress.* Grand Rapids: Eerdmans, 2014.

———. *The Problem of Pain.* New York: Harper One-Harper Collins, 1996.

———. *Surprised by Joy.* New York: Inspirational Press, 1994.

———. *The Weight of Glory.* Sermon. Church of St. Mary the Virgin. Oxford, England. June 8, 1942. Accessed December 3, 2023. https://www.wheelersburg.net/Downloads/Lewis%20Glory.pdf.

Lindsley, Arthur W. "C. S. Lewis's Seven Key Ideas." C. S. Lewis Institute. January 1, 2010. https://www.cslewisinstitute.org/resources/c-s-lewis-seven-key-ideas.

Longnecker, Dwight. "Nostalgia and Desire in C. S. Lewis and T. S. Eliot." The Imaginative Conservative. November 19, 2013. https://theimaginativeconservative.org/2013/11/looking-for-another-country-c-s-lewis-and-t-s-eliot.html.

M

Maus, Cynthia Pearl. *Christ and the Fine Arts.* Rev. ed. New York: Harper, 1959.

McNutt, Francis, *Deliverance from Evil.* Grand Rapids: Chosen Books, 2009.

McReynolds, Kathy. *Catherine Marshall.* Ada, MI: Bethany House, 1999.

Moltmann, Jürgen. *The Theology of Play.* Translated by Reinhard Ulrich. New York: Harper, 1972.

Motley, Daniel. "C. S. Lewis' Ingenious Apologetic of Longing." *Logos* (blog). August 7, 2015. https://www.logos.com/grow/c-s-lewis-ingenious-apologetic-of-longing.

Murray, Abdu. *Saving Truth: Finding Meaning and Clarity in a Post-Truth World*. Grand Rapids: Zondervan, 2018.

N

National Geographic Book Service. *Everyday Life in Bible Times*. Washington, DC: National Geographic Society, 1967.

Nouwen, Henri, *The Dance of Life: Weaving Sorrows and Blessings into One Joyful Step*. Edited by Michael Ford. Notre Dame, IN: Ave Maria Press, 2006.

O

O'Connor, Flannery. *Mystery and Manners*. New York: Farrar, Straus and Giroux, 1970.

P

"Paul Tillich Quotes." *BrainyQuote*. Accessed February 2, 2023, https://www.brainyquote.com/quotes/paul_tillich_114351.

Payne, J. B. *The Encyclopedia of Biblical Prophecy*. Ada, MI: Baker Publishing Group, 1980. Accessed August 29, 2023, https://www.gotquestions.org/Bible-prophecy.html.

Perry, Madison. 8@8 Prayer Group. Facebook Public Group. Accessed April 22, 2020. https://facebook.com/groups/8at8pm.

Petro, Bill. 2021. "History of Herod Antipas: Why Jesus Called Him 'That Fox.'" *Medium* (blog). March 24, 2021. https://billpetro.com/history-herod-antipas.

Piper, John. "God Filled Your Bible with Poems." *Desiring God*. August 16, 2016. https://www.desiringgod.org/articles/god-filled-your-bible-with-poems.

Pitts, Jonathan. "How to Trust God Even When Your Heart Is Broken." *The Christy Wright Show* (podcast). August 11, 2020. https://www.facebook.com/watch/?v=287091792584448.

Plimpton, George, and Frank H. Crowther, "E. B. White, The Art of the Essay No. 1." *The Paris Review* 48 (Fall 1969). Accessed August 18, 2023. https://www.theparisreview.org/interviews/4155/the-art-of-the-essay-no-1-e-b-white.

Prater, Lisa Foust. "26 Bible Verses for Farmers: Farming Is Fueled by Science, but It Is Rooted in Faith." *Successful Farming*, April 16, 2022. https://www.agriculture.com/family/26-bible-verses-for-farmers.

R

"Resourcefulness." *Metro Family Magazine*. Accessed August 21, 2021. https://www.metrofamilymagazine.com/resourcefulness.

Rhodes, Suzanne U. "Advent." In *What a Light Thing, This Stone*. Abingdon, VA: Sow's Ear Press, 1999.

Rodale, Maria. "Pigs Prefer Music for Optimal Growth." October 18, 2010. http://www.mariasfarmcountrykitchen.com/pigs-prefer-music-for-optimal-growth.

Rusten, E. Michael, and Sharon O. Rusten. *The One Year Christian History*. Carol Stream, IL: Tyndale House, 2003.

S

Saferstein, Mark, ed. "Where Does That Hole Go?" *Oh! Ranger! True Stories from Our National Parks*. New York: American Park Network, 2007.

"Saint Augustine Quotes." *BrainyQuote*. Accessed June 20, 2019. https://www.brainyquote.com/quotes/saint_augustine_148548.

Sandburg, Carl. *Abraham Lincoln: The Prairie Years*. Vol. 1. New York: Harcourt, Brace, and World, 1926.

Sandburg, Helga. *A Great and Glorious Romance: The Story of Carl Sandburg and Lilian Steichen*. New York: Harcourt, Brace, Jovanovich, 1978.

Scazerro, Peter. *Emotionally Healthy Leadership*. Grand Rapids: Zondervan Reflective, 2015.

Schaeffer, Francis. *No Little People*. Wheaton, IL: Crossway, 2003.

Schnall, Marianne. "An Interview with Maya Angelou." *The Guest Room* (blog). *Psychology Today*. February 17, 2009. https://www.psychologytoday.com/us/blog/the-guest-room/200902/interview-maya-angelou.

Shaffer, Mary Ann, and Annie Barrows. *The Guernsey Literary and Potato Peel Pie Society*. New York: The Dial Press, 2008.

Sims, Michael. *The Story of Charlotte's Web*. Reprint ed. London, UK: Bloomsbury Publishing, 2012.

Snow, Blake. "James Song." *Costco Connections*. April 2019.

Spurgeon, Charles. *Morning and Evening*. Rev. and updated ed. New Kensington, PA: Whitaker House, 2002.

———. "A Psalm for the New Year." Sermon. In *Spurgeon's Sermons*, Vol. 8. Accessed July 13, 2023. https://ccel.org/ccel/spurgeon/sermons08/sermons08.i.html.

———. *Prayer and Spiritual Warfare*. New Kensington, PA: Whitaker House, 1998.

Stanley, Charles. *Life Principles Daily Bible*. Nashville: Thomas Nelson, 2011.

Stephens, R. Paul, *Seven Days of Faith: Every Day Alive with God*. Colorado Springs, CO: NavPress, 2001.

Stovall, Jim. "Horse Sense." *Get Motivation* (blog). Accessed January 16, 2020. https://www.getmotivation.com/motivationblog/2012/06/horse-sense-by-jim-stovall.

Sweet, Melissa. *Some Writer!: The Story of E. B. White*. Boston: Houghton Mifflin Harcourt, 2016.

T

Tenney, Merrill C., ed. *Zondervan Pictorial Bible Dictionary*. Grand Rapids: Zondervan, 1967.

Thomas, Jay. "Purpose Driven Death." Sermon. Chapel Hill Bible Church. Chapel Hill, North Carolina. Spring 2020.

Tripp, Valerie. *Josefina's Short Story Collection*. Middleton, WI: American Girl Publishing, 2001.

V

Von Helms, Todd. *Before You Leave.* New York: King's College Press, 2020.

W

Warren, Rick. "Faith Is Thanking God in Advance." *Pastor Rick's Daily Hope.* June 21, 2021. https://pastorrick.com/faith-is-thanking-god-in-advance.

Watkins, H. W. "Commentary on John 2:11." In *Ellicott's Commentary for English Readers.* Edited by Charles John Ellicott. London: Cassell and Company, Ltd. 1905. Accessed September 30, 2021. https://biblehub.com/commentaries/john/2-11.htm.

West, Steve. "Home Calling." *Out Walking* (blog). August 23, 2020. https://www.outwalking.net/2020/08/index.html.

White, E. B., *Charlotte's Web.* New York: Harper & Brothers, 1952.

———. "Bye Low Baby," *New Yorker*, March 17, 1928. https://www.newyorker.com/magazine/1928/03/17/bye-low-baby.

———. "Death of a Pig," *The Atlantic,* January 1948. https://www.theatlantic.com/magazine/archive/1948/01/death-pig/309203.

———. *One Man's Meat.* New York: Harper & Brothers, 1942.

———. "Sabbath Morn." In *One Man's Meat.* Thomaston, ME: Tilbury House, 1982.

———. *Stuart Little.* New York: Harper & Brothers, 1945.

———. "What Am I Saying to My Readers?" *New York Times.* May 14, 1961. https://archive.nytimes.com/www.nytimes.com/books/97/08/03/lifetimes/white-readers.html.

White, E. B., and Edmund Ware Smith. *Chickens, Gin, and a Maine Friendship.* Lanham, MD: Down East Books, 2020.

Wright, N. T. *Paul for Everyone: The Prison Letters.* Louisville, KY: Westminster John Knox Press, 2004. Quoted in a sermon (untitled). One Harbor Church, Morehead, North Carolina. September 4, 2022.

Y

Yates, John. Sermon. Holy Trinity Anglican Church. Raleigh, North Carolina. May 9, 2021.

INDEX

Aging – November
Aloneness – February
Animals – October
Anointing: Dew – May
Anxiety: Dizziness – September
Appearances: Deception, Perception, and Fraud – April
Apples: – September
Asking Questions – July
Autumn – October
Bad News – March
Balance – May
Baptism – April
Barns – August
Barnyard Disciples – March
Belonging and Adoption – February
Blood – April
Boards – April
Boundaries: Charlotte's Outlook on Emotions, Time, and Talents – January
Boundaries: Fern's Fences – January
Boundaries: Templeton under the Trough – January
Boundaries: Wilbur's Pen – January
Calling: "Here Pig" – March
Calling: The Writer – October
Captured: Sin – April
Changed – April
Charlotte's Entanglements – June
Charlotte's Web: Tips for Writing – October
Cheerleaders – September
Childlike – July
Choices – September
Christmas – December
Clean and White: Moral Freedom – July
Coming Kingdom – December
Communication in Community – March
Contentment – November
Courage and Risk – June
Crisis: God Gives Wisdom – March
Darkness: God Gives Light – March
Death – April
Death of a Vison – September
Decisiveness – August

Direction – May
Disappointment – March
Discipline – April
Distractions – July
Division of Responsibility – March
Dreams – March
Dump, The – July
Easter: The Gospel in *Charlotte's Web* – April
Eggs and the Art of Hatching – May
Emotional Self-Control: God Gives Self-Discipline – March
Emotions and Motivations: Fern's Heart – January
Emotions and Motivations: The Heart of Charlotte – January
Emotions and Motivations: The Rat's Nest – January
Emotions and Motivations: Wilbur's Achy-Breaky Heart – January
Enemies – March
Enemy Territory – April
Energy and Hope – May
Equipping and Design – May
Established – December
Ethnic Barriers Broken – December
Evenings – November
Expectations of Others: Do What? – February
Failure – September
Faith – April
Faithfulness – July
Fame – September
Farmers – August
Fear – March
Fences: Boundaries – August
Fern: Apples and Growth – December
Fern's Puddles – June
Ferris Wheel – June
Finances – November
Finding the Good in the Bad – February
Fishing – October
Flight – May
Food and Feasting I – November
Food and Feasting II – November
Foxes – October
Friendship – February
Frogs – June
Generations and Descendants – December
Generosity – November
Glory! - June
Glory of the Ordinary – October

Glory of Story, The – October
Goodbyes – September
Goodness – June
Grace – August
Gratitude I – November
Gratitude II: Collected Prayers of Thanksgiving – November
Greed and Bribes – November
Grief – November
Harvest – September
Harvest of Gluttony – November
Hero: The Protector – August
Holy Spirit – April
Home – June
Honey of Wisdom, The: Accepting God's Point of View – June
Humble – February
Humor – July
Identity – February
Identity: Charlotte's Will, Purposes, and Preferences – January
Identity: Fern's Will, Purposes, and Preferences – January
Identity: Templeton's Will, Purposes, and Preferences – January
Identity: Wilbur's Will, Purposes, and Preferences—Hoof Am I? – January
Imagination – July
Initiative – August
Insignificance – February
Journeys – July
Joy I – December
Joy II – December
Justice – July
Lament to Creativity: From the "Dung and the Dark" – May
Land – August
Last Day, The – September
Legacy that Lasts, A – September
Liberty: Toward the Merry-Go-Round – July
Life – July
Life and Health – July
Life Goals – May
Listening: The Discarded Milking Stool – April
Loneliness – February
Longing – October
Look Up! – June
Love – February
Magnum Opus – September
Management Tips from Charlotte – August
Marriage – February
Memories – December

Milk and Meat – November
Mission: Specific Assignments – March
More Dreams – May
Mornings – April
Motherhood – May
Mud and Manure – March
Murder and Betrayal – April
Music – June
Mustard Seed's Journey I, The – November
Mustard Seed's Journey II, The – November
Myth – October
Names – May
Naysayers – August
Opus – October
Parables – October
Passion: Fire in the Tennis Shoes – May
Patience – August
Peace – November
Perseverance – August
Place – June
Planning – September
Play – July
Plot and Providence – November
Poetry – October
Power of One – May
Presence – December
Presumption – October
Prophecy – December
Provision – November
Puddle Jumping – June
Purpose I: Why Are You Alive? – May
Purpose II: You Have Been My Friend – May
Purpose III: Working It Out – May
Purpose IV: Oops – May
Purpose V: It Could Be Right in Front of You – May
Radiance and Light – December
Radiant – February
Rain – June
Reading, Education, and Vocabulary – October
Relationships: Charlotte's Web – January
Relationships: Fern's Who – January
Relationships: Pork Links – January
Relationships: Strings Attached – January
Renewal of Vision – September
Rest – October

Reviews Quarterly (end of March, June, September, and December
Review Yearly (end of December)
Rewards – September
Rooting Around – October
Routines and Rhythms of Life – August
Rudeness – August
Runtiness – February
Scatter – July
Scraps and Slops – November
Scriptures on Death (God Gives Hope with New Life) – April
Scriptures on Writing – October
Seed Life – May
Self-Control Scriptures – November
Self-Sacrifice – February
Servanthood – July
Shadows of Death (God Gives Hope with New Life) – April
Shame – October
Signs and Wonders I – December
Signs and Wonders II – December
Sin, Captured – April
Singing – June
Small Things – February
Smelling – March
Some Pig! – February
Specific Goals – August
Suffering: God Gives Grace – March
Surprising Deliverers– April
Tears – September
Teamwork: The Power of Together – February
Temple Ton: Physical Growth – December
Templeton's Obstacles: TemPest Stations – June
Terrific – February
Thinking – July
Thoughts and Beliefs: Fern's Mind – January
Thoughts and Beliefs: Pig Brains – January
Thoughts and Beliefs: Templeton's Dump – January
Thoughts and Beliefs: Thinking Upside Down with Charlotte – January
Time and Seasons: God – August
Time and Seasons: Man – August
Transportation: The Farm Truck – August
Trapping: Rat Persuasion (Bribes) – July
Trials before Triumph – September
Trough, The – December
Truth: Swinging – July
Uncertainty – August

Uninvited – March
Unseen – June
Unstuck with an Updraft: Out of the Deep Freeze – April
Utopia – December
Victory – September
Vision: God Gives Guidance for Timing – March
Voice – June
Waiting – March
Waiting for the Dawn – February
Weakness – February
Weapons – April
Weaving – July
Weight of Glory – September
Wilbur Force: Growth from the Appeal of the Squeal to the Real Deal – December
Wilbur's Wobblestacles – June
Wisdom, The Honey of: Accepting God's Point of View – June
Words – October
Work and Diligence – August

ENDNOTES

Frontmatters

1. E. B. White, "Sabbath Morn," in *One Man's Meat* (New York: Harper & Row, 1944; Thomaston, ME: Tilbury House, 1982), 40–41. Citations refer to the Tilbury House edition.
2. White, "Sabbath," 41.
3. White, "Sabbath," 48.
4. E. B. White and Edmund Ware Smith, *Chickens, Gin, and a Maine Friendship* (Lanham, MD: DownEast Books, 2020), 18.
5. Quoted in Melissa Sweet, *Some Writer!: The Story of E. B. White* (Boston: Houghton Mifflin Harcourt, 2016), 74.
6. C. S. Lewis, *The Problem of Pain* (New York: Harper One-Harper Collins, 1996).
7. Dorothy Lobrano Guth, ed. *Letters of E. B. White*, rev. and updated by Martha White (New York: Harper, 2007), 543, and Scott Elledge, *E. B. White: A Biography* (New York: Norton, 1984), 271, 294. See also E. B. White, "Death of a Pig," *The Atlantic*, January 1948, https://www.theatlantic.com/magazine/archive/1948/01/death-pig/309203. Elledge explains, "This experience gave White the vision for writing a book about a pig, which he wrote about in the 90th anniversary issue of the *Atlantic Monthly* in an article named 'Death of a Pig' . . . [White wrote, 'I spent several days and nights in mid-September with an ailing pig and I feel driven to account for this stretch of time, more particularly since the pig died at last, and I lived and things might easily have gone the other way round.' The animal had become precious to him."
8. White, "Death of a Pig," n.p.
9. Guth, *Letters*, 509.
10. White, *Charlotte's Web* (New York: Harper & Brothers, 1952). Note: the book will be referenced as *CW* in all subsequent footnotes.), 90.
11. See October devotional, "Ordinary."
12. E. B. White, "What Am I Saying to My Readers?" *New York Times*, May 14, 1961. https://archive.nytimes.com/www.nytimes.com/books/97/08/03/lifetimes/white-readers.html.
13. *CW*, 183.
14. The Bible abounds with many other references to God's glory as seen in creation. See Pss. 8:1–4; 19:1; 95:3–5; 104:24–25; Isa. 40:26; John 1:3; Col 1:16.
15. Internet definition from Google search.
16. *CW*, 85.
17. In considering what Jesus said about miracles, the reader may want to start with the real "parable of the Arables," In Mark 4, Jesus taught about the "arable" heart.
18. The premise that time is the most valuable asset is taken from Jim Kwik, "3 Simple Hacks to Remember Everything You Read," YouTube Video, September 14, 2019. https://youtube.com/watch?v=BTip4HCO2Lk.

19 The metaphor is an appropriate one, for the tree's roots go down into the earth, and the branches in somewhat the same shape reach up to heaven, representing the wholeness of life and connecting an earth-based story to heavenly truths. Consider also that there were two trees in Eden: the Tree of Knowledge of Good and Evil and the Tree of Life. It's the Tree of Life that will be in the new Jerusalem. (Notes from Paul Blackham, "Touch and Skin," Creative Christianity Summit, June 18, 2021, https://www.youtube.com/watch?v=LHpE08PoFLY.

20 White, "Death of a Pig."

21 Written in the eighteenth century, the hymn first appeared in *Spiritual Magazine* in 1761 as "The Tree of Life My Soul Hath Seen," *Hymnary.org*, accessed December 6, 2023, https://hymnary.org/text/the_tree_of_life_my_soul_hath_seen.

January

1 Carl Sandburg, *Abraham Lincoln: The Prairie Years*, Vol. 1 (New York: Harcourt, Brace, and World, 1926), 475.
2 *CW*, 2.
3 *CW*, 126.
4 *CW*, 126.
5 *CW*, 156.
6 *CW*, 4.
7 *CW*, 106.
8 Henry Cloud and John Townsend, *Boundaries* (Grand Rapids: 1996), 102–3.
9 *CW*, 8.
10 *CW*, 51.
11 *CW*, 32.
12 *CW*, 56.
13 *CW*, 62.
14 *CW, 114.*
15 *CW*, 31.
16 *CW*, 17.
17 *CW*, 50.
18 *CW*, 89–90.
19 *CW*, 99.
20 *CW*, 89.
21 "Resourcefulness," *Metro Family Magazine*, accessed August 21, 2021. https://www.metrofamilymagazine.com/resourcefulness.
22 *CW*, 122.
23 Charles Dickens, *A Christmas Carol* (Simon and Schuster Paperbacks: New York, 2007), 7.
24 *CW*, 138.
25 *CW*, 168.
26 *CW*, 65.
27 *CW*, 40.

28 *CW*, 184.
29 *CW*, 163; italics in original.
30 *CW*, 60.
31 *CW*, 143.
32 *CW*, 89.

February

1 *CW, 101.*
2 *CW*, 81.
3 *CW*, 81.
4 *CW*, 96.
5 *CW*, 115.
6 *CW*, 140.
7 "Saint Augustine Quotes," *BrainyQuote*, accessed June 20, 2019, https://www.brainyquote.com/quotes/saint_augustine_148548.
8 *CW*, 3.
9 *CW*, 177.
10 Justin Whitmel Early, *The Common Rule: Habits of Purpose for an Age of Distraction* (Downers Grove, IL: InterVarsity Press, 2019), 164.
11 Early, *The Common Rule*, 164.
12 *CW*, 81.
13 *CW*, 1.
14 *CW*, 30.
15 David Brooks, Lydia Dugdale, and Andy Crouch, "Coronavirus and Quarantine: What Big Questions Can We Be Asking?" Veritas Forum, YouTube video, 1:25:22, March 26, 2020, https://www.youtube.com/watch?v=3RP4BKCKGwI.
16 Brian Frost (sermon, Providence Baptist Church, Raleigh, NC), November 29, 2020.
17 *CW*, 163.
18 E. B. White, *Here Is New York* (New York: Harper Brothers, 1948).
19 Bill Johnson, *Strengthen Yourself in the Lord* (Shippenburg, PA: Destiny Image Publishing, 2007), 19.
20 *CW*, 122.
21 Kathy Koch, interview, Focus on the Family Broadcast, February 4, 2020, https://www.focusonthefamily.com/episodes/broadcast/are-your-five-core-needs-being-met-part-1-of-2.
22 Jim Stovall, "Horse Sense," *Get Motivation* (blog), accessed January 16, 2020, https://www.getmotivation.com/motivationblog/2012/06/horse-sense-by-jim-stovall.
23 As quoted in Drew Greenblatt, "5 Leadership Principles from UVA Basketball Coach Tony Bennett," January 14, 2015, https://www.inc.com/drew-greenblatt/five-core-principles-coach-tony-bennett-taught-for-basketball-will-help-your-lea.html.
24 *CW*, 31.
25 *CW*, 184.

26 *CW*, 27.
27 https://hymnary.org/text/o_love_that_wilt_not_let_me_go.
28 *CW, 120.*
29 *CW*, 66.
30 *CW*, 35.
31 Koch interview, Focus on the Family.
32 *CW*, 39.
33 Flannery O'Connor, *Mystery and Manners* (New York: Farrar, Straus and Giroux, 1970), 174.
34 *CW*, 164.
35 *CW*, 33–34.
36 *CW,* 33–34.
37 *CW*, 114.

March

1 *CW*, 124.
2 Nick Craig and Scott Snook, "From Purpose to Impact," *Harvard Business Review* (Spring 2020), 95.
3 *CW, 40.*
4 Dianne Bundt, *Blessings for Your New Year 50-pack: A Prayer Journey to Bethlehem*, 1 Kings 4:29; Prov. 2:6; Dan. 5:12 (Carol Stream, IL: NavPress cards, 2006).
5 *CW*, 51.
6 Charles Spurgeon, *Morning and Evening*, Rev. and Updated Edition (New Kensington, PA: Whitaker House, 2002), 318.
7 David Brooks, *The Road to Character* (New York: Random House, 2015), 94.
8 Stephen Davey, "The Truth about Trouble" (Sermon, Colonial Baptist Church, Raleigh, North Carolina), March 22, 2020.
9 *CW*, 31.
10 *CW*, 2.
11 For his discerning and in-depth analysis of the biblical story, see Timothy Keller, *The Prodigal God* (New York: Random House-Penguin Books, 2008).
12 Lincoln biographer Carl Sandburg wrote these telling words about Mary Todd Lincoln in *Abraham Lincoln*, 258.
13 *CW*, 49.
14 *CW*, 148.
15 *CW*, 166.
16 *CW*, 45.
17 *CW*, 115.
18 The quote appears in an interview with E. B. White in George Plimpton and Frank H. Crowther, "The Art of the Essay No. 1," *The Paris Review* 48 (Fall 1969), accessed August 18, 2023, http://theparisreview.org/interviews/4155/the-art-of-the-essay-no-1-e-b-white.
19 *CW*, 12.

20. Elledge, *White*, 302. The quote is found in White's *One Man's Meat* (New York: Harper & Brothers, 1950), 212.
21. See monologue by White, "Bye Low Baby," *New Yorker*, March 17, 1928, https://www.newyorker.com/magazine/1928/03/17/bye-low-baby, as quoted in Elledge, *White*, 153–54. The bird is disgusted when his suffering ends and he has to stop languishing.
22. *CW*, 61.
23. Elledge, *White*, 302.
24. *CW*, 61.
25. *CW*, 12.
26. *CW*, 60.
27. *CW*, 176.
28. *CW*, 49.
29. *CW*, 118.
30. E. B. White, *Stuart Little* (New York: Harper and Row, 1945), 92–93.
31. *CW*, 61.
32. *CW*, 55.
33. *CW*, 138.
34. Blake Snow, "James Song," *Costco Connections* (April 2019), 21.
35. Snow, "James Song," 21.
36. For the spiritual gifts inventory, go to https://www.lifeway.com/en/articles/women-leadership-spiritual-gifts-growth-service. For the Enneagram, http://truity.com/test/enneagram-personality-test.
37. *CW*, 19.
38. Kenneth Acha, "Calling vs. Vision: What Is the Difference Between Calling and Vision?" Wise Christians Ministries (blog), May 2, 2016, https://www.wisechristians.com/calling-vs-vision-what-is-the-difference-between-calling-and-vision.
39. https://www.kennethacha.org/.
40. *CW*, 1.
41. *CW*, 116.

April

1. *CW*, 148.
2. *CW*, 87.
3. Available at fighterverses.com.
4. *CW*, 164.
5. *CW*, 46.
6. *CW*, 90.
7. Guth, *Letters*, 562.
8. Elledge, *White*, 10.
9. O'Connor, *Mystery*, 167.
10. Quoted in Peter Scazerro, *Emotionally Healthy Spirituality* (Grand Rapids: Zondervan, 2007), 174.
11. *Book of Common Prayer, Rite 2* (Nashville: Abingdon, 1979).
12. *CW*, 23.

13 https://www.celebraterecovery.com.
14 *CW*, 146.
15 *CW*, 49.
16 White, "Death of a Pig."
17 *CW*, 50.
18 Peter Drucker, *The Effective Executive* (New York: HarperCollins Business, 2006), ix.
19 *CW*, 157.
20 Bill Johnson, *Strengthening Yourself in the Lord* (Shippenburg, PA: Destiny Image Publishers, 2007), 143.
21 Rick Warren, "Faith Is Thanking God Ahead of Time," *Pastor Rick's Daily Hope*, August 12, 2020, https://pastorrick.com/thanking-god-ahead-of-time.
22 *CW*, 159.
23 E. Michael Rusten and Sharon O. Rusten, *The One Year Christian History* (Carol Stream, IL: Tyndale House, 2003), 588–89.
24 *CW*, 39.
25 *CW*, 164.
26 *CW*, 150.
27 *CW*, 183.
28 *CW*, 165.
29 Christy Wright, "Stop Looking Back: How to Be You" (blog), May 2020, christywright.com.
30 Madeleine L'Engle, *The Rock That Is Higher: Story as Truth* (Colorado Springs, CO: Convergent Books, 2018), 291.
31 Jay Thomas, "Purpose Driven Death" (Sermon, Chapel Hill Bible Church, Chapel Hill, North Carolina, Spring 2020).
32 "Easter Wings" is an exquisite example of shaped verse and was written by the acclaimed English poet and Anglican priest, George Herbert. The poem is from *The Temple*, and its shape reflects the diminished state of sinners and the spiritual advancement of believers, who are joined to Christ and His victory. "Easter Wings," in *The Works of George Herbert* (Hertfordshire, UK: Wordsworth Editions, Ltd., 1994), 35.
33 *CW*, 178.
34 Gerard Manley Hopkins, author of "God's Grandeur," was a Jesuit priest whose use of poetical language was highly inventive, spiritually passionate, and influential to poets, even those of today. The poem is a sonnet. With its wondrous use of sound and imagery, we are reminded that the earth is the Lord's, and no matter how humans spoil and degrade it with industry and indifference, the Spirit lovingly watches over and preserves it like a mother bird her young. "God's Grandeur" in *Modern American & Modern British Poetry*, ed. Louis Untermeyer (New York: Harcourt, Brace & World, 1955), 429.
35 *CW*, 31.
36 John Brownlie, "The King Shall Come when Morning Dawns," Hymnary.org.
37 C. S. Lewis, *The Last Battle* (New York: Harper Collins, 1956), 210.
38 Kathy McReynolds, *Catherine Marshall* (Ada, MI: Bethany House, 1999), 51–52.

39 James Weldon Johnson was a leading voice of the Harlem Renaissance in New York City in the 1920s and '30s that revived and celebrated African American intellectual and cultural expressions of literature, music, dance, art, scholarship, and other works. A leader in civil rights activism, he wrote the lyrics for the Black national anthem, "Lift Every Voice and Sing." Johnson's "Prayer at Sunrise" in *Fifty Years & Other Poems* (Boston: The Cornhill Company, 1917), accessed December 4, 2023, https://poets.org/poem/prayer-sunrise.
40 *CW*, 15.
41 Henri Nouwen, *The Dance of Life: Weaving Sorrows and Blessings into One Joyful Step*, ed. Michael Ford (Notre Dame, IN: Ave Maria Press, 2006), 106.
42 "Paul Tillich Quotes," *BrainyQuote*, accessed February 2, 2023, https://www.brainyquote.com/quotes/paul_tillich_114351.
43 *CW*, 166.
44 *CW*, 179.
45 Cloud and Townsend, *Boundaries*, 271.
46 https://www.celebraterecovery.com.
47 *CW*, 4.

May

1   *CW*, 2.
2   Bianco da Siena, "Come Down, O Love Divine," trans. Richard Frederick Littledale, Hymnary.org, accessed December 4, 2023, https://hymnary.org/text/come_down_o_love_divine. Bianco da Siena was an Italian poet and wool worker (born ca. 1350, died ca. 1434) who entered a community of lay brothers, the Order of Jesuates, that followed the rule of St. Augustine.
3   *CW*, 147.
4   Francis A. Schaeffer, *No Little People* (Wheaton, IL: Crossway, 2003), 66.
5   *CW*, 171.
6   *CW*, 20.
7   *CW*, 51.
8   *CW*, 61.
9   C. S. Lewis, *The Weight of Glory* (sermon, Church of St. Mary the Virgin, Oxford, UK, June 8, 1942), accessed December 3, 2023, https://www.wheelersburg.net/Downloads/Lewis%20Glory.pdf.
10 L'Engle, *The Rock*, 206.
11 *CW*, 26.
12 Spurgeon, *Morning and Evening*, 104.
13 *CW*, 164.
14 *CW*, 26.
15 https://on-purpose.com.
16 *CW*, 25.
17 *CW*, 27.
18 Warren, "Faith Is Thanking God."
19 *CW*, 170.
20 "Here, Where You Stand," *Magnolia Journal*, Spring 2020, 83.

21 Bundt, *Blessings*, Pss. 25:12; 139:16; Jer. 29:11.
22 *CW*, 60.
23 Ken Boa writes that "knowledge is sometimes translated skill." (*Reflections Ministries*, February, 2014, https://kenboa.org.)
24 Spurgeon, *Morning and Evening*, 104.
25 *CW*, 35.
26 Sandburg, *Abraham Lincoln*, 305.
27 *CW*, 44.
28 *CW*, 17.
29 Michael Sims, *The Story of Charlotte's Web*, reprint ed. (London, UK: Bloomsbury Publishing, 2012), 131.
30 Sims, *Story of Charlotte's Web*, 29.
31 White said this to a group of sixth graders in Los Angeles on May 20, 1973. Quoted in *Letters of E. B. White*, rev. ed. (NY: Harper Perennial, 2007), 596–97.
32 *CW*, 173.
33 *CW*, 101.
34 The Old Testament, like the New, is replete with affirmations of God's personal and possessive love for His children. As examples see Ex. 19:5–6; Deut. 4:20; 7:6; Zeph. 3:17; and Mal. 3:17.
35 *CW*, 7.
36 Robin Bates, "Charlotte's 'Web Poetry' Saves Lives," December 20, 2013, *Better Living through Beowulf*, http://betterlivingthroughbeowulf.com/charlottes-web-poetry-saves-lives.
37 John Yates (sermon, Holy Trinity Anglican Church, Raleigh, North Carolina, May 9, 2021). See also Matt. 16:18; John 21:15–17.
38 *CW*, 168.
39 Andy Crouch, "Lament Is the Seed of Creativity," Veritas Forum, YouTube video, April 28, 2020, https://www.youtube.com/watch?v=URZBI7ycJa0.
40 *CW*, 115, emphasis in original.
41 Mari Fitz-Wynn. Holy Trinity Healing Prayer Training, Raleigh, NC, April 27, 2021.
42 *CW*, 178.

June

1 *CW*, 110.
2 Ken Boa, *Reflections*, February, 2018, https://kenboa.org.
3 *CW*, 39.
4 *CW*, 48.
5 Maria Rodale, "Pigs Prefer Music for Optimal Growth," October 18, 2010, http://www.mariasfarmcountrykitchen.com/pigs-prefer-music-for-optimal-growth.
6 Kim McNeal is a friend in the author's writers' group. She said that the Lord spoke these words to her at her home in Raleigh, North Carolina.
7 The quote appears in a letter to Arthur Greeves, June 20, 1916, and is included in C. S. Lewis, *Collected Letters (1905–1931)*, vol. 1, ed. Walter Hooper (New York: Harper Collins, 2000), 196.

8   *CW*, 104.
9   *CW*, 104.
10 *CW*, 183.
11 *CW*, 63.
12 *CW*, 51.
13 *CW*, 51.
14 *CW*, 173.
15 T. S. Eliot, *Four Quartets* (New York: Harcourt, 1943).
16 *CW*, 25.
17 *CW*, 1.
18 *CW*, 12.
19 Steve West, "Home Calling," *Out Walking* (blog), August, 2020, http://outwalking.net/2020/08/index.html.
20 Vance Havner, "Home Before Dark" (Sermon), YouTube video, *Christian Library*, accessed November 18, 2023, https://www.youtube.com/watch?v=2tk4Hp0okGs30:55.
21 *CW*, 142.
22 Lewis, *The Problem of Pain*, 28–32.
23 Lewis, *The Problem of Pain*, 34.
24 Lewis, *The Problem of Pain*, 34.
25 *CW*, 129.
26 *CW*, 176.
27 *CW*, 3.
28 *CW*, 1.
29 Todd Von Helms, *Before You Leave* (New York: King's College Press), 222–23.
30 *CW*, 126.
31 *CW*, 140.
32 John Koessler, "Shrewd and Innocent," *Today in the Word* (blog), November 25, 2020.
33 *CW*, 142.
34 *CW*, 36.
35 *CW*, 183.
36 Folliot S. Pierpoint, "For the Beauty of the Earth," 1864, hymn. https://my.hymnary.org/song/dynamic/78/for_the_beauty_of_the_earth.
37 Fanny Crosby, "Blessed Assurance," 1873, hymn. https://www.google.com/search?client=safari&rls=en&q=lyrics+blessed+assurance&ie=UTF-8&oe=UTF-8.

July

1   *CW*, 131.
2   *CW*, 122.
3   O'Connor, *Mystery*, 115.
4   *CW*, 68.
5   Abdu Murray, *Saving Truth: Finding Meaning and Clarity in a Post-Truth World* (Grand Rapids: Zondervan, 2018), 184.

6   Samuel A. Alito, Jr., Commencement Speech, Franciscan University of Steubenville 76th Annual Commencement, May 11, 2024.
7   *CW*, 54.
8   *CW*, 54.
9   *CW*, 56.
10 A Google search for the definition of imagination will turn this one up on multiple sites.
11 *CW*, 18.
12 Randy Alcorn, *Heaven* (Carol Stream, IL: Tyndale House, 2004), 395.
13 R. Paul Stephens, *Seven Days of Faith: Every Day Alive with God* (Colorado Springs, CO: NavPress, 2001), 211.
14 Jürgen Moltmann, *The Theology of Play*, trans. Reinhard Ulrich (New York: Harper, 1972), 17.
15 Stephens, *Seven Days*, 212.
16 Moltmann, *Theology*, 31–33.
17 *CW*, 170.
18 *CW*, 162.
19 Sandburg, *Abraham Lincoln*, 305.
20 Mary Ann Shaffer and Annie Barrows, *The Guernsey Literary and Potato Peel Pie Society* (New York: The Dial Press, 2008), 33.
21 Bundt, *Blessings*, Prov. 17:22; Eccl. 9:7; Jer. 31:13.
22 *CW*, 63.
23 *CW*, 33.
24 *CW*, 97.
25 *CW*, 51.
26 *CW*, 51.
27 *CW*, 89.
28 *CW*, 90.
29 *CW*, 55.
30 Murray, *Saving Truth*, 184.
31 *CW*, 43.
32 *CW*, 64.
33 *CW*, 175.
34 Sarah Arthur, *The Year of Small Things: Radical Faith for the Rest of Us* (Ada, MI: Brazos Press, 2017), 177.
35 Bundt, *Blessings*, Job 11:18; Ps. 12:5; Proverbs 1:33; Acts 24ff.
36 See book by Shantel Ellis: *Metanoia: (n.) The Journey of Changing One's mind, Heart, Self or Way of Life*
37 *CW*, 179.
38 *CW*, 84.
39 J. D. Greear, "Distinguishing Good and Bad Distraction" (sermon, Summit Church, Raleigh-Durham, North Carolina, July 29, 2018. Also see Luke 10. https://summitchurch.com/GetFile.ashx?Guid=f288eff1-5e1c-4bba-b606-aacb89061537.
40 *CW*, 168.

41 *CW*, 3.
42 Elledge, *White*, 188–89.
43 *CW*, 182.

August

1 *CW*, 70.
2 *CW*, 13.
3 Sims, *The Story*, 207.
4 Sims, *The Story*, 206.
5 White is quoted in "Some Book! *Charlotte's Web* Turns 60," NPR, *All Things Considered*, October 15, 2012.
6 *CW*, 178–79.
7 Claudia Greggs, Sermon Twenty-Four, Holy Trinity Anglican Church, Raleigh, North Carolina, 2021.
8 *CW*, 183.
9 Henry David Thoreau, *Walden* (New York: Harper Large Print Classics, 2000), 17.
10 *CW*, 183.
11 *CW*, 1.
12 Donnie Greggs, "Healthy Rest" (sermon, One Harbor Church, Morehead City, August 26, 2018).
13 Valerie Tripp, *Josefina's Short Story Collection* (Middleton, WI: American Girl Publishing, 2001), 14.
14 *CW*, 66.
15 Spurgeon, *Morning and Evenings*, 104.
16 *CW*, 115.
17 *CW*, 65.
18 *CW*, 64.
19 *CW*, 89.
20 *CW*, 93.
21 *CW*, 93.
22 *CW*, 61.
23 *CW*, 89.
24 *CW*, 164.
25 *CW*, 63.
26 Institute of Basic Life Principles, *Advanced Seminar Textbook* (Oak Brook, IL, 1986), 323.
27 Dianne Bundt, quoted in Whispers of Angels (blog), accessed August 22, 2023, http://www.whispersofangels.org/2012/01/blessings-for-your-new-year-by-dianne.html.
28 *CW*, 63.
29 Charles Stanley, *Life Principles Daily Bible*, Nashville: Thomas Nelson, 2011.
30 *CW*, 76.
31 Dwight Longnecker, "Nostalgia and Desire in C. S. Lewis and T. S. Eliot," *The Imaginative Conservative*, November 19, 2013. https://theimaginativeconservative.org/2013/11/looking-for-another-country-c-s-lewis-and-t-s-eliot.html.

32 Bundt, *Blessings*, Ps. 128:2; Eccl. 2:24.
33 *CW*, 5.
34 L'Engle, *The Rock*, 263.
35 *CW*, 103.
36 *CW*, 57–58.
37 *CW*, 61.
38 *CW*, 61.
39 *CW*, 148.
40 *CW*, 105.
41 *CW*, 42.
42 Lisa Foust Prater, "26 Bible Verses for Farmers: Farming Is Fueled by Science, but It Is Rooted in Faith," *Successful Farming*, April 16, 202211/30/2019, accessed September 8, 2021, https://www.agriculture.com/family/26-bible-verses-for-farmers.
43 *CW*, 174.
44 Thomas Ken, "All Praise to Thee, My God, This Night," *The Hymnal of the Protestant Episcopal Church in the United States of America* (New York: Church Pension Fund, 1940), 165.
45 *CW*, 124.
46 *CW*, 155.
47 *CW*, 63–64.

September

1 *CW*, 127. For other episodes of Wilbur being dizzy and fainting, see pages 155 and 159.
2 *CW*, 148.
3 Kim McNeal shared these words with the author and a writing group to which they belong.
4 *CW*, 20.
5 "How Firm a Foundation," authorship uncertain, but attributed to George Keith or R. Keen, from Rippon's *A Selection of Hymns* (first printed 1787). https://www.hymnal.net/en/hymn/h/339.
6 *CW*, 58.
7 Marianne Schnall, "An Interview with Maya Angelou, *The Guest Room* (blog), *Psychology Today*, February 17, 2009, https://www.psychologytoday.com/us/blog/the-guest-room/200902/interview-maya-angelou.
8 Jennifer Latson, "How Edison Invented the Light Bulb—and Lots of Myths about Himself," *Time Magazine*, October 21, 2014, https://time.com/3517011/thomas-edison.
9 Megan Basham, "Denzel Washington Advises Crowd at Christian Event to 'Stay on Your Knees,' Says 'Strength and Leadership' Are Part of God's Role for Men," Dailywire.com, September 24, 2021.
10 Both quotes supposedly by Churchill are found on goodreads.com and various other internet sites.
11 *CW*, 72.

12 *CW*, 168.
13 *CW*, 25.
14 *CW*, 173.
15 *CW*, 172.
16 *CW*, 183.
17 Quoted in David Jeremiah, *Ever Faithful* (Nashville: Thomas Nelson, 2018), 95.
18 *CW*, 183.
19 *CW*, 145.
20 *CW*, 151.
21 *CW*, 174.
22 C. S. Lewis, *The Weight of Glory* (sermon, the Church of St. Mary the Virgin, Oxford, England, June 8, 1942), ellipsis in original, accessed December 3, 2023, https://www.wheelersburg.net/Downloads/Lewis%20Glory.pdf.
23 Spurgeon, *Morning and Evening*, 104.
24 *CW*, 160.
25 *CW*, 160.
26 *CW*, 171.
27 *CW*, 55.
28 *CW*, 172.
29 *CW*, 17.

October

1 As quoted in Elledge, *White*, 205 (in a postcard to James Thurber, September 25, 1937).
2 Guth, *Letters*, 155.
3 *CW*, 184.
4 Katherine White wrote to a *New York Times* critic in 1943, saying, "They are not words that should be applied to anyone who is an honest man and an honest writer. Andy is both." Quoted in Linda Davis, *Onward and Upward: A Biography of Katherine S. White* (New York: Harper, 1987), 140.
5 L'Engle, *The Rock*, 218.
6 White's words to a student, quoted in Sims, *The Story of Charlotte's Web*, 229.
7 *CW*, 122.
8 *CW*, 90.
9 C. S. Lewis, *Miracles* (New York: Touchstone, 1996), 176.
10 Arthur W. Lindsley, "C. S. Lewis's Seven Key Ideas," C. S. Lewis Institute, January 1, 2010, https://www.cslewisinstitute.org/resources/c-s-lewis-seven-key-ideas.
11 Quoted in Elledge, *White*, 251.
12 Glossary, ESV.org.
13 F. C. Fensham, *The New Bible Dictionary* (Grand Rapids: Eerdmans, 1962), 932.
14 Merrill Tenney, ed., *Zondervan Pictorial Bible Dictionary* (Grand Rapids: Zondervan, 1967), 621.
15 *CW*, 106.

16 Vanessa Boris, "What Makes Storytelling So Effective for Learning?, Havardbusinessreview.org, December 20, 2017, https://www.harvardbusiness.org/what-makes-storytelling-so-effective-for-learning/.
17 Bates, "Charlotte's 'Web Poetry.'"
18 Quoted in Helga Sandburg, *A Great and Glorious Romance: The Story of Carl Sandburg and Lilian Steichen* (New York: Harcourt, Brace, Jovanovich, 1978), 204.
19 Bates, "Charlotte's 'Web Poetry'"; *CW*, 149.
20 John Piper, "God Filled Your Bible with Poems," *Desiring God*, August 16, 2016, https://www.desiringgod.org/articles/god-filled-your-bible-with-poems.
21 *CW*, 164.
22 *CW*, 116.
23 *CW*, 98.
24 Shaffer and Barrows, *Guernsey Literary*, 53.
25 Elledge, *White*, 58.
26 *CW*, 113.
27 *CW*, 113.
28 Matt Cardin, "Autumn Longing: C. S. Lewis," *The Teeming Brain* (blog), October 16, 2006, https://www.teemingbrain.com/2006/10/16/autumn-longing-cs-lewis.
29 Lewis, *Pilgrim's Regress* (Grand Rapids: Eerdmans, 2014), 212.
30 Quoted in Guth, *Letters*, 155.
31 C. S. Lewis, *Surprised by Joy* (New York: Inspirational Press, 1994), 41.
32 C. S. Lewis, *Mere Christianity* (New York: Harper Collins, 1952), 136–37.
33 Daniel Motley, "C. S. Lewis' Ingenious Apologetic of Longing," *Logos* (blog), September 17, 2018, https://www.logos.com/grow/c-s-lewis-ingenious-apologetic-of-longing.
34 Motley, "Lewis' Ingenious Apologetic."
35 Motley, "Lewis' Ingenious Apologetic."
36 *CW*, 46.
37 *CW*, 46.
38 Guth, *Letters*, 562.
39 *CW*, 173.
40 Institute in Basic Youth Conflicts, *Character Sketches*, vol. 1 (Big Sandy, TX: IBLP, 1976), 372.
41 *CW*, 9.
42 *CW*, 57.
43 *CW*, 58.
44 *CW*, 28.
45 Brené Brown quote in Goodreads, from *The Gifts of Imperfection* (Center City, MN: Hazelden Publishing, 2010), accessed July 17, 2023, https://www.goodreads.com/quotes/8765518-shame-resilience-101-here-are-the-first-three-things-that.
46 Francis McNutt, *Deliverance from Evil* (Grand Rapids: Chosen Books, 2009), 124–25.
47 Abdu Murray, "Honor and Shame Culture," RZIM Founders Weekend Conference: "And He Gave Some Evangelists" (CD set No. 8), October 25–27, 2019, Miami, Florida.

48 *CW*, 42.
49 *CW*, 91.
50 L'Engle, *The Rock*, 204.
51 Ken, "All Praise to Thee, My God, This Night," *The Hymnal of the Protestant Episcopal Church in the United States of America* (New York: Church Pension Fund, 1940), 165.
52 *CW*, 109.
53 Cynthia Maus, *Christ and the Fine Arts* (New York: Harper and Brothers, 1959), 8–9.
54 Diane Langberg, "The Ministry of Small Things" (lecture, Biblical Theological Seminary, Hatfield, PA), March 2009, http://wrfnet.org/resources/2009/05/ministry-small-things-wrf-member-dr-diane-langberg.
55 N. T. Wright, *Paul for Everyone: The Prison Letters* (Louisville, KY: Westminster John Knox Press, 2004). Quoted in a sermon, One Harbor Church, Morehead, North Carolina, September 4, 2022.

November

1 *CW*, 174.
2 Institute of Basic Life Principles calendar, November 2019.
3 The first two entries were collected by Blair Donovan, "Collected Prayers," CountryLiving.com. October 1, 2020.
4 *CW*, 12.
5 *CW*, 174.
6 Spurgeon, *Morning and Evening*, 104.
7 *CW*, 43.
8 *CW*, 123.
9 *CW*, 9.
10 Spurgeon, "A Psalm for the New Year" (sermon, the Metropolitan Tabernacle, Newington, London, January 5, 1862), in *Spurgeon's Sermons*, Vol. 8, accessed July 13, 2023, https://ccel.org/ccel/spurgeon/sermons08/sermons08.i.html.
11 *CW*, 174–75.
12 *CW*, 175.
13 *CW*, 168.
14 *CW*, 122.
15 Geoff, "Why Is Covetousness Idolatry?" *Geoff's Miscellany* (blog), September 24, 2017, https://geoffsmiscellany.com/why-is-covetousness-idolatry.
16 *CW*, 26.
17 The twelve baskets of scraps may even represent the fruitfulness of the work of each of the apostles as they fulfilled their missions. John Yates (sermon, Holy Trinity Anglican Church, Raleigh, North Carolina, May 9, 2021).
18 R. G. LeTourneau, *Mover of Men and Mountains* (Chicago: Moody Publishers, 1967).
19 *CW*, 118.
20 Spurgeon, *Morning and Evening*, 104.
21 *CW*, 11.

22 *CW*, 72.
23 Floyd Barackman, *Practical Christian Theology* (Grand Rapids: Kregel, 2001), 81.
24 *CW*, 172.
25 *CW*, 183.
26 *CW*, 176.
27 Spurgeon, *Morning and Evening*, 318.
28 *CW*, 115.
29 Cardinal John Henry Newman, quoted in Jo Jones, *Friends in the Kitchen* (Chesapeake, VA: Jo Jo Publications, 2003), 112.
30 *CW*, 165.
31 Jonathan Pitts, "What to Do When Your Heart Is Broken," *The Christy Wright Show* (podcast), August 11, 2020, https://www.facebook.com/watch/?v=287091792584448; quoting 2 Cor. 6:10.
32 *CW*, 3.

December

1 *CW*, 85.
2 Darren Carlson, "When Muslims Dream of Jesus," The Gospel Coalition, May 31, 2018, https://www.thegospelcoalition.org/article/muslims-dream-jesus.
3 Ken Boa, "Modern Pensees," from a sermon in *Reflections Newsletter*, November 2021.
4 *CW*, 77–78.
5 H. W. Watkins, "Commentary on John 2:11 in *Ellicott's Commentary for English Readers*, ed. Charles John Ellicott, 1905, accessed September 30, 2021, https://biblehub.com/commentaries/john/2-11.htm.
6 *CW*, 99.
7 *CW*, 117.
8 *CW*, 5.
9 *CW*, 82.
10 *CW*, 164.
11 *CW*, 148.
12 *CW*, 183.
13 *CW*, 183.
14 *CW*, 173.
15 This is the fourth stanza of "O Little Town of Bethlehem" by Phillips Brooks, *The Hymnal of the Protestant Episcopal Church in America* (New York: Church Pension Fund, 1940).
16 *CW*, 183.
17 *CW*, 183.
18 *CW*, 183.
19 *CW*, 113.
20 J. B. Payne, *The Encyclopedia of Biblical Prophecy* (Ada, MI: Baker Publishing Group, 1980), 674–75, accessed August 29, 2023, https://www.gotquestions.org/Bible-prophecy.html.
21 *CW*, 184.

22 "Then Samuel took a stone and set it up between Mizpah and Shen and called its name Ebenezer; for he said, 'Till now the Lord has helped us'" (1 Sam. 7:12).
23 Sandburg, *Abraham Lincoln*, 308.
24 Charles Spurgeon, *Prayer and Spiritual Warfare* (New Kensington, PA: Whitaker House, 1998), 12.
25 *CW*, 41.
26 *CW*, 182.
27 Madison Perry, 8@8 Prayer Group, Facebook Public Group, accessed April 22, 2020, https://facebook.com/groups/8at8pm.
28 *CW*, 182.
29 *CW*, 163.
30 *CW*, 23.

www.ingramcontent.com/pod-product-compliance
Lightning Source LLC
Chambersburg PA
CBHW070607170426
43200CB00012B/2610